1972 /1st

D1346222

The Observer's Pocket Series

ASSOCIATION FOOTBALL

The Observer Books

A POCKET REFERENCE SERIES
COVERING NATURAL HISTORY, TRANSPORT,
THE ARTS, ETC.

Natural History

BIRDS
BIRDS' EGGS
BUTTERFLIES
LARGER MOTHS
COMMON INSECTS
WILD ANIMALS
ZOO ANIMALS
WILD FLOWERS
GARDEN FLOWERS
FLOWERING TREES
              AND SHRUBS
HOUSE PLANTS
CACTI
TREES
GRASSES
FERNS
COMMON FUNGI
LICHENS
POND LIFE
FRESHWATER FISHES
SEA FISHES
SEA AND SEASHORE
GEOLOGY
ASTRONOMY
WEATHER
CATS
DOGS
HORSES AND PONIES

Transport

AIRCRAFT
AUTOMOBILES
COMMERCIAL VEHICLES
SHIPS
MANNED SPACEFLIGHT

The Arts etc.

ARCHITECTURE
CATHEDRALS
CHURCHES
HERALDRY
FLAGS
PAINTING
MODERN ART
SCULPTURE
FURNITURE
MUSIC
POSTAGE STAMPS

Sport

ASSOCIATION FOOTBALL

The Observer's Book of
Association
FOOTBALL

ALBERT SEWELL

WITH 16 COLOUR PLATES AND
42 BLACK AND WHITE ILLUSTRATIONS

FREDERICK WARNE & CO LTD
FREDERICK WARNE & CO INC
LONDON NEW YORK

Library of Congress
Catalog Card No.: 72–81144
ISBN 7232 1511 1

Filmset by Keyspools Ltd, Golborne, Lancs
Printed in Great Britain by
C Tinling & Co Ltd, Prescot

1022.472

Contents

Acknowledgements

The authors and publishers wish to thank the following for their kind permission to reproduce photographs: Syndication International, page 7, page 130 (both), 131 (both), 132 (both), 133 (left), 134 (both), 135 (left), 136 (both), 137 (right), 138 (both), 139 (both, and Plate 13; The Press Association Ltd, page 140 (left), 156 and Plates 3, 8, 9, 10, 11, 12 and 14; The Associated Press Ltd, pages 133 (right), 140 (right) and Plate 7; Hayters, page 135 (right), 137 (left) and Plate 15 (left and right); Sports Press Pictures, page 159; Topix, page 162; W. Pilkington, Plate 1; Colorsport, Plate 2; Arsenal Football Club, Plate 4; Sport and General Press Agency Ltd, Plate 5; Central Press Photos Ltd, Plate 6; Fox Photos Ltd, Plate 15 (centre); Sports Press Pictures, Plate 16.

Foreword
by Sir Alf Ramsey
(England Team Manager)

For many years I have admired *The Observer's Pocket Series* because of the visual and technical detail which the books provide for those anxious to widen their knowledge. Yet I have sometimes thought it a pity that such a diverse and compact library of information did not embrace sport in its varying aspects.

Clearly, others held similar views and so I was naturally pleased that, in acknowledging the demand for an extension of their work into this field, the publishers should choose to kick off, so to speak, with Association Football.

The game, for me, has been a way of life since my formative years as a lad at school in Essex. Indeed, outside my home it is my constant companion.

Football is one of the truly international sports and its growth is reflected in the enormous appeal which the World Cup competitions now make among the 138 member countries which form the *Fédération Internationale de Football Association*.

Each era produces its own greatness, and comparisons between players of different periods are profitless exercises. Nevertheless, there has been a notable advance in the scientific development of football tactics during the past decade. The trained condition of players at top professional level has never been higher; their equipment, supervision and rewards are all first class and the modern footballers are now very much an integral part of the community.

I have been fortunate to know closely many of these players, more particularly, of course, those who have represented England since I was appointed team manager in

October 1962. Their qualities of loyalty, responsibility and, above all, self-control in testing circumstances, provide me with some of my most rewarding memories.

From time to time I read and hear criticism that some of the players selected for international duty are getting on in years. I would say that the age of a player is not important in itself. Far more important, to my mind, is his performance. I shall always insist if players become less effective than others available, they will be replaced. Having said that I must emphasize that football at the highest reaches is a game which demands *experience*. You need only examine the most consistently successful teams in our own League competition to realize that.

Clearly it is too early to predict how we shall fare in the next World Cup tournament, the final rounds of which are not played until 1974. All I will say is that we have some outstanding players and it will take a very good team to stop us from achieving the ultimate goal—the return of the world crown to England.

Meanwhile I hope your interest will be stimulated by this *Observer Book of Association Football*, with its International, European and other splendidly informative sections, not least the club histories and well-tabulated records.

Most of all I commend its sensible size and illustrative format which is a hallmark of this particular series. It deserves to become the pocket companion of all those who enjoy and support this great game of ours.

The History of the Game

It is impossible to say exactly when football began because its origins are lost, literally, in the mists of time. Some say men (and women) first began kicking 'an object' around, as far back as the twelfth century. Perhaps they did, but it took a long time for the game to become organized.

The first real stirrings were in the middle of last century, when boys at established English public schools, and at universities such as Cambridge, began to play a form of soccer which at least bore some resemblance to our modern game. It is surprising that a game thought of mainly as a working man's pastime should have originated in the very bastions of the so-called privileged classes.

However, such was the popularity of football that it was not long before it appealed to a wider audience. The oldest Football League club was founded in 1862—26 years before the inauguration of the League itself—Notts County, who came into existence three years before their arch-rivals Nottingham Forest.

The following year, 1863, saw the formation of the Football Association—in a public house in central London. This was the world's first organized attempt at controlling the game at national level, and it was from the new body's title that Association football, or soccer, got its name.

Many people north of the Border believe that Scotland, not England, gave football to the world. With due respect to the Scots, who have contributed so much to the game, this is not so. The first Scottish club, the famous and once powerful Queen's Park, did not appear on the field until 1867, and the Scottish Football Association waited until 1873 for its inception.

One major difference between Notts County and Queen's Park was that while both started life as amateur organizations, the English club had turned professional by 1885. The Scots remained amateur, and today they alone among Britain's League clubs play strictly 'for fun'. Incidentally, it is an odd twist that they also play in Britain's biggest stadium, the 135,000-capacity Hampden Park in Glasgow.

Brazil, West Germany, Hungary may come and go. England and Scotland go on for ever in the International soccer sense, despite misguided attempts in the past to belittle the annual clash between these two. The first match was played in November 1872, in Glasgow, and resulted in a goalless draw (it was to be 98 years before the next similar result).

Irish soccer is one province in which that country's traditional luck usually deserts it. A small country to start with, Ireland suffers even more by having to supply players for two International sides—Northern Ireland and the Republic of Ireland. In February 1882, long before the partition, an all-Ireland side played England for the first time and crashed by the improbable score of 13–0 in Belfast. This is still a record for any British International match, and is not likely to be broken.

At this period, new developments in the game were coming thick and fast as its popularity spread rapidly. The official Home International Championship was first played for in the season 1883–84 and Scotland had a clean sweep, winning all three matches. In 1885 professionalism was legalized in English soccer, and a year later Arbroath carved their own slice of history by winning a Scottish Cup tie 36–0 against the luckless, and long-since defunct Bon Accord. This remains the highest score in any official senior football match in Britain. The present-day off-side law and the system of early-round elimination of weak teams both help to ensure that this kind of farce will never be seen again.

In October 1887, Preston North End made a brave effort to challenge Arbroath's feat when they annihilated Hyde 26–0 in an F.A. Cup match. Whether the Preston players had their eye on the record will never be known, but they certainly had no mercy on poor Hyde.

Soccer moved fast in the eighties. The Football League was formed in 1888 and for those who wonder why it should be honoured with the title *The* Football League, and not the English Football League, the answer is that it was the first such body in the world.

How many of today's soccer followers can reel off the names of those famous twelve clubs which formed the basis of what has become the world's greatest league competition? They were Accrington, Aston Villa, Blackburn Rovers, Bolton Wanderers, Burnley, Derby County, Everton, Notts County, Preston North End, Stoke City, West Bromwich Albion and Wolverhampton Wanderers. Of that number, only Accrington are not still members; they left the League in March 1962, after struggling through the years since the Second World War as Accrington Stanley, and are now to be found playing in the Lancashire Combination.

In 1970 two other founder members, Aston Villa and

Preston, were relegated to Division Three for the first time in their history. The following year Blackburn Rovers went down for the first time, along with Bolton, another of the famous originals. Such is the swing of fortune in soccer across the decades.

Modern fans think of Tottenham Hotspur in 1961 and Arsenal ten years later as the 'double clubs', i.e. those which have won both the League Championship and the F.A. Cup in the same season. But as long ago as 1888–89, the year in which the League began, Preston won the Cup without conceding a goal, and the Championship without losing a game. This was quite an achievement, even if competition was a lot less fierce in those days, and Aston Villa were the only other side before Tottenham, in 1960–61, to win both trophies in one season. They did it in the season 1896–97.

Floodlights are regarded as one of the wonders of modern soccer. But how many people realize that matches were being played under artificial light long before the end of last century? The first reference to a 'floodlit' game is found in records dated 1887, which tells of a game being played at Sheffield by *candlelight*! This is a difficult scene to imagine, but the players must have managed somehow.

As the nineteenth century drew to a close, the game continued to boom. Attendances rose each year, and while there was no sign yet of international competition against foreign opponents, the game was slowly being introduced abroad.

It is impossible to tell when football was first taught to other countries—to the Brazilians for example—but we do know that British sailors had a lot to do with it. The British Navies, Royal and Merchant, were at the height of their power and influence in the fifty years between 1875 and 1925, and it was during this half century that the game was taken round the world. Sailors on leave abroad often played football among themselves; local inhabitants watched with interest, learned quickly, and soon challenged the soccer 'missionaries' and sometimes beat them.

The first International match between England and a foreign country took place on 6 June 1908. England met Austria in Vienna and won handsomely 6–1. Two days later the teams met again at the same venue and this time the Austrians were beaten 11–1. England then went on to Budapest, and crushed Hungary 7–0, before moving finally to Prague and soundly defeating Bohemia (now Czechoslovakia) 4–0 to end a highly successful first professional tour abroad.

The following year the Austrians invited England back, no doubt hoping for revenge. This time they lost 8—1, so in three games in twelve months against the Austrians, all of them in Vienna, England piled up an aggregate of 25 goals and lost only three. However, and significantly in terms of the improvement in soccer standards abroad, when the teams next met, in May 1930—again in Vienna—there was a goalless draw, and when Austria first played here (at Chelsea in December 1932) England only just scraped home 4—3.

England should have been warned during the year between those two games, when the Scots crashed by a humiliating 5—0 in Vienna!

Despite that 1908 England tour, international football with overseas countries competing did not become established until the early thirties. The 1914—18 War had much to do with that, and throughout the twenties the total of matches played abroad by England was no more than fifteen.

It was not until the summer of 1950 that any British country played a team from the Americas. This was when England participated in the World Cup for the first time. They beat Chile 2—0 in their opening match of the final series in Brazil, but 29 June marked the blackest day in the entire playing history of British soccer. From Belo Horizonte came what must rate as the most fantastic scoreline in the international game: England 0, U.S.A. 1. It was a result which rocked the footballing world. Perhaps the least excited country was the United States itself, so little interest did they show in the game of Association Football.

To the North Americans soccer was, and to a large extent still is, a minority sport, and that freak result was as unlikely as, say England beating the U.S.A. at baseball. But it happened!

This match belongs, however, to soccer's comparatively modern history, and there is reason here to go back to the turn of the century. In the season 1898—99 a feat occurred which almost certainly will never be repeated in British soccer. Rangers, who over the years have been Scotland's most successful club despite the recent dominance of Celtic, took the Scottish League title in a canter. They won every one of the 18 games they played in the competition, and even allowing for the relatively low standard of Scottish club soccer, it was a tremendous achievement.

The overall standards of play in Scotland are certainly low. A look at past winners of the Scottish League Championship tells the tale. In 1932 Motherwell won the title for the first and only time. Apart from that year, the championship was shared between Rangers and Celtic from 1904, when it was won by Third Lanark, to 1948 when Hibernian took it. During those years the title went to Rangers no fewer than 20 times, and to Celtic 15. Indeed Motherwell's surprise victory in 1932 interrupted a run of eight consecutive successes for Rangers.

Occasionally, in Scotland, other sides have made temporary challenges. Airdrieonians for example, were runners-up in the League in 1923–24–25–26—a frustrating experience. The Edinburgh clubs Hibernian (three times) and Heart of Midlothian (twice) have won the Championship since the war.

Aberdeen have challenged strongly in recent years. But for the good of club soccer in Scotland it remains a sad fact that in the past 75 years the Scottish title has failed to reach Rangers or Celtic on only eleven occasions. Compare that with the situation in England, where at the start of each season the ultimate winners could come from any of a dozen clubs.

But if Scottish football tended to stagnate because of the great strength of Rangers and Celtic, the game elsewhere grew in power. The development that was to make soccer a world game came in 1904, when F.I.F.A.—the Federation of International Football Associations—was founded in Paris. Seven countries—France, Belgium, Holland, Switzerland, Spain, Denmark and Sweden—were the original members. Today there are 138 members of the world body.

Amateur soccer, or rather a twentieth century version of the original amateur game, came along in 1907 when the Amateur F.A. was formed and the following year Britain put a team in the Olympic Games and won the final at London's White City, beating Denmark 2–0.

The 1914–18 War inevitably caused a major disruption in sport, and football suffered along with the rest. Unlike the 1939–45 War, when unofficial soccer continued as a means of giving the population something else to think about, there was virtually nothing organized. But when the war ended the game soon got back into its stride. A look at the 1920s tells us that. . . . *In 1923* Wembley staged its first Cup Final, with an attendance of 126,000, many of whom stormed the gates and broke in. *In 1926* Huddersfield Town won the League Championship for the third successive year, the first team to do so, and a feat as yet emulated only by Arsenal in 1933–34–35. Huddersfield were also runners-up in 1927, and again in

1928, the greatest period in their history.

In 1927 Cardiff City beat Arsenal 1–0 at Wembley and became the first, and only, side to take the F.A. Cup out of England. This feat is still reckoned to be the most outstanding in Welsh soccer, which has always had to take second place in popularity to rugby. *In 1929* England lost for the first time on foreign soil, Spain triumphing 4–3 in Madrid, and the following year the World Cup was launched.

Uruguay beat Argentina 4–2 in the Final, and South America was on the world soccer map. And so into the thirties.

The record individual number of goals in any British senior League or Cup match was set in April 1936 when Joe Payne, Luton Town centre-forward, scored ten in his club's 12–0 win against Bristol Rovers in a Division 3 match.

A year later the largest crowd ever to watch a match in Britain squeezed into Hampden Park for the Scotland–England International. The official attendance was 149,547, and unless a new stadium is built it is a British record which will never be broken. Still in Scotland, Celtic's Jimmy McGrory retired in 1938 after scoring an all-time record 550 goals in first-class soccer. This was a record for Britain; overseas players have scored more—Brazil's Pele has topped the 1000 mark.

If Scottish club soccer was often overshadowed on the field by its English counterpart, the largest crowds were to be found north of the Border. Manchester United and Arsenal set up the still-existing record for an English League match—82,950. That was on 17 January 1948, at Maine Road (United were still using Manchester City's ground while their own at Old Trafford was being restored after bomb damage during the War). In March of the same year Rangers and Hibernian met in the Scottish Cup semi-final at Hampden Park in front of 143,570. Then, in the Final, nearly a quarter of a million fans saw the two matches Rangers needed to beat Greenock Morton. Those were the days of the great crowds, after years when people had been starved of top-class competitive football.

Coming more up to date—although that depends to a large extent on the age of the reader—in 1953 Stanley Mortensen scored a hat-trick in the Coronation Year F.A. Cup Final against Bolton Wanderers. He was the first man to achieve such a feat, but even his success was over-shadowed by that of his partner, Stanley (now Sir Stanley) Matthews.

Bolton, led by Nat Lofthouse, were 3–1 ahead well into the second half. It seemed all over for Blackpool, and for the great Matthews who had never won a Cup-winners' medal, and was playing in what was to be his last Final. Then the two Stanleys broke loose. Matthews mesmerized a Bolton side playing one short after injury—there were no substitutes then —and Blackpool triumphed 4–3.

It was a sad ending for Bolton, who have never been quite the same since, but a fairy-tale finish for Blackpool and Stanley Matthews in one of the great all-time F.A. Cup Finals.

The 'Matthews Final' could be regarded as almost the end of an era in British football. Six months later, at Wembley in November 1953, came the 6–3 slaughter of England by Hungary—those magnificent Magyars—which led to a vast re-thinking on the game's tactics and economics. The sequel has been that, in less than 20 years since, football has made its greatest strides within Britain's shores, as indeed it had to do if it was to keep up with the growth of soccer abroad.

A new competitive dimension was brought to the game in 1955 with the launching of the European Cup, and both in that and the two other big European tournaments—the Cup-Winners' Cup and Fairs Cup (now the U.E.F.A. Cup) British clubs have figured prominently among the honours, as will be seen from reference to the European section of this book.

One of the most important factors in the revolution within British football was the removal of the maximum wage in 1961. This ensured that our stars did not need to go to Italy to earn salaries commensurate with their skills, as world-class players like John Charles, Denis Law, Jimmy Greaves and others had been disposed to do.

In 1965 came the long-overdue acceptance of substitutes in League football. A year later came the greatest achievement of all for British soccer, with England's triumph at Wembley as host nation in the World Cup. And now Sir Alf Ramsey is busy planning how that world crown, which was handed over to Brazil in Mexico in 1970, can be won back in Munich in 1974.

Guide to the 92 Football League Clubs in England and Wales

as at the end of the 1971–72 season

Aldershot

Recreation Ground,
High St., Aldershot.
Aldershot 20211

Shirts: Red
Shorts: Red
Stockings: Red

The years of the Second World War provided Aldershot with the most colourful teams in their history. Many of the game's best names were on military service in the garrison town and appeared as guests for the club. Among them were Frank Swift, Tommy Lawton, Matt Busby, Denis Compton, and the full England half-back line of that era, Cliff Britton, Stan Cullis and Joe Mercer.

In more settled times Aldershot have rarely achieved much of distinction. Indeed in seasons in the old Third Division South they never figured higher than tenth. That was in 1938–39.

Since then their most successful season was in 1969–70 when they were sixth in Division Four. That was the season, too, when they attracted their record attendance to the Recreation Ground, 19,138 watching their fourth round F.A. Cup replay against Carlisle.

Another notable Cup triumph occurred in 1963–64 when they defeated Aston Villa, then a Division One team, 2–1 after a goalless draw at Villa Park. Aldershot can claim a share of at least one record—that of the quickest goal. Albert Mundy scored six seconds after the kick-off at Hartlepool on 25 October 1958.

Record attendance: 19,138 v. Carlisle (F.A. Cup), January 1970
Modern Capacity: 20,000.
Entered Football League: 1932—Div. 3 (South).
Biggest win: 8–1 v. Gateshead (Div. 4), September 1958.
Heaviest defeat: 0–9 v. Bristol City (Div. 3 South), December 1946.
Highest final League position: 6th in Div. 4, 1969–70.
Best in F.A. Cup: 5th Round, 1932–33.
Best in Football League Cup: 2nd Round, 1960–61, 1962–63, 1963–64, 1965–66, 1966–67, 1970–71, 1971–72.
Pitch measurements: $117\frac{1}{2} \times 76$ yd.
Highest League Scorer in Single Season: R. Fogg—24 in 1963–64 (Div. 4).
Transfers—
    Highest fee paid: £9000—Jimmy Melia (from Southampton), November 1968.
    Highest fee received: £50,000—Joe Jopling (to Leicester), September 1970.

Arsenal

Arsenal Stadium,
Highbury, London, N5.
01—226—3312

Shirts: Red, White Sleeves
Shorts: White
Stockings: Red, with Thin
White Band

By performing the League Championship—F.A. Cup double in 1971, Arsenal not only caught up with their illustrious past—they exceeded it. They became the first club to win the Championship eight times, and the 'double' was signalled by Bertie Mee being voted 'Manager of the Year' and captain Frank McLintock winning the 'Footballer of the Year' award.

Arsenal have been constant members of Division One since 1919, and their greatest era until the seventies occurred during the 1930's when they 'came to power' under the managership of Herbert Chapman. They were League Champions in 1931, 1933, 1934, 1935, and 1938, and won the F.A. Cup in 1930 and 1936.

After the war they won the First Division title in 1948 and 1953, and the F.A. Cup again in 1950. But then came a long period of non-success from which the way back to former glory followed two losing appearances in the Football League Cup Final.

In the 1970 Fairs Cup they achieved their first European prize; a year later they completed the double and, in a bid to add to their laurels, in December 1971 Arsenal paid a new British record transfer fee of £220,000 for Alan Ball, from Everton.

League Champions: 1930—31, 1932—33, 1933—34, 1934—35, 1937—38, 1947—48, 1952—53, 1970—71.
F.A. Cup Winners: 1929—30, 1935—36, 1949—50, 1970—71.
European Fairs Cup Winners: 1969—70.
The Double (League and F.A. Cup Winners): 1970—71.
Record attendance: 73,295 v. Sunderland (League), March 1935.
Modern Capacity: 63,000.
Entered Football League: 1893—Div. 2.
Biggest win: 12—0 v. Loughborough T. (Div. 2), March 1900.
Heaviest defeat: 0—8 v. Loughborough T. (Div. 2), December 1896.
Best in Football League Cup: Runners-up 1967—68, 1968—69.
Pitch measurements: 110 × 71 yd.
Highest League Scorer in Single Season: E. Drake—43 in 1934—35 (Div. 1).
Transfers—
  Highest fee paid: £220,000—Alan Ball (from Everton), December 1971.
  Highest fee received: £100,000—Jon Sammels (to Leicester), July 1971.

Aston Villa

Villa Park,
Trinity Road,
Birmingham 6, 6HE.
021–327–6604

Shirts: Claret, Light Blue
  Collar and Sleeves
Shorts: White
Stockings: White

The deeds of few clubs are written as deeply into the game's history as those of Aston Villa. They were among the 12 founder members of the Football League in 1888; they were Champions 6 times between 1894 and 1910, and in 1897 achieved the 'double' of League title and F.A. Cup, a feat previously performed by Preston N.E. in 1888–89 and which Tottenham Hotspur (1960–61) and Arsenal (1970–71) have since equalled. When they finished runners-up to Arsenal in 1930–31, they scored 128 League goals, which remains a record for a First Division club. In addition, Villa won the Football League Cup in 1961, its inaugural year.

Certainly, those lads of the Aston Villa Wesleyan Church could never have realized in 1874 what glories the club they formed would achieve! It would need many pages to record Villa's great players: Charlie Wallace, Harold Halse, Harry Hampton, Clem Stephenson and Joe Bache (the 1913 Cup Final attack); Sam Hardy, Frank Barson, Andy Ducat, Frank Moss, 'Pongo' Waring, Billy Walker, Jimmy Hagan, Alex Massie, Trevor Ford, Peter McParland. These are but a few.

League Champions: 1893–94, 1895–96, 1896–97, 1898–99, 1899–1900, 1909–10.
Division 2 Champions: 1937–38, 1959–60.
Division 3 Champions: 1971–72.
F.A. Cup Winners: 1886–87, 1894–95, 1896–97, 1904–05, 1912–13, 1919–20, 1956–57.
League Cup Winners: 1960–61.
The Double (League and F.A. Cup Winners): 1896–97.
Record attendance: 76,588 v. Derby County (F.A. Cup), March 1946.
Modern Capacity: 64,000.
Entered Football League: 1888—Div. 1.
Biggest win: 13–0 v. Wednesbury Old Athletic (F.A. Cup), 1886–87.
Heaviest defeat: 1–8 v. Blackburn R. (F.A. Cup), 1888–89.
Pitch measurements: 115 × 75 yd.
Highest League Scorer in Single Season: T. Waring—49 in 1930–31 (Div. 1).
Transfers—
  Highest fee paid: £100,000—Bruce Rioch (from Luton), July 1969.
  Highest fee received: £100,000—Tony Hateley (to Chelsea), October 1966.

Barnsley

Oakwell Ground,
Grove Street, Barnsley.
Barnsley 4113

Shirts: Red
Shorts: White
Stockings: Red

Ever since their formation, Barnsley have known the extremes of fortune. Often, it must be said, the emphasis has been on the struggle to make ends meet. Yet there have been great occasions such as winning the F.A. Cup as a Second Division side in 1912 after herculean efforts against West Bromwich Albion. The teams met first at the old Crystal Palace in a goalless draw, and Barnsley snatched victory by the only goal during extra time in the replay at Bramall Lane, Sheffield. This was deserved compensation for their 2—0 defeat by Newcastle, in the Final two years earlier, when a second match was also required to decide the outcome.

One of their biggest disappointments was missing promotion to Division One in 1922 on goal average. Three times Barnsley were Third Division North Champions: in 1933—34, when they scored 118 goals; in 1938—39, when they won 30 and drew 7 of their 42 League games; and in 1954—55.

Like other clubs living in the shadows of better-known neighbours, Barnsley have discovered many stars, among them Eric Brook and Fred Tilson, who together played in Manchester City's 1934 F.A. Cup-winning team; George Hunt, Wilf Copping, Dick Spence, Danny Blanchflower and Tommy Taylor, who lost his life in the Munich air disaster involving Manchester United in February, 1958.

F.A. Cup Winners: 1911—12.
Division 3 (North) Champions: 1933—34, 1938—39, 1954—55.
Record attendance: 42,056 v. Stoke (F.A. Cup), February 1935.
Modern Capacity: 38,500.
Entered Football League: 1898—Div. 2.
Biggest win: 9—0 v. Loughborough T. (Div. 2), January 1899 and 9—0 v. Accrington Stanley (Div. 3 North), February 1934.
Heaviest defeat: 0—9 v. Notts County (Div. 2), November 1927.
Best in Football League Cup: 3rd Round, 1962—63.
Pitch measurements: 110 × 74 yd.
Highest League Scorer in Single Season: C. McCormack—33 in 1950—51 (Div. 2).
Transfers—
    Highest fee paid: £20,000 (joint fee)—Frank Sharp and Leslie Lea (from Cardiff), August 1970.
    Highest fee received: £40,000—Stuart Barraclough (to Newcastle), July 1970.

Barrow

Holker Street,
Barrow-in-Furness.
Barrow 20346/23061

Shirts: White
Shorts: Royal Blue
Stockings: White

Honours have always been elusive for Barrow since they were one of the original members of the old Division Three North in 1921. In fact, their one season of triumph came in 1966–67 when, by finishing third with 59 points, they won promotion to the reconstituted Third Division. But, unhappily for them, their stay was comparatively brief, and they were relegated in 1970.

If present-day followers of football do not associate Barrow with goalscoring feats, those who supported the club in pre-war days will remember the 1933–34 season with particular relish. That season Barrow scored 116 goals, more than any other club in the land except Barnsley (118), the Third Division North champions that year. Their 19 League wins included a 12–1 trouncing of Gateshead. Barrow who finished in eighth place, might have won promotion but for conceding 94 goals. J. Shankly scored 39 of those League goals, which remains a club record.

The rare days of large crowds at Holker Street are moments to be savoured by the hard core of Barrow enthusiasts. Such an occasion was 9 January 1954 when 16,840 squeezed into the ground for an F.A. Cup-tie. They saw Swansea Town, then a Second Division club, held to a 2–2 draw. But Barrow lost the replay 4–2.

Record attendance: 16,840 v. Swansea (F.A. Cup), January 1954.
Modern Capacity: 16,500.
Entered Football League: 1921—Div. 3 (North).
Biggest win: 12–1 v. Gateshead (Div. 3 North), May 1934.
Heaviest defeat: 1–10 v. Hartlepool (Div. 4), April 1959.
Highest final League position: 3rd in Div. 4, 1966–67.
Best in F.A. Cup: 3rd Round, 1945–46, 1947–48, 1953–54, 1955–56, 1958–59, 1963–64, 1966–67, 1967–68.
Best in Football League Cup: 3rd Round, 1962–63, 1967–68.
Pitch measurements: 111 × 76 yd.
Highest League Scorer in Single Season: J. Shankly—39 in 1933–34 (Div. 3, North).
Transfers— ·
  Highest fee paid: £7000—David Storf (from Rochdale), July 1967.
  Highest fee received: £20,000—George Smith (to Portsmouth), May 1967.

Birmingham City

St Andrew's,
Birmingham, B9 4NH.
021—772—0101/2689

Shirts: Royal Blue, Broad
     White Stripe on Front
Shorts: White
Stockings: Royal Blue

Although the League Championship, F.A. Cup and European prizes still elude them, Birmingham City have seldom been short of class players in one or more key positions. Their speciality has been goalkeepers of international calibre, among them Dan Tremelling, Harry Hibbs, Gil Merrick and Jim Herriot.

As Small Heath, the club were founder members of Division Two in 1892. They stepped into Division One in 1894, but slipped back two years later. Promotion came once more in 1901, but this time they lasted only one season. They climbed again in 1903; the name Small Heath was dropped in favour of Birmingham in 1905, and a year later they moved to their present St Andrew's home from Muntz Street.

Another spell in Division Two was from 1908 until 1921, when they took the Championship on goal average. Then followed an 18-year spell in the top grade that lasted until 1939 and included their first, but unsuccessful, F.A. Cup visit to Wembley in 1931.

After the 1939—45 war they had another unsettled period under the new title of Birmingham City, with promotion in 1948, relegation in 1950, promotion in 1955, and relegation again in 1965.

Division 2 Champions: 1892—93, 1920—21, 1947—48, 1954—55.
League Cup Winners: 1962—63.
Record attendance: 66,844 v. Everton (F.A. Cup), Feb. 1939.
Modern Capacity: 52,500.
Entered Football League: 1892—Div. 2.
Biggest win: 12—0 v. Walsall Town Swifts (Div. 2), December 1892 and 12—0 v. Doncaster Rovers (Div. 2), April 1903.
Heaviest defeat: 1—9 v. Sheffield Wednesday (Div. 1), December 1930.
Best in F.A. Cup: Final, 1930—31, 1955—56.
Pitch measurements: 115 × 74 yd.
Highest League Scorer in Single Season: J. Bradford—29 in 1927—28 (Div. 1).
Transfers—
    Highest fee paid: £80,000—Bob Hatton (from Carlisle), October 1971.
    Highest fee received: £100,000—Jimmy Greenhoff (to Stoke), August 1969.

Blackburn Rovers

Ewood Park,
Blackburn, BB2 4JF.
Blackburn 55432/3

Shirts: Blue and White Halves
Shorts: White
Stockings: White with Blue Rings

The F.A. Cup was almost the exclusive property of Blackburn Rovers during the latter part of the last century. They won the trophy in three successive years, 1884–86, and again in 1890 and 1891, then had to wait 37 years to win it for the sixth time by beating Huddersfield 3–1 at Wembley in 1928.

Rovers were original members of the Football League in 1888 and carried off the First Division Championship in 1912 and 1914. They remained continuously in the top flight of League clubs until 1936. Since then, however, they have had varying spells in the Second Division and their fortunes slumped to a new low in 1970–71 when, together with Bolton Wanderers, another Lancashire club steeped in tradition, they dropped into Division Three.

Many chroniclers of the game—and certainly those old enough to remember—maintain that Bob Crompton was the finest full-back of any era. In the early part of the century he was capped 34 times for England and played for Rovers for 23 years. Another fine full-back Bill Eckersley, served England with distinction, winning 17 caps in the early 1950s, and Rovers must sigh today for a marksman in the mould of Ted Harper who scored 43 goals in Division One in 1925–26.

League Champions: 1911–12, 1913–14.
Second Division Champions: 1938–39.
F.A. Cup Winners: 1883–84, 1884–85, 1885–86, 1889–90, 1890–91, 1927–28.
Record attendance: 61,783 v. Bolton (F.A. Cup), March 1929.
Modern Capacity: 52,000.
Entered Football League: 1888—Div. 1.
Biggest win: 11–0 v. Rossendale United (F.A. Cup), 1884–85.
Heaviest defeat: 0–8 v. Arsenal (Div. 1), February 1933.
Best in Football League Cup: Semi-final 1961–62.
Pitch measurements: 116 × 72 yd.
Highest League Scorer in Single Season: E. Harper—43 in 1925–26 (Div. 1).
Transfers—
    Highest fee paid: £60,000—Jimmy Kerr (from Bury), May 1970.
    Highest fee received: £95,000—Mike England (to Tottenham), August 1966.

Blackpool

Bloomfield Road,
Blackpool, FY1 6JJ.
Blackpool 46118

Shirts: Tangerine
Shorts: White
Stockings: Tangerine

Their appearances at Wembley in the years immediately after the Second World War will remain treasured memories for all associated with the Blackpool club. They went down 4–2 to Manchester United in the 1948 F.A. Cup Final, which has a place among Wembley's finest games; then they lost 2–0 to Newcastle in 1951 and finally came their memorable 4–3 triumph over Bolton in 1953. That was the match in which Stanley Matthews inspired his team-mates to snatch victory.

Stanley Mortensen, who achieved a hat-trick in the Bolton final, scored nearly 200 League goals for the club he later managed. Another notable personality of that era was the captain, Harry Johnston, who received the 'Footballer of the Year' award in 1951—of which Matthews was the first holder in 1948.

Blackpool came closest to taking the First Division title in 1956 when they finished runners-up. They continued as a power through the fifties when much of the credit was due to their astute manager Joe Smith, the former England and Bolton inside forward who served from 1935 to 1958.

After being relegated in 1967, they bounced back again in 1970, but their comeback lasted only one season as they finished bottom of Division One—a sad ending to the Blackpool career of one of their finest ever players, Jimmy Armfield, who made more than 550 League appearances for the club and was capped 43 times at full-back for England.

F.A. Cup Winners: 1952–53.
Second Division Champions: 1929–30.
Record attendance: 39,118 v. Man. Utd. (League), April 1952.
Modern Capacity: 38,000.
Entered Football League: 1896—Div. 2.
Biggest win: 8–4 v. Charlton Ath. (Div. 1), September 1952.
Heaviest defeat: 1–10 v. Huddersfield Town (Div. 1), December 1930.
Best in Football League Cup: Semi-final 1961–62.
Pitch measurements: 111 × 73 yd.
Highest League Scorer in Single Season: J. Hampson—45 in 1929–30 (Div. 2).
Transfers—
   Highest fee paid: £60,000—Alan Suddick (from Newcastle), December 1966.
   Highest fee received: £150,000—Tony Green (to Newcastle), October 1971.

Bolton Wanderers

Burnden Park,
Bolton, BL3 2QR.
Bolton 21101

Shirts: White
Shorts: Navy Blue
Stockings: White

Three times between 1923—the first Wembley F.A. Cup Final—
and 1929, Bolton Wanderers won the game's most coveted
domestic trophy. They did so without conceding a single goal at
Wembley, and those were indeed golden years for one of the
founder members of the Football League. So it was a matter of
particular regret to many far beyond Bolton when this famous
club was relegated to Division Three, in 1971, for the first time.
Five Wanderers players took part in each of those successful
Finals—against West Ham in 1923 (2—0), Manchester City 1926
(1—0) and Portsmouth 1929 (2—0). They were Pym in goal,
Haworth, Nuttall, Seddon and Butler. Bolton won the Cup again
in 1958 and were losing finalists in 1894, 1904 and 1953.
Curiously, for all their Cup-fighting prowess and many years in
Division One, Bolton have never won the League Championship.
No one ever typified the fighting spirit of Wanderers better
than centre-forward Nat Lofthouse, the club's most-capped
player. He played 33 times for England and, between 1946—61,
scored 255 League goals—the club record.
Tragedy struck Burnden Park on 9 March 1946, when crush
barriers broke at an F.A. Cup-tie between Bolton and Stoke City.
Thirty-three people were killed and more than four hundred
injured in the worst football disaster ever known in England.

F.A. Cup Winners: 1922—23, 1925—26, 1928—29, 1957—58.
Second Division Champions: 1908—09.
Record attendance: 69,912 v. Manchester City (F.A. Cup),
February 1933.
Modern Capacity: 60,000.
Entered Football League: 1888—Div. 1.
Biggest win: 13—0 v. Sheffield United (F.A. Cup), February
1890.
Heaviest defeat: 0—7 v. Manchester City (Div. 1), March 1936.
Best in Football League Cup: 4th Round, 1960—61, 1971—
72.
Pitch measurements: $112\frac{1}{2} \times 76$ yd.
Highest League Scorer in Single Season: J. Smith—38 in
1920—21 (Div. 1).
Transfers—
   Highest fee paid: £70,000—Terry Wharton (from Wolves),
   October 1967.
   Highest fee received: £80,000—Wyn Davies (to New-
   castle), October 1966.

Bournemouth and Boscombe Athletic

Dean Court,
Bournemouth.
Bournemouth 35381

Shirts: Red and Black
  Stripes
Shorts: Black
Stockings: Black, with
  Red and White Tops

No era has been more exciting or rewarding for Bournemouth than the start of the seventies. Their promotion from the Fourth Division at the end of the 1970–71 season was followed by another year of splendid achievement in the Third.

During this time Ted MacDougall, a centre-forward sought by many prominent clubs, broke several Bournemouth goal-scoring records, among them most goals in a season, previously held by Ron Eyre with 32 in season 1928–29. During the successful 1970–71 season MacDougall was the Football League's highest scorer with 42, and the following season scored nine goals in a match—a new F.A. Cup record—when Bournemouth beat Margate 11–0 in the first round, their record victory.

Under the vibrant managership of the former West Ham United full-back John Bond, and an enthusiastic board of directors, Bournemouth's attractive football has recently drawn large crowds to Dean Court.

The club was originally known simply as Boscombe, but when elected to the Third Division (South) in 1923, Bournemouth was incorporated in the title. Apart from finishing runners-up in this section in 1947–48, the 'Cherries' have often figured prominently without attaining the heights of more recent times. During a thrilling F.A. Cup run in 1957, which took them to the sixth round, the club knocked out Wolves (1–0) and Spurs (3–1).

Record attendance: 28,799 v. Manchester United (F.A. Cup), March 1957.
Modern Capacity: 24,000.
Entered Football League: 1923—Div. 3 (South).
Biggest win: 11–0 v. Margate (F.A. Cup), November 1971.
Heaviest defeat: 1–8 v. Bradford City (Div. 3), January 1970.
Highest final League position: 2nd in Div. 3 South, 1947–48.
Best in F.A. Cup: 6th Round 1956–57.
Best in Football League Cup: 4th Round 1961–62, 1963–64.
Pitch measurements: 115 × 75 yd.
Highest League Scorer in Single Season: E. MacDougall—42 in 1970–71 (Div. 4).
Transfers—
  Highest fee paid: £30,000 Bobby Howe (from West Ham), January 1972.
  Highest fee received: £30,000—Roger Jones (to Blackburn), January 1970.

Bradford City

Valley Parade,
Bradford, BD8 7DY.
Bradford 2656

Shirts: Claret and Amber
Stripes
Shorts: Black
Stockings: Black with
Amber Tops

Bradford City are striving hard to keep first-class Association football alive in the area now that their neighbours, Bradford Park Avenue, have lost their membership of the Football League.

Yet most of City's glories belong to the past. They were in Division One between 1908 and 1922, and became the first holders of the present F.A. Cup in 1911 when they defeated Newcastle United 1–0 at Old Trafford, after a goalless draw at the old Crystal Palace. During seasons 1910–11 and 1911–12, Bradford City played 12 consecutive F.A. Cup ties without conceding a goal.

When they won the Third Division North title in season 1928–29, City scored 128 goals and obtained 63 points, by far their best statistics in League football.

Not surprisingly in an area noted for the handling game, Bradford City F.C. developed in 1903 from a Rugby club—Manningham. Since then a number of fine players have worn City's colours, among them Sam Barkas, Alf Quantrill, Tommy Cairns, Arthur Whitehurst (who scored seven goals v. Tranmere in 1929) Dicky Bond, Peter Logan, Willie Watson and Trevor Hockey.

F.A. Cup Winners: 1910–11.
Division 2 Champions: 1907–08.
Division 3 (North) Champions: 1928–29.
Record attendance: 39,146 v. Burnley (F.A. Cup), March 1911.
Modern Capacity: 24,000.
Entered Football League: 1903—Div. 2.
Biggest win: 11–1 v. Rotherham (Div. 3 North), August 1928.
Heaviest defeat: 1–9 v. Colchester Utd. (Div. 4), December 1961.
Best in Football League Cup: 5th Round 1964–65.
Pitch measurements: 112 × 71 yd.
Highest League Scorer in Single Season: D. Layne—34 in 1961–62 (Div. 4).
Transfers—
    Highest fee paid: £10,000—Ken Leek (from Northampton), November 1965.
    Highest fee received: £23,000—Bruce Bannister (to Bristol Rovers), November 1971.

Brentford

Griffin Park,
Braemar Road,
Brentford, Middlesex.
01—560—2021

Shirts: Red and White
Stripes
Shorts: Black, White
Striped Seams
Stockings: Black, Red and
White Hooped Tops.

A small band of sporting enthusiasts met in 1888 to discuss the formation of a Rugby club. Instead, by a single vote, they decided in favour of Association football—and that is how Brentford F.C. came into existence.

They became professional in 1900, and after successes in the Southern League became founder members of the Third Division in 1920, and under the progressive management of Harry Curtis they began a long period of success which took them into Division One in 1935. Among their achievements was to win all 21 home League matches in the Third Division (South) in season 1929—30 but, curiously, they failed to win promotion that year, finishing runners-up to Plymouth. In those days only the Champions went up. But in 1932—33 they took the title and added the Second Division crown just two seasons later.

After the Second World War, Brentford slipped from First to Fourth Division. In January 1967 they were near to going out of existence, but they resisted a take-over bid by Queen's Park Rangers, and by November 1971 they had cleared a debt of £104,000.

Division 2 Champions: 1934—35.
Division 3 (South) Champions: 1932—33.
Division 4 Champions: 1962—63.
Record attendance: 39,626 v. Preston N.E. (F.A. Cup), March 1938.
Modern Capacity: 38,000.
Entered Football League: 1920—Div. 3.
Biggest win: 9—0 v. Wrexham (Div. 3), October 1963.
Heaviest defeat: 0—7 v. Swansea (Div. 3 South), November 1924 and 0—7 v. Walsall (Div. 3 South), January 1957.
Best in F.A. Cup: 6th Round 1937—38, 1945—46, 1948—49.
Best in Football League Cup: 3rd Round 1960—61, 1968—69.
Pitch measurements: 114 × 75 yd.
Highest League Scorer in Single Season: J. Holliday—36 in 1932—33 (Div. 3 South).
Transfers—
  Highest fee paid: £17,500—John Dick (from West Ham), September 1962.
  Highest fee received: £30,000—Roger Cross (to Fulham), September 1971.

27

Brighton and Hove Albion

Goldstone Ground,
Old Shoreham Road,
Hove 4,
Sussex, BN3 7DE.
Brighton 739535

Shirts: Blue and White
Stripes
Shorts: White
Stockings: White, Blue
Trimmed Top

When Brighton and Hove Albion became Champions of the old Division Three (South) in 1958, there were hopes that a major club could develop in the popular seaside town. The crowd-drawing potential in the district is unlimited, as was illustrated on 27 December that year, when nearly 37,000 packed into the Goldstone Ground for the visit of Fulham. Unfortunately for Albion, they could not produce the players capable of surviving in a higher division for more than four seasons before the team was relegated.

Cup competitions have certainly produced some memorable occasions. In 1932 the Football Association made Brighton play through all the early qualifying rounds because application for exemption had been overlooked. And in a first round proper tie in November 1965, they recorded their biggest victory—a 10–1 beating of Wisbech.

While a Third Division club, Albion provided Tommy Cook to lead the England attack against Wales in 1925. Cook's marksmanship earned him 113 League goals between 1922–29.

Division 3 (South) Champions: 1957–58.
Division 4 Champions: 1964–65.
Record attendance: 36,747 v. Fulham (League), December 1958.
Modern Capacity: 38,000.
Entered Football League: 1920—Div. 3.
Biggest win: 10–1 v. Wisbech (F.A. Cup), November 1965.
Heaviest defeat: 0–9 v. Middlesbrough (League), August 1958.
Best in F.A. Cup: 5th Round 1929–30, 1932–33, 1945–46, 1959–60.
Best in Football League Cup: 4th Round 1966–67.
Pitch measurements: 112 × 75 yd.
Highest League Scorer in Single Season: A. Vallance—30 in 1929–30 (Div. 3 South).
Transfers—
    Highest fee paid: £25,000—Chris (Kit) Napier (from Newcastle), August 1967; £25,000—Ken Beamish (from Tranmere), March 1972.
    Highest fee received: £15,000—Bill Curry (to Derby), September 1960.

Bristol City

Ashton Gate,
Bristol, BS3
Bristol 664093

Shirts: Red, White Trim
Shorts: White
Stockings: Red and White

Nothing they have achieved since can compare with Bristol City's performances before the First World War. In their first season in Division One, in 1906–07, they finished runners-up to Newcastle, and two years later reached the F.A. Cup Final for the only time in their history. Playing in that match at the old Crystal Palace which Manchester United won 1–0 was Billy Wedlock, probably the greatest of all City's servants. He was only five feet four, but as a centre-half he represented England for six successive seasons.

In more recent times John Atyeo, a Second Division striker good enough to win England caps, made 645 League and F.A. Cup appearances between 1951 and 1966, scoring 350 goals.

Since those heady early years Bristol City have never been able to regain First Division status, which they surrendered in 1911. They have alternated between Divisions Two and Three during the past 60 years with seasons of occasional brilliance, such as 1954–55 when they strode away with the old Third Division (South) title. They obtained 70 points—nine more than the second club.

In September 1971 they received their record transfer fee of £100,000, when Chris Garland signed for Chelsea.

Divison 2 Champions: 1905–06.
Division 3 (South) Champions: 1922–23, 1926–27, 1954–55.
Record attendance: 43,335 v. Preston N.E. (F.A. Cup), February 1935.
Modern Capacity: 40,500.
Entered Football League: 1901—Div. 2.
Biggest win: 11–0 v. Chichester (F.A. Cup), November 1960.
Heaviest defeat: 0–9 v. Coventry City (League), April 1934.
Best in F.A. Cup: Final 1908–09.
Best in Football League Cup: Semi-final 1970–71.
Pitch measurements: 115×78 yd.
Highest League Scorer in Single Season: D. Clark—36 in 1946–47 (Div. 3 South).
Transfers—
    Highest fee paid: £35,000—Bobby Kellard (from Portsmouth), July 1968.
    Highest fee received: £100,000—Chris Garland (to Chelsea), September 1971.

Bristol Rovers

Bristol Stadium,
Eastville,
Bristol 5, BS5 6NN.
Bristol 558620

Shirts: Blue
Shorts: White
Stockings: White

Twice during the 1950s Bristol Rovers finished sixth in Division Two. That is the closest they have been to joining the élite of the Football League. For most of their existence, which grew out of the picturesquely named Black Arabs club, Rovers have spent their days in the more modest company of the Third Division (South) and the Third Division. They won the old South section convincingly enough in 1953, losing only eight of their 46 matches, and with centre-forward Geoff Bradford setting a new club record by scoring 33 League goals that season.

Rovers have always had a reputation for developing their own players, and Ronnie Dix, Phil Taylor, Roy Bentley and Larry Lloyd are just a few who have achieved distinction elsewhere.

Unlike their neighbours, Bristol City, the Rovers have never reached the Final of the F.A. Cup. The furthest they have gone is the sixth round, in 1951 and 1958—the year in which they knocked out Burnley, then a First Division side.

Division 3 (South) Champions: 1952—53.
Record attendance: 38,472 v. Preston N.E. (F.A. Cup), January 1960.
Modern Capacity: 40,000.
Entered Football League: 1920—Div. 3.
Biggest League win: 7—0 v. Swansea (Div. 2), October 1954; 7—0 v. Brighton (Div. 3 South), November 1952; 7—0 v. Shrewsbury (Div. 3), March 1964.
Heaviest defeat: 0—12 v. Luton Town (Div. 3 South), April 1936.
Best in F.A. Cup: 6th Round 1950—51, 1957—58.
Best in Football League Cup: 5th Round 1970—71, 1971—72.
Pitch measurements: 112 × 76 yd.
Highest League Scorer in Single Season: G. Bradford—33 in 1952—53 (Div. 3 South).
Transfers—
    Highest fee paid: £25,000—Brian Godfrey (from Aston Villa), May 1971.
    Highest fee received: £50,000—Larry Lloyd (to Liverpool), April 1969.

Burnley

Turf Moor,
Burnley.
Burnley 27777

Shirts: Claret, Blue Collar and Cuffs.
Shorts: White
Stockings: White, Claret and Blue
Hooped Turnover

Burnley shattered all records in the Football League in season 1920–21, by playing 30 consecutive matches without defeat. This memorable League record from 6 September to 25 March read: played 30, won 21, drawn 9, goals 68–17, points 51. Thus Burnley won the First Division title for the first time in their history, and their record unbeaten sequence was not surpassed until 1969–70 when Leeds played 34 matches before losing.

Burnley, one of the League's founder clubs in 1888, lost their place in Division One for season 1897–98, when they were Second Division Champions. They dropped again from 1900–13, and the following year won the F.A. Cup for the only time so far.

Another successful period for Burnley, who have astutely operated the transfer market to survive in the shadow of the two glamour clubs of Manchester, occurred in the early 1960s. They won the League Championship for the second time in 1960, and two years later finished runners-up both in Division One and in the F.A. Cup. But by 1971 their playing fortunes slumped and relegation ended a spell of 24 years in the First Division.

League Champions: 1920–21, 1959–60.
Division 2 Champions: 1897–98.
F.A. Cup Winners: 1913–14.
Record attendance: 54,775 v. Huddersfield Town (F.A. Cup), February 1924.
Modern Capacity (while under alteration): 39,000.
Entered Football League: 1888—Div. 1.
Biggest League win: 9–0 v. Darwen (Div. 1), January 1892; 9–0 v. Crystal Palace (F.A. Cup), 1908–09; 9–0 v. New Brighton (F.A. Cup), January 1957.
Heaviest League defeat: 0–10 v. Aston Villa (Div. 1), August 1925 and 0–10 v. Sheffield United (Div. 1), January 1929.
Best in Football League Cup: Semi-final 1960–61, 1968–69.
Pitch measurements: $115\frac{1}{2} \times 73$ yd.
Highest League Scorer in Single Season: G. Beel—35 in 1927–28 (Div. 1).
Transfers—
  Highest fee paid: £60,000—Paul Fletcher (from Bolton), March 1971.
  Highest fee received: £190,000—Ralph Coates (to Tottenham), May 1971.

Bury

Gigg Lane,
Bury, BL9 9HR.
061—764—4881/2

Shirts: White
Shorts: Royal Blue
Stockings: Royal Blue,
White Band

Bury, nicknamed 'The Shakers', have certainly stirred the football world in their time, starting from season 1894—95, when they won the Second Division championship in their first year as League members. Five years later they defeated Southampton 4—0 in the F.A. Cup Final at the old Crystal Palace, and in 1903 they caused an even bigger stir by winning the trophy again without conceding a single goal in any of their ties. They trounced Derby County on the same ground by six goals to nil— which remains the biggest winning margin in the Final.

Bury stayed in the First Division for seventeen seasons; they dropped to the Second Division in 1912 and regained higher status in 1924, but this time they survived for only five seasons. Since then they have achieved occasional periods of glory such as winning the Division Three title in 1960—61 by a margin of six points. They reached the semi-final of the Football League Cup in season 1962—63 before losing 4—3 on aggregate to Birmingham City, the eventual winners of the trophy. Bury showed their tenacity as Cup fighters in 1955 when they played Stoke City for a record 9 hours 22 minutes, in five meetings in the F.A. Cup third round before Stoke won 3—2 at Old Trafford. But in recent times 'The Shakers' have themselves been shaken as they slipped back to the Third Division in 1967 and then to the Fourth.

F.A. Cup Winners: 1899—1900, 1902—03.
Division 2 Champions: 1894—95.
Division 3 Champions: 1960—61.
Record attendance: 35,000 v. Bolton Wanderers (F.A. Cup), January 1960.
Modern Capacity: 35,000.
Entered Football League: 1894—Div. 2.
Biggest win: 12—1 v. Stockton (F.A. Cup), 1896—97.
Heaviest defeat: 0—10 v. Blackburn Rovers (F.A. Cup), 1887—88.
Best in Football League Cup: Semi-final 1962—63.
Pitch measurements: 116 × 80 yd.
Highest League Scorer in Single Season: N. Bullock—31 in 1925—26 (Div. 1).
Transfers—
    Highest fee paid: £25,000—Alf Arrowsmith (from Liverpool), December 1968.
    Highest fee received: £60,000—Alec Lindsay (to Liverpool), March 1969.

Cambridge United

The Abbey Stadium,
534 Newmarket Road,
Cambridge.
Teversham 2170

Shirts: White, Amber and
    Black Neck and Cuffs
Shorts: White
Stockings: White

The remarkable rise of Cambridge United should serve as an inspiration to all those clubs seeking Football League status. From the moment they turned professional in 1946, Cambridge United rapidly established a reputation as a progressive-thinking club while playing in the Cambridgeshire, Eastern Counties and Southern Leagues. They won the Southern League Championship in successive years, 1968—69 and 1969—70, and by then their credentials had so impressed Football League clubs that at the annual meeting, in June 1970, they were elected to the Fourth Division in place of Bradford Park Avenue.

Understandably the switch to higher class football produced many fresh challenges for Cambridge and the first season in the League was very much one of trial and error. The team displayed reasonably consistent form at the Abbey Stadium, losing only five of their 23 League matches, but points were seldom easy to obtain on opponents' grounds. In the end, Cambridge finished only just clear of the four re-election places.

One of the highlights of their inaugural year as a Football League club was a friendly fixture with Chelsea, in May 1970, which attracted a ground record of 14,000. The match was Chelsea's 'thank you' for signing Ian Hutchinson, who had joined them from Cambridge in July 1968 and quickly won England Under-23 honours.

Record attendance: 14,000 v. Chelsea (Friendly), May 1970.
Modern Capacity: 16,000.
Entered Football League: 1970—Div. 4.
Biggest League win: 6—0 v. Darlington (Div. 4), September 1971.
Heaviest defeat: 0—5 v. Colchester (League Cup), August 1970.
Highest final League position: 18th in Div. 4, 1970—71.
Best in F.A. Cup: 2nd Round 1953—54, 1970—71, 1971—72.
Best in Football League Cup: 1st Round 1970—71, 1971—72.
Pitch measurements: 112 × 75 yd.
Highest League Scorer in Single Season: I. Hollett—11 in 1970—71 (Div. 4).
Transfers—
    Highest fee paid: £6,000—John Collins (from Luton), February 1971.
    Highest fee received: £5,000—Ian Hutchinson (to Chelsea), July 1968.

Cardiff City

Ninian Park,
Cardiff, CF1 8SX.
Cardiff 28501 & 33230

Shirts: Blue
Shorts: White
Stockings: Blue

The most memorable event in Cardiff City's history occurred in 1927, when they became the first non-English club to win the F.A. Cup. That year they beat Arsenal 1–0 at Wembley and the drama of the occasion was heightened by the fact that the Arsenal goalkeeper, Dan Lewis, whose error allowed Cardiff to triumph, was himself a Welshman.

Three years earlier another mistake—this time by a City player—cost Cardiff the First Division Championship. They needed two points from their final match against Birmingham, but missed a penalty late in the game and could only draw.

In the Cardiff goal, during their First Division days of the 1920s, was Tom Farquharson their longest-serving player. He made nearly 450 League appearances between 1922 and 1935.

Cardiff's star waned, however, and the club slipped into the Second Division in 1929 and the Third (South) two seasons later, but re-emerged as Southern Section Champions in 1947.

As regular Welsh Cup winners, Cardiff (founded in 1899) have made six appearances in the European Cup-Winners' Cup and become one of Britain's most travelled clubs. In 1967–68 they reached the semi-finals but lost 4–3 on aggregate to S.V. Hamburg. The club's most-capped player was full-back Alf Sherwood, who represented Wales in 41 full Internationals between seasons 1946–47 and 1956–57.

F.A. Cup Winners: 1926–27.
Division 3 (South) Champions: 1946–47.
Record attendance: 61,566 Wales v. England (International), October 1961.
Modern Capacity: 62,500.
Entered Football League: 1920—Div. 2.
Biggest win: 9–2 v. Thames (Div. 3 South), February 1932.
Heaviest defeat: 2–11 v. Sheffield United (Div. 1), January 1926.
Best in Football League Cup: Semi-final 1965–66.
Pitch measurements: 112 × 76 yd.
Highest League Scorer in Single Season: S. Richards—31 in 1946–47 (Div. 3 South).
Transfers—
    Highest fee paid: £45,000—Barrie Jones (from Plymouth), September 1964; £45,000—Alan Warboys (from Sheffield Wednesday), December 1970.
    Highest fee received: £110,000—John Toshack (to Liverpool), November 1970.

Carlisle United

Brunton Park,
Carlisle, CA1 1LL.
Carlisle 26237

Shirts: Blue
Shorts: White
Stockings: Blue

Carlisle United's progress was unspectacular following their formation in 1903, when Carlisle Red Rose F.C. and Shadongate United amalgamated. In 1928 they were elected to Division Three (North) in place of Durham City and finished eighth in their first campaign. But they had to seek re-election in 1934—35 after finishing bottom, nine points behind the next club.

They were third in 1951, but when Division Four was formed from the bottom 12 clubs of each section of the Third in 1958, Carlisle were among them.

They gained promotion in 1962, dropped straight back the following season, but immediately went up again, with Hugh McIlmoyle scoring 39 out of a grand total of 113 League goals in that 1963—64 season.

McIlmoyle made a rich, though interrupted, contribution to Carlisle's continued progress, moving to Wolves after promotion from Division Four, then returning to be top scorer again in 1968—69 before going to Middlesbrough for £50,000.

Carlisle, situated so close to the Border that at one time there was speculation about their joining the Scottish League, swept on into Division Two in 1965, just twelve months after leaving the Fourth Division.

Division 3 (North) Champions: 1964—65.
Record attendance: 27,500 v. Birmingham City (F.A. Cup), January 1957, and 27,500 v. Middlesbrough (F.A. Cup), February 1970.
Modern Capacity: 30,000.
Entered Football League: 1928—Div. 3 (North).
Biggest win: 8—0 v. Hartlepool (Div. 3 North), September 1928, and 8—0 v. Scunthorpe Utd (Div. 3 North), December 1952.
Heaviest League defeat: 1—11 v. Hull City (Div. 3 North), January 1939.
Best in F.A. Cup: 5th Round 1963—64, 1969—70.
Best in Football League Cup: Semi-final 1969—70.
Pitch measurements: 117 × 78 yd.
Highest League Scorer in Single Season: J. McConnell—42 in 1928—29 (Div. 3 North).
Transfers—
  Highest fee paid: £22,500—Hugh McIlmoyle (from Bristol City), September 1967.
  Highest fee received: £80,000—Bob Hatton (to Birmingham), October 1971.

Charlton Athletic

The Valley,
Floyd Road, Charlton,
London, SE7 8AW.
01–858–3711/2

Shirts: Red
Shorts: White
Stockings: Red

Charlton Athletic was a name to conjure with between 1935 and 1947 when the London club distinguished themselves in League and Cup. They came within touching distance of a memorable League hat-trick after winning the Division Three (South) Championship in 1935. The following season they gained promotion to Division One, and twelve months later they were runners-up for the Championship itself. They were beaten in extra time in the F.A. Cup Final of 1946 by Derby. Charlton returned to Wembley the following season and won the Cup by beating Burnley 1–0 after extra time.

But after the glories of the forties came the slump of the fifties, with Charlton falling into Division Two in 1957. On several occasions since then they have had to struggle to avoid a further drop.

Among Charlton's best-known players were Sam Bartram, who kept goal for them in 583 League games from 1934–56, and South Africans John Hewie (capped 19 times by Scotland at full-back) and Stuart Leary, who holds the club scoring record with 153 goals between 1953–62.

In December 1957 Charlton staged one of the most amazing recoveries in football history. With 20 minutes left in a Second Division match at home to Huddersfield, they were losing 5–1 and reduced to ten men—yet finished winners by 7–6, with Johnny Summers scoring five of the goals.

F.A. Cup Winners: 1946–47.
Division 3 (South) Champions: 1928–29, 1934–35.
Record attendance: 75,031 v. Aston Villa (F.A. Cup), February 1938.
Modern Capacity: 67,000.
Entered Football League: 1921—Div. 3 (South).
Biggest win: 8–1 v. Middlesbrough (Div. 1), September 1953.
Heaviest defeat: 1–11 v. Aston Villa (Div. 2), November 1959.
Best in Football League Cup: 4th Round 1962–63, 1964–65.
Pitch measurements: 114 × 73 yd.
Highest League Scorer in Single Season: R. Allen—32 in 1934–35 (Div. 3 South).
Transfers—
    Highest fee paid: £50,000—Eamonn Rogers (from Blackburn), October 1971.
    Highest fee received: £80,000—Len Glover (to Leicester), November 1967.

Chelsea

Stamford Bridge Grounds,
Fulham Road,
London, SW6.
01-385-5545/6

Shirts: Royal Blue
Shorts: Royal Blue, White
   Seam
Stockings: White

For the first fifty years of their existence Chelsea did not win a single prize. Then they celebrated their golden jubilee by taking the League Championship of 1954–55 under the managership of Ted Drake. Under his successor, Tommy Docherty, they won the League Cup in 1964–65 and, guided by Dave Sexton, they have become one of modern football's most successful clubs.

In 1970 Chelsea at last lifted the F.A. Cup, dramatically beating Leeds 2–1 in extra time at Old Trafford in the first replayed Final since 1912. That victory qualified them for the Cup-Winners' Cup, and led them a year later to their first European prize, Real Madrid being beaten in the replayed Final in Athens. In 1972 they reached their third successive Final—this time in the League Cup.

No other club ever gained election to the Football League without taking part in any competition or so much as a friendly match, as Chelsea did in 1905. Apart from season 1962–63, they have been permanent members of the First Division since 1930.

Having established a place among the élite, Chelsea have embarked on a multi-million pound ground reorganization that, by the late 1970s, will put Stamford Bridge among Europe's finest homes of football.

League Champions: 1954–55.
F.A. Cup Winners: 1969–70.
League Cup Winners: 1964–65.
Winners of European Cup-Winners' Cup: 1970–71.
Record attendance: 82,905 v. Arsenal (League), October 1935.
Modern Capacity: 62,000.
Entered Football League: 1905—Div. 2.
Biggest win: 13–0 v. Jeunesse Hautcharage, Luxembourg (European Cup-Winners' Cup), September 1971.
Heaviest defeat: 1–8 v. Wolves (Div. 1), September 1953.
Pitch measurements: 114 × 71½ yd.
Highest League Scorer in Single Season: J. Greaves—41 in 1960–61 (Div. 1).
Transfers—
   Highest fee paid: £170,000—Steve Kember (from Crystal Palace), September 1971.
   Highest fee received: £100,000—Alan Birchenall (to Crystal Palace), June 1970; £100,000—Keith Weller (to Leicester City), September 1971.

Chester

The Stadium,
Sealand Road,
Chester, CH1 4LW.
Chester 21048

Shirts: Sky Blue
Shorts: Sky Blue
Stockings: Sky Blue

For Chester F.C., proximity to those two great Merseyside clubs, Everton and Liverpool, has always meant severe competition for players and supporters. The club was formed in 1884—four years before the Football League began—but did not gain election to the old Third Division North until 1931. The early seasons were full of promise. The team finished third in their début year, fourth the following season, third in 1934—35, were runners-up in 1935—36, and third in 1936—37.

A number of International players, among them Tommy Lawton and Don Welsh, assisted the club while on military service during the Second World War. On the resumption of peace-time League football in 1946—47, Chester filled third place once more, but since then a succession of managers, including John Harris, who as a player had helped Chelsea to their first Championship in 1955, have not been able to bring the Cheshire club much success.

In the F.A. Cup, Chester have never gone beyond the fourth round, but for a brief period in the winter of 1952 they attracted attention in the competition by holding First Division Chelsea to a 2—2 draw in the third round at Stamford Bridge. A record crowd of 20,500 saw Chester lose the replay 3—2.

Record attendance: 20,500 v. Chelsea (F.A. Cup), January 1952.
Modern Capacity: 20,000.
Entered Football League: 1931—Div. 3 (North).
Biggest win: 12—0 v. York City (Div. 3 North), February 1936.
Heaviest defeat: 2—11 v. Oldham Athletic (Div. 3 North), January 1952.
Highest final League position: 2nd in Div. 3 (North), 1935—36.
Best in F.A. Cup: 4th Round 1932—33, 1936—37, 1938—39, 1946—47, 1947—48, 1969—70.
Best in Football League Cup: 3rd Round 1962—63, 1964—65.
Pitch measurements: 114 × 75 yd.
Highest League Scorer in Single Season: R. Yates—36 in 1946—47 (Div. 3 North).
Transfers—
  Highest fee paid: £8,000—Ian Moir (from Blackpool), May 1967.
  Highest fee received: £11,000—Billy Foulkes (Newcastle), October 1951.

Chesterfield

Recreation Ground,
Chesterfield.
Chesterfield 2318

Shirts: Royal Blue, White
Trims
Shorts: White
Stockings: Royal Blue,
White Tops

Membership of Chesterfield F.C. in their formation year of 1866 cost a couple of shillings or ten new pence. Exactly 100 years later the club's most distinguished product, Gordon Banks, kept goal for England in their World Cup Final victory over West Germany at Wembley. Banks, later of Leicester City and Stoke City, has always acknowledged the value of those early days with Chesterfield. He is one of two outstanding goalkeepers developed post-war by the club. The other was Ray Middleton, who became a Justice of the Peace following his work for local youth organizations. Other well-known players in the town of the Crooked Spire have included members of the Milburn family, 'Legs' Linacre, Tommy Capel and Gordon Dale.

Chesterfield played in Division Two between 1899 and 1909 but then dropped out of the League until 1921, when they re-entered as members of Division Three (North), a section which they won in 1931 and 1936.

They have spent two separate periods in Division Two since those early days, and in 1947 finished fourth—the highest final placing they have attained in the Football League. More recently they have alternated between the Third and Fourth Divisions while pursuing a policy of trying to discover their own youngsters —including perhaps, another Banks. . . .

Division 3 (North) Champions: 1930–31, 1935–36.
Division 4 Champions: 1969–70.
Record attendance: 30,143 v. Tottenham (F.A. Cup), February 1938.
Modern Capacity: 28,500.
Entered Football League: 1899—Div. 2.
Biggest win: 10–0 v. Glossop N.E. (Div. 2), January 1903.
Heaviest defeat: 1–9 v. Port Vale (Div. 2), September 1932.
Best in F.A. Cup: 5th Round 1932–33, 1937–38, 1949–50.
Best in Football League Cup: 4th Round 1964–65.
Pitch measurements: 114×73 yd.
Highest League Scorer in Single Season: J. Cookson—44 in 1925–26 (Div. 3 North).
Transfers—
Highest fee paid: £8,000—George Smith (from Manchester City), October 1951.
Highest fee received: £50,000—Alan Stevenson (to Burnley), January 1972.

Colchester United

Layer Road Ground,
Colchester.
Colchester 74042

Shirts: Royal Blue, White
Trim
Shorts: Royal Blue
Stockings: White

Colchester United first made an impact on soccer in England in 1948, when they achieved a series of astonishing F.A. Cup giant-killing acts. While still members of the Southern League, they knocked out Huddersfield Town and Bradford (who had previously defeated Arsenal) before finally falling at Blackpool in the fifth round. Their manager then was Ted Fenton, who later guided West Ham back to the First Division.

Not surprisingly after such impressive evidence of their talents, Colchester were elected to the Football League in 1950. And 21 years later, in the fifth round of season 1970–71, they celebrated their 'coming of age' with another incredible Cup triumph. This time they defeated Leeds United, probably the most powerful club side in Europe, 3–2, at Layer Road. By now even Wembley seemed a possibility for manager Dick Graham's team of Fourth Division enthusiasts, but in the quarter-finals Colchester were drawn away to Everton and were soundly beaten 5–0.

Their most impressive season to date in the League came in 1961–62, when they were runners-up to Millwall in the Fourth Division, scoring 104 goals in 44 matches. That season Colchester's 23 League victories included their record 9–1 win over Bradford City.

Record attendance: 19,072 v. Reading (F.A. Cup), November 1948.
Modern Capacity: 16,000.
Entered Football League: 1950—Div. 3 (South).
Biggest win: 9–1 v. Bradford City (Div. 4), December 1961.
Heaviest defeat: 0–7 v. Leyton Orient (Div. 3 South), January 1952; 0–7 v. Reading (Div. 3 South), September 1957.
Highest final League position: 2nd in Div. 4, 1961–62.
Best in F.A. Cup: 6th Round 1970–71.
Best in Football League Cup: 4th Round 1963–64.
Pitch measurements: 110 × 74 yd.
Highest League Scorer in Single Season: R. Hunt—37 in 1961–62 (Div. 4).
Transfers—
    Highest fee paid: £15,000—Dave Simmons (from Aston Villa), December 1970.
    Highest fee received: £15,000—Bobby Hunt (to Northampton), March 1964; £15,000—Duncan Forbes (to Norwich), September 1968.

Coventry City

Highfield Road Ground,
Coventry.
Coventry 57171

Shirts: Sky Blue, Dark
Blue Neck and Cuff
Shorts: Sky Blue
Stockings: Navy Blue

The rise of Coventry City from the obscurity of the Fourth Division in 1959, to the glamour of the First Division eight years later, is one of the success stories of modern soccer.

From the old Southern League, they gained admission to the Football League in 1919 and just avoided relegation from the Second Division in their first season. They dropped down to the Third Division in 1925 and took eleven seasons to get back into the Second, finishing 1935—36 as Third Division South Champions.

Coventry slipped again in 1952 and became founder members of the Fourth Division in 1958. After only one season in the Fourth, however, the new-look City gained promotion to the Third and began the thrilling climb that took them into the First Division in 1967.

Derrick Robins, a progressive-minded chairman, and his ebullient manager of that era, Jimmy Hill, led the Sky Blue Revolution of the sixties and, having reached the 'promised land' of the First Division, City had to survive a two-season threat of relegation before they could breathe more comfortably in the top section.

Divison 2 Champions: 1966—67.
Division 3 (South) Champions: 1935—36.
Division 3 Champions: 1963—64.
Record attendance: 51,455 v. Wolves (League), April 1967.
Modern Capacity: 52,000.
Entered Football League: 1919—Div. 2.
Biggest win: 9—0 v. Bristol City (Div. 3 South), April 1934.
Heaviest defeat: 2—10 v. Norwich City (Div. 3 South), March 1930.
Best in F.A. Cup: 6th Round 1962—63 (also reached last eight in old 4th Round 1909—10).
Best in Football League Cup: 5th Round 1964—65, 1970—71.
Pitch measurements: 110×72 yd.
Highest League Scorer in Single Season: C. Bourton—49 in 1931—32 (Div. 3 South).
Transfers—
    Highest fee paid: £100,000—Wilf Smith (from Sheffield Wednesday), August 1970.
    Highest fee received: £99,000—Bobby Gould (to Arsenal), February 1968.

Crewe Alexandra

Gresty Road,
Crewe.
Crewe 3014

Shirts: Red
Shorts: White
Stockings: Black, Red and
White Tops

The club owes its origins to the game of cricket. In 1876 a local cricket team decided to form a football section, and only 12 years later, while still amateurs, Crewe Alexandra—derived from the name of the town and the hotel they used—had reached the semi-final of the F.A. Cup.

They turned professional in 1893, the year after becoming a founder member of Division Two of the Football League. Unhappily, they were not re-elected in 1896 and remained in comparative obscurity until after the First World War when they re-entered the League in Division Three (North) in 1921.

Since then the story of Crewe has almost always been one of hard struggle and dedication by all connected with the club. Promotion from Division Four in 1962—63, when they were third, and again in 1967—68 (fourth) have provided brief periods of reward, and another was the club's remarkable 2—1 F.A. Cup third round win at Chelsea in January 1961.

The most melancholy period in Crewe's long history occurred during 1956—57 when they played 30 League matches without a win. One of the finest players produced by Crewe was Frank Blunstone, who moved to Chelsea as a boy winger in February 1953 and went on to gain five full caps for England.

Record attendance: 20,000 v. Tottenham (F.A. Cup), January 1960.
Modern Capacity: 16,000.
Entered Football League: 1892—Div. 2.
Biggest win: 8—0 v. Rotherham Utd (Div. 3 North), October 1932.
Heaviest defeat: 2—13 v. Tottenham (F.A. Cup), February 1960.
Highest final League position: 3rd in Div. 4, 1962—63.
Best in F.A. Cup: Semi-final 1887—88.
Best in Football League Cup: 3rd Round 1960—61.
Pitch measurements: 112×75 yd.
Highest League Scorer in Single Season: T. Harkin—35 in 1964—65 (Div. 4).
Transfers—
　Highest fee paid: £5000—Gordon Wallace (from Liverpool), October 1967.
　Highest fee received: £20,000—John Mahoney (to Stoke), March 1967.

42

Crystal Palace

Selhurst Park,
London, SE25 6JU.
01—653—2223

Shirts: White, Broad Claret
and Blue Stripe down
centre front and back
Shorts: White
Stockings: Light Blue,
Claret Tops

The progress of Crystal Palace to First Division status became
more than a dream from April 1966, when they appointed Bert
Head as manager. He joined them from Bury, but first made his
mark in football management at Swindon, where he built a star-
studded team from nothing, and by 1969 Palace were in the top
division. They kept pace off the field, too, as Arthur Wait, their
energetic chairman, embarked upon a big redevelopment scheme.

Back in 1905 when the club was formed, matches were played
on the famous Crystal Palace ground where 20 Cup Finals were
staged from 1895 to 1914. That was in the club's Southern
League days.

The club were elected to the Football League in 1920 and
celebrated by finishing at the top of the Third Division, but that
was the only notable landmark in Palace history until 1961,
when they climbed out of the Fourth Division and began their
rise to the top. After a bad start to season 1971—72, Palace sold
Steve Kember to Chelsea for £170,000 and Alan Birchenall to
Leicester for £100,000. The money was used to buy new players
in a spectacular bid to hold their First Division place.

Division 3 Champions: 1920—21.
Record attendance: 49,498 v. Chelsea (League), December
1969.
Modern Capacity: 52,000.
Entered Football League: 1920—Div. 3.
Biggest win: 9—0 v. Barrow (Div. 4), October 1959.
Heaviest defeat: 4—11 v. Manchester City (F.A. Cup), February
1926.
Best in F.A. Cup: 6th Round 1964—65 (also reached last eight
in old 4th Round 1906—07).
Best in Football League Cup: 5th Round 1968—69, 1970—71.
Pitch measurements: 110 × 75 yd.
Highest League Scorer in Single Season: P. Simpson—46
in 1930—31 (Div. 3 South).
Transfers—
    Highest fee paid: £100,000—Alan Birchenall (from Chel-
sea), June 1970.
    Highest fee received: £170,000—Steve Kember (to
Chelsea), September 1971.

Darlington

Feethams Ground,
Darlington.
Darlington 65097/6771

Shirts: White, Black Hoops
Shorts: Black, White Seam
Stockings: White, Black Hoop

Eighty pounds would not buy a complete set of team kit today. Yet in season 1924—25 Darlington won the Third Division North title with a team, collected by Jack English, for just that modest sum. They finished five points ahead of the next two clubs, Nelson and New Brighton, neither of whom are now members of the Football League. Unfortunately they survived only two seasons before being relegated.

Darlington are one of the comparatively few League clubs to have used only one ground—the Feethams—since their formation in 1883. In their early years they played in the Northern League and became professional in 1908, when they joined the North-Eastern League. The club was reformed after the First World War, and in 1921 bècame one of the original members of the old Division Three North.

They remained there until Division Four was created in 1958, and in season 1965—66 they delighted their supporters by finishing runners-up with the same number of points (59) as the champions, Doncaster Rovers. A year later, however, they were relegated. Darlington's best-known players have included centre-forward Doug Brown (74 League goals in 97 matches from 1923—26) and Ken Furphy, who has gone on to manage Workington, Watford and Blackburn.

Division 3 (North) Champions: 1924—25.
Record attendance: 21,023 v. Bolton Wanderers (League Cup), November 1960.
Modern Capacity: 21,000.
Entered Football League: 1921—Div. 3 (North).
Biggest win: 13—1 v. Scarborough (F.A. Cup), 1886.
Heaviest defeat: 0—10 v. Doncaster (Div. 4), January 1964.
Best in F.A. Cup: 5th Round 1957—58.
Best in Football League Cup: 5th Round 1967—68.
Pitch measurements: 110 × 74 yd.
Highest League Scorer in Single Season: D. Brown—39 in 1924—25 (Div. 3 North).
Transfers—
  Highest fee paid: £6000—Bobby Cummings (from Newcastle), October 1965.
  Highest fee received: £17,000—Bryan Conlon (to Millwall), November 1967.

Derby County

Baseball Ground,
Shaftesbury Crescent,
Derby, DE3 8NB.
Derby 40105

Shirts: White
Shorts: Black
Stockings: White

The revival of Derby County began with the appointment of Brian Clough, former Middlesbrough and England centre-forward, in May 1967. Under his inspiring managership (and, on the field, rallied by the captaincy and playing skill of Dave Mackay, who had been one of the architects of Tottenham Hotspur's success in the sixties) Derby roared back into the First Division two years later. In season 1971–72 they became League Champions for the first time.

Why do Derby County—one of the original 12 Football League clubs in 1888—have a home with the unlikely name of the Baseball Ground? In 1895 a wealthy businessman, Sir Francis Ley, formed a baseball club in the town and built a fine ground, but the American game did not catch on. After a few months, the baseball club was disbanded, and County moved in. Previously they had played at the Derby racecourse ground.

In 1946 Derby, with world-class inside-forwards in Raich Carter and Peter Doherty, won their first major trophy, beating Charlton 4–1 in extra time in the F.A. Cup Final. But between 1953 and 1955 they slumped from First to Third Division North. They climbed back into the Second Division by 1957, but it was another ten years before Clough arrived and launched the real recovery.

League Champions: 1971–72.
Division 2 Champions: 1911–12, 1914–15, 1968–69.
Division 3 (North) Champions: 1956–57.
F.A. Cup Winners: 1945–46.
Record attendance: 41,826 v. Tottenham (League), September 1969.
Modern Capacity: 42,000.
Entered Football League: 1888—Div. 1.
Biggest win: 9–0 v. Wolves (Div. 1), January 1891; 9–0 v. Sheffield Wednesday (Div. 1), January 1899.
Heaviest defeat: 2–11 v. Everton (F.A. Cup), 1889–90.
Best in Football League Cup: Semi-final 1967–68.
Pitch measurements: 110 × 71 yd.
Highest League Scorer in Single Season: J. Bowers—37 in 1930–31 (Div. 1); R. Straw—37 in 1956–57 (Div. 3 North).
Transfers—
    Highest fee paid: £170,000—Colin Todd (from Sunderland), February 1971.
    Highest fee received: £45,000—Willie Carlin (to Leicester), October 1970.

Doncaster Rovers

Belle Vue Ground,
Doncaster, DN4 5HT.
Doncaster 55281

Shirts: White
Shorts: Red
Stockings: White

Doncaster Rovers' past is crowded with players of distinction: the Keetley brothers, Frank, Harold, Joe and Tom (who still holds the club record for the most League goals—178); Fred Emery, later manager; Sam Cowan who won England caps with Manchester City; Jack Lambert, Arsenal's centre-forward in the 1930 and 1932 F.A. Cup Finals; Peter Doherty, rated by many as the most skilful inside-forward of his era; Clarrie Jordan (42 League goals in 1946—47); Manchester United and Northern Ireland goalkeeper Harry Gregg; England Under-23 forward Alick Jeffrey, with 36 goals, was the League's top scorer in 1964—65.

The Belle Vue ground, opposite Doncaster racecourse, is at 118½ by 79 yards the largest pitch in the League and no more notable performances have been achieved on it than in 1946—47. That season Rovers won the old Third Division North title with the astonishing total of 72 points from 42 League matches, including 37 from away games. Not surprisingly, that points tally has remained a League record. At that time interest in the Rovers pulled big crowds to Belle Vue and, in October 1948, 37,149 saw a League match against Yorkshire rivals, Hull City, which illustrates the crowd potential this long-established club can attract when on a winning streak.

Division 3 (North) Champions: 1934—35, 1946—47, 1949—50.
Division 4 Champions: 1965—66, 1968—69.
Record attendance: 37,149 v. Hull (League), October 1948.
Modern Capacity: 40,000.
Entered Football League: 1901—Div. 2.
Biggest win: 10—0 v. Darlington (Div. 4), January 1964.
Heaviest defeat: 0—12 v. Small Heath (Div. 2), April 1903.
Best in F.A. Cup: 5th Round 1951—52, 1953—54, 1954—55, 1955—56.
Best in Football League Cup: 3rd Round 1960—61, 1964—65, 1966—67.
Pitch measurements: 118½ × 79 yd.
Highest League Scorer in Single Season: C. Jordan—42 in 1946—47 (Div. 3 North).
Transfers—
    Highest fee paid: £10,000—John Flowers (from Stoke), July 1966.
    Highest fee received: £30,000—Paul Gilchrist (to Southampton), March 1972.

Everton

Goodison Park,
Liverpool, L4 4EL.
051–525–5263/4

Shirts: Royal Blue
Shorts: White
Stockings: White

In 1888 Everton became one of the original members of the Football League and were Division ·One champions in 1890–91. Fifteen years later they won the F.A. Cup for the first time. Everton stayed in the First Division for 42 years until 1930, then spent only one season in the Second before returning to win the First Division twice more (1932 and 1939) before the Second World War. By a fractional goal average, the club went down again in 1951, and it took them three years to get back.

Never was promotion more timely. As Everton went up, Liverpool went down, so the record remained that Merseyside has never been without a First Division club. A new and glorious era began for Everton when pools millionaire John Moores became a director and, in April 1961, Harry Catterick was appointed manager. Twice since then—in 1963 and 1970— Everton have won the ·Championship, making seven League titles in all, and in 1966 they took the F.A. Cup for the third time.

Bill 'Dixie' Dean, one of the club's most famous players, created League history in 1927–28 by scoring 60 goals in 39 First Division games, a feat that has never been equalled.

League Champions: 1890–91, 1914–15, 1927–28, 1931–32, 1938–39, 1962–63, 1969–70.
Division 2 Champions: 1930–31.
F.A. Cup Winners: 1905–06, 1932–33, 1965–66.
Record attendance: 78,299 v. Liverpool (League), September 1948.
Modern Capacity: 60,000.
Entered Football League: 1888—Div. 1.
Biggest win: 11–2 v. Derby County (F.A. Cup), 1889–90.
Heaviest defeat: 4–10 v. Tottenham (Div. 1), October 1958.
Best in Football League Cup: 5th Round 1960–61.
Pitch measurements: 112 × 75 yd.
Highest League Scorer in Single Season: W. R. Dean—60 in 1927–28 (Div. 1).
Transfers—
  Highest fee paid: £150,000—Henry Newton (from Nottingham Forest), October 1970.
  Highest fee received: £220,000—Alan Ball (to Arsenal), December 1971.

Exeter City

St James's Park,
Exeter, EX4 6PX.
0392–54073

Shirts: Red and White Stripes
Shorts: Red
Stockings: Red, White Tops

No one would suggest that life has been easy for the City club which has never journeyed beyond the Third Division. Nevertheless, a number of distinguished players began their careers at St James's Park. They include left-winger Cliff Bastin, who became an England international and collected F.A. Cup-winning and First Division Championship medals with Arsenal before he was 20; Dick Pym, Bolton's goalkeeper in three successful Cup Finals at Wembley in the 1920s; and Harold Blackmore, who scored one of Bolton's goals in the 1929 F.A. Cup victory over Portsmouth.

Who among Exeter's older supporters will forget the wonderful Cup run in 1931? After fighting through to the competition proper, they beat First Division Derby 3–2 at Exeter; next they won 2–1 at Bury and then, back in front of their own followers again, defeated Leeds United 3–1. That victory put Exeter in the last eight and when they held another Division One side, Sunderland 1–1 at Roker Park, it seemed they were heading for the semi-finals. But before a record crowd of nearly 21,000 the replay was lost by four goals to two.

Record attendance: 20,984 v. Sunderland (F.A. Cup), March
    †931.
Modern Capacity: 18,500.
Entered Football League: 1920—Div. 3.
Biggest win: 8–1 v. Coventry City (Div. 3 South), December
    1926; 8–1 v. Aldershot (Div. 3 South), May 1935.
Heaviest defeat: 0–9 v. Notts County (Div. 3 South), October
    1948; 0–9 v. Northampton (Div. 3 South), April 1958.
Highest final League position: Runners-up Division 3
    (South) 1932–33.
Best in F.A. Cup: 6th Round 1930–31.
Best in Football League Cup: 3rd Round 1966–67, 1968–69.
Pitch measurements: 115 × 75 yd.
Highest League Scorer in Single Season: F. Whitlow—34
    in 1932–33 (Div. 3 South).
Transfers—
    Highest fee paid: £6000—Alan Banks (from Cambridge
        City), October 1963.
    Highest fee received: £9000—Bruce Stuckey (to Sunderland), October 1967.

LEAGUE CLUBS: COLOUR GUIDE

Aldershot

Arsenal

Aston Villa

Barnsley

Barrow

Birmingham City

Blackburn Rovers

Blackpool

LEAGUE CLUBS: COLOUR GUIDE

Bolton Wanderers

Bournemouth & B.A.

Bradford City

Brentford

Brighton &
Hove Albion

Bristol City

Bristol Rovers

LEAGUE CLUBS: COLOUR GUIDE

Burnley

Bury

Cambridge United

Cardiff City

Carlisle United

Charlton Athletic

Chelsea

Chester

LEAGUE CLUBS: COLOUR GUIDE

Chesterfield   Colchester United   Coventry City

Crewe Alexandra   Crystal Palace

Darlington   Derby County   Doncaster Rovers

LEAGUE CLUBS: COLOUR GUIDE

Everton

Exeter City

Fulham

Gillingham

Grimsby Town

Halifax Town

Hartlepool

LEAGUE CLUBS: COLOUR GUIDE

Huddersfield Town   Hull City   Ipswich Town

Leeds United   Leicester City

Lincoln City   Liverpool   Luton Town

LEAGUE CLUBS: COLOUR GUIDE

Manchester City   Manchester United   Mansfield Town

Middlesbrough   Millwall

Newcastle United   Newport County   Northampton Town

LEAGUE CLUBS: COLOUR GUIDE

Norwich City

Notts County

Nottingham Forest

Oldham Athletic

Orient

Oxford United

Peterborough United

LEAGUE CLUBS: COLOUR GUIDE

Plymouth Argyle   Portsmouth   Port Vale

Preston North End   Queen's Park Rangers

Reading   Rochdale   Rotherham United

LEAGUE CLUBS: COLOUR GUIDE

Scunthorpe United

Sheffield United

Sheffield Wednesday

Shrewsbury Town

Southampton

Southend United

Southport

Stockport County

LEAGUE CLUBS: COLOUR GUIDE

Stoke City   Sunderland

Swansea City   Swindon Town   Torquay United

Tottenham Hotspur   Tranmere Rovers

LEAGUE CLUBS: COLOUR GUIDE

Walsall

Watford

West Bromwich
Albion

West Ham United

Wolverhampton
Wanderers

Workington

Wrexham

York City

Celtic

Rangers

Hearts

Hibernian

Aberdeen

Dundee

GOALKEEPERS' COLOURS

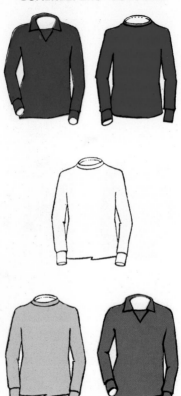

Internationals only

INTERNATIONAL SHIRTS

England

Scotland

Wales

Northern Ireland

Republic of Ireland

INTERNATIONAL BADGES

England

Scotland

Wales

Northern Ireland

Republic of Ireland

Fulham

Craven Cottage,
Stevenage Road,
Fulham, London, SW6.
01–736–5621/7035

Shirts: White
Shorts: Black
Stockings: Red

Although this Thames-side club has fielded many outstanding players, among them the former England captain Johnny Haynes and George Cohen, one of England's 1966 World Cup-winning team, has never won the League Championship or, in fact, reached an F.A. Cup Final.

Twice Fulham have experienced brief spells of First Division football, but after losing top status for the second time in 1968, they dropped straight into the Third Division which they had left in 1932. They returned to Division Two as runners-up in 1971.

In 1907 they became Southern League Champions and were elected to the Second Division of the Football League. In their first season, they were only four points away from promotion to the First and they reached the F.A. Cup semi-final.

From 1928 to 1932, Fulham were in the Third Division but then returned to the Second with centre-forward Frank Newton scoring 41 of their 111 goals that season. Although F.A. Cup semi-finalists three more times, Fulham still could not reach Wembley, despite the assistance of such players as Ronnie Rooke, Arthur Rowley, holder of the League scoring record, Bedford Jezzard, Tony Macedo, Roy Bentley and Jimmy Hill.

Division 2 Champions: 1948–49.
Division 3 (South) Champions: 1931–32.
Record attendance: 49,335 v. Millwall (League), October 1938.
Modern Capacity: 45,000.
Entered Football League: 1907—Div. 2.
Biggest win: 10–1 v. Ipswich (Div. 1), December 1963.
Heaviest defeat: 0–9 v. Wolves (Div. 1), September 1959.
Best in F.A. Cup: Semi-final 1907–08, 1935–36, 1957–58, 1961–62.
Best in Football League Cup: 5th Round 1967–68, 1970–71.
Pitch measurements: 110 × 75 yd.
Highest League Scorer in Single Season: F. Newton—41 in 1931–32 (Div. 3 South).
Transfers—
    Highest fee paid: £35,000—Allan Clarke (from Walsall), March 1966; £35,000—Vic Halom (from Orient), October 1968.
    Highest fee received: £150,000—Allan Clarke (to Leicester), June 1968.

Gillingham

Priestfield Stadium,
Gillingham, Kent.
Medway 51854

Shirts: Blue
Shorts: White
Stockings: Blue

When Gillingham were voted out of the Football League in 1938 and replaced by Ipswich Town, their existence as a senior club seemed to be over. But after the war, under an energetic and far-seeing management, they became a force in the Southern League. When, in 1950, the Football League decided to increase membership from 88 to 92 clubs, by extending each Third Division section (North and South) from 22 to 24 teams, 'The Gills' were readmitted.

The club started life as New Brompton Excelsior, changing their name to Gillingham in 1913. The subsequent playing years until they left the League provided little of distinction. In fact, the club had to wait until season 1963–64 for their first major success—the Championship of the Fourth Division. They lost only nine of their 46 matches and beat Carlisle United to the title on goal average, each club obtaining 60 points. But at the end of the 1970–71 season they were relegated.

Gillingham have rarely made much impact in the F.A. Cup (they have only once reached the fifth round), but in the last qualifying round in December, 1924, they lost to Barrow after nine hours and five meetings.

Division 4 Champions: 1963–64.
Record attendance: 23,002 v. Queen's Park Rangers (F.A. Cup), January 1948.
Modern Capacity: 22,000.
Entered Football League: 1920—Div. 3.
Biggest win: 10–1 v. Gorleston (F.A. Cup), November 1957.
Heaviest defeat: 2–9 v. Nottingham Forest (Div. 3 South), November 1950.
Best in F.A. Cup: 5th Round 1969–70.
Best in Football League Cup: 4th Round 1963–64.
Pitch measurements: 114 × 75 yd.
Highest League Scorer in Single Season: E. Morgan—31 in 1954–55 (Div. 3 South).
Transfers—
  Highest fee paid: £8000—Rodney Green (from Bradford City), July 1964.
  Highest fee received: £20,000—Charlie Crickmore (to Rotherham), November 1967.

Grimsby Town

Blundell Park,
Cleethorpes, Lincs.
Cleethorpes 61420/61803

Shirts: Black and White
   Stripes
Shorts: Black
Stockings: Red

In the period between the two wars Grimsby Town, whose ground is situated in the town of Cleethorpes, played in all four sections of the Football League—the Third Division and Third North section, as well as the First and Second Divisions.

They were still in Division One immediately after the Second World War, but finished bottom in 1948, and until recently there had been a gradual decline in the club's playing performances, culminating in their having to seek re-election after finishing 91st on the League ladder in season 1968—69.

The club was founded as Grimsby Pelham in 1878, but after a year dropped the name Pelham. They won the Division Two Championship in 1901 and again in 1934. Two years later they lost to Arsenal by the only goal in the semi-final of the F.A. Cup. They again reached the last four in 1939, this time crashing 5—0 to Wolverhampton Wanderers.

Grimsby have produced many first-class forwards, none better than Ernest (Pat) Glover, who scored 42 League goals in 1933—34, and Jackie Bestall, the finest creator of attacks in the club's history.

Division 2 Champions: 1900—01, 1933—34.
Division 3 (North) Champions: 1925—26, 1955—56.
Division 4 Champions: 1971—72.
Record attendance: 31,650 v. Wolves (F.A. Cup), February 1937.
Modern Capacity: 28,000.
Entered Football Leauge: 1892—Div 2.
Biggest win: 9—2 v. Darwen (Div. 2), April 1899.
Heaviest defeat: 1—9 v. Arsenal (Div. 1), January 1931.
Best in F.A. Cup: Semi-final 1935—36, 1938—39.
Best in Football League Cup: 5th Round 1965—66.
Pitch measurements: 111 × 74 yd.
Highest League Scorer in Single Season: E. Glover—42 in 1933—34 (Div. 2).
Transfers—
   Highest fee paid: £10,000—Ron Foster (from Leyton Orient), December 1962.
   Highest fee received: £20,000—Doug Collins (to Burnley), September 1968.

Halifax Town

Shay Ground,
Halifax.
Halifax 53423

Shirts: Tangerine
Shorts: Blue
Stockings: Tangerine

The seasons of reward have been strictly limited for Halifax Town since their early days in the Yorkshire Combination and Midland League. So there was understandable excitement in 1971 when the club made a sustained bid to bring Second Division football to The Shay for the first time. In the end, they had to be content with third place behind Preston (managed ironically enough by their previous chief, Alan Ball, senior) and Fulham.

Two seasons earlier the Town side had won their way into the Third Division as runners-up to Doncaster Rovers after an unbroken sequence as members of the Third Division (North) and then the Fourth Division. In those bleak days Halifax often had to seek re-election, and it says much for their perseverance that League clubs repeatedly voted them back.

The Shay bulged at its sides one February day in 1953, when nearly 37,000 turned up to watch Tottenham Hotspur in the F.A. Cup fifth round. Halifax had made the most of their luck in being drawn at home in every tie, and after dealing with Ashton and Southport, they put out First Division 'giants' Cardiff and Stoke. But for all the urgings of their record crowd they went down 3–0 to Spurs.

Record attendance: 36,885 v. Tottenham (F.A. Cup), February 1953.
Modern Capacity: 38,000.
Entered Football League: 1921—Div. 3 (North).
Biggest win: 7–0 v. Bishop Auckland (F.A. Cup), January 1967.
Heaviest defeat: 0–13 v. Stockport County (Div. 3 North), January 1934.
Highest final League position: Runners-up Div. 3 (North) 1934–35; runners-up Div. 4 1968–69.
Best in F.A. Cup: 5th Round 1932–33, 1952–53.
Best in Football League Cup: 4th Round 1963–64.
Pitch measurements: 110 × 70 yd.
Highest League Scorer in Single Season: A. Valentine—34 in 1934–35 (Div. 3 North).
Transfers—
    Highest fee paid: £14,000—Fred Kemp (from Blackpool), January 1972.
    Highest fee received: £30,000—Chris Nicholl (to Luton), August 1969; £30,000—Dave Lennard (to Blackpool), October 1971.

Hartlepool

Victoria Ground,
Scarborough Street,
Hartlepool.
Hartlepool 2584/3492

Shirts: Blue
Shorts: White
Stockings: Blue and
White Hoops

Overshadowed throughout their existence by their powerful north-eastern neighbours, Newcastle and Sunderland, the Hartlepool club have known more of life's struggles than success. Indeed, they have had to apply ten times for re-election.

They joined the old Division Three North on its formation in 1921, and stayed in this section until they moved into the newly created Fourth Division in 1958. They did finish runners-up in 1956—57, but in those days only one club gained promotion from each Third Division section. They scored 90 goals in their 46 matches that season, and on that form they were unlucky to miss a higher grade.

They had to wait another 11 years, until 1968, before they experienced promotion. Then they took third place in Division Four behind Luton and Barnsley. Unfortunately, at the end of the following season they were relegated. In April 1959, they briefly commanded attention by thrashing Barrow 10—1; three years later they lost by the same margin to Wrexham.

One of Hartlepool's longest-serving managers was Fred Westgarth in the after-war years, and the club also launched Brian Clough on a managerial career that developed so successfully with Derby County.

Record attendance: 17,420 v. Manchester United (F.A. Cup), January 1959.
Modern Capacity: 18,000.
Entered Football League: 1921—Div. 3 (North).
Biggest win: 10—1 v. Barrow (Div. 4), April 1959.
Heaviest defeat: 1—10 v. Wrexham (Div. 4), May 1962.
Highest final League position: Runners-up Div. 3 (North) 1956—57.
Best in F.A. Cup: 4th Round 1954—55.
Best in Football League Cup: 2nd Round 1965—66, 1967—68, 1969—70.
Pitch measurements: 113 × 76 yd.
Highest League Scorer in Single Season: W. Robinson—28 in 1927—28 (Div. 3 North).
Transfers—
    Highest fee paid: £10,000—Ambrose Fogarty (from Sunderland), November 1963.
    Highest fee received: £8000—Terry Bell (to Reading), March 1970.

Huddersfield Town

Leeds Road,
Huddersfield, HD1 6PE.
Huddersfield 20335/6

Shirts: Royal Blue and
   White Stripes
Shorts: White
Stockings: White, Royal
   Blue Band

In the mid-twenties Huddersfield reigned supreme as First Division Champions for three successive years (1924—25—26), the greatest era in their history. Yet not many years earlier the club had struggled through periods of financial crisis. But a playing revival brought Huddersfield a phenomenal run of success in the 1919—20 season. They not only won promotion, but also reached the F.A. Cup Final.

The appointment of Herbert Chapman as manager (1922—25) heralded the club's dominant period. In that great team of the twenties which Chapman created were the captain Clem Stephenson, who had played for Aston Villa, winger Billy Smith, who made nearly 500 appearances in 15 years, full-backs Roy Goodall and Sam Wadsworth.

Huddersfield just failed to win the League title four years running, finishing second in 1927. The following season, 1927—28, they came close to doing the double, but finished runners-up again in the League and lost to Blackburn Rovers in the F.A. Cup Final. They stayed in Division One until 1952, then won back their place first time. In 1956 they dropped again and spent 14 years in the Second Division.

League Champions: 1923—24, 1924—25, 1925—26.
Division 2 Champions: 1969—70.
F.A. Cup Winners: 1921—22.
Record attendance: 67,037 v. Arsenal (F.A. Cup), February 1932.
Modern Capacity: 52,000.
Entered Football League: 1910—Div. 2.
Biggest win: 10—1 v. Blackpool (Div. 1), December 1930.
Heaviest defeat: 1—7 v. Bolton Wanderers (Div. 1), January 1930; 1—7 v. Wolves (Div. 1), October 1948.
Best in Football League Cup: Semi-final 1967—68.
Pitch measurements: 116 × 76 yd.
Highest League Scorer in Single Season: S. Taylor—35 in 1919—20 (Div. 2); G. Brown—35 in 1925—26 (Div. 1).
Transfers—
   Highest fee paid: £45,000—Dick Krzywicki (from W.B.A.), March 1970.
   Highest fee received: £80,000—Derek Parkin (to Wolves), February 1968.

Hull City

Boothferry Park,
Hull, HU4 6EU.
0482—52195/6

Shirts: Amber
Shorts: Black
Stockings: Amber

Hull City, in more recent seasons, have been noted for scoring potential. In winning the Third Division Championship in 1965–66 they totalled 109 goals. In 1969–70 they got 72 goals—only Sheffield United, with 73, scored more in the Second Division—and between them Ken Houghton, Chris Chilton and Ken Wagstaff netted 52 of them.

Hull City was formed as an amateur club in 1904 and gained admission to the Second Division in 1905. Four times up to 1960 they dropped into the Third Division, then regained their status in the higher grade.

They came closest to promotion to Division One in 1910 when Oldham Athletic pipped them for second place by ·286 of a goal. During the Second World War Hull's ground in Anlaby Road was hit by enemy bombs, and in 1946 the club was reformed and acquired their present impressive home, Boothferry Park, which has its own railway station.

Hull have often been impressive F.A. Cup fighters. They were semi-finalists in 1930 [despite being on their way down to the Third Division (North)], and as a Second Division side in 1921 sprang a sensation in the third round by beating Burnley 3–0.

That season Burnley won the First Division title and, their defeat by Hull apart, played 30 matches between September and March without being beaten.

Division 3 (North) Champions: 1932–33, 1948–49.
Division 3 Champions: 1965–66.
Record attendance: 55,019 v. Man. Utd. (F.A. Cup), Feb. 1949.
Modern Capacity: 42,000.
Entered Football League: 1905—Div. 2.
Biggest win: 11–1 v. Carlisle (Div. 3 North), January 1939.
Heaviest defeat: 0–8 v. Wolves (Div. 2), November 1911.
Best in F.A. Cup: Semi-final 1929–30.
Best in Football League Cup: 3rd Round 1961–62, 1962–63, 1963–64, 1969–70.
Pitch measurements: 113 × 73 yd.
Highest League Scorer in Single Season: W. McNaughton —39 in 1932–33 (Div. 3 North).
Transfers—
    Highest fee paid: £60,000—Ken Knighton (from Blackburn), March 1971.
    Highest fee received: £92,000—Chris Chilton (to Coventry), August 1971.

Ipswich Town

Portman Road,
Ipswich, IP1 2DA.
Ipswich 51306/57107

Shirts: Royal Blue
Shorts: White
Stockings: Royal Blue

Football fame came to Ipswich in 1962 when they won the League Championship in their first season in Division One. Under the guidance of Alf Ramsey, later knighted for his services to football as England's manager, the club had a remarkable rise.

Ramsey took over as manager in August 1955, after Town had gone down to the Third Division. Two years later they were back in the Second Division. They won promotion to the First as Champions after three more seasons, and a year later surprised the whole soccer world by winning the League Championship.

After their shock Championship triumph in 1962, with Ray Crawford (33) and Ted Phillips (28) scoring 61 of their 93 goals, Ipswich slipped down to the Second Division in 1964 and it took them four seasons to fight their way back into the First.

Crawford holds the aggregate goal record (203) for Ipswich and Phillips, who also played a great part in their meteoric rise to fame, set a new club record for the most goals in a season—41 in the Third Division South, 1956–57. But the man above all others who put Ipswich on the soccer map was Sir Alf Ramsey, and his feeling for the little East Anglian town is reflected in the fact that throughout his reign as England manager he has continued to live there.

League Champions: 1961–62.
Division 2 Champions: 1960–61, 1967–68.
Division 3 (South) Champions: 1953–54, 1956–57.
Record attendance: 30,837 v. Manchester United (League), February 1969.
Modern Capacity: 30,500.
Entered Football League: 1938—Div. 3 (South).
Biggest win: 10–0 v. Floriana, Malta (European Cup), September, 1962.
Heaviest defeat: 1–10 v. Fulham (Div. 1), December 1963.
Best in F.A. Cup: 5th Round 1953–54, 1958–59, 1966–67, 1970–71.
Best in Football League Cup: 5th Round 1965–66.
Pitch measurements: 112 × 75 yd.
Highest League Scorer in Single Season: E. Phillips—41 in 1956–57 (Div. 3 South).
Transfers—
    Highest fee paid: £65,000—Allan Hunter (from Blackburn), September 1971.
    Highest fee received: £88,000—Danny Hegan (to W.B.A.), May 1969.

Leeds United

Elland Road,
Leeds, LS11 0ES.

Shirts: White
Shorts: White
Stockings: White

Since the late sixties, Leeds have established a reputation as one of the most consistent and powerful clubs in Europe. Yet in 1962 they finished only two places away from Third Division football, at which point player-manager Don Revie took over as the full-time boss.

Revie rebuilt the team, and a new era began for Leeds in 1964 with their return to the First Division. In their first season back in the top bracket, Leeds came near to a great double, being beaten to the First Division title by Manchester United on goal average and losing the F.A. Cup Final to Liverpool in extra time. They achieved the League Cup and Fairs Cup double in 1968, and at last won the Championship in 1969. But the F.A. Cup still eluded them, despite leading Chelsea three times in the 1970 Final—twice at Wembley and again in the Old Trafford replay. By 1971 they were fielding a full team of Internationals.

At last, in May 1972, Leeds United won the F.A. Cup, beating the holders Arsenal, but, two nights later, they were foiled in their other great bid, losing the final Championship match at Wolverhampton where a point would have given them the Double.

League Champions: 1968–69.
Division 2 Champions: 1923–24, 1963–64.
F.A. Cup Winners: 1971–72.
League Cup Winners: 1967–68.
European Fairs Cup Winners: 1967–68, 1970–71.
Record attendance: 57,892 v. Sunderland (F.A. Cup), March 1967.
Modern Capacity: 50,000.
Entered Football League: 1905—Div. 2 (as Leeds City).
Biggest win: 10–0 v. Lyn Oslo (European Cup), September 1969.
Heaviest defeat: 1–8 v. Stoke City (Div. 1), August 1934.
Pitch measurements: 115 × 76 yd.
Highest League Scorer in Single Season: J. Charles—42 in 1953–54 (Div. 2).
Transfers—
    Highest fee paid: £165,000—Allan Clarke (from Leicester), June 1969.
    Highest fee received: £80,000—Mike O'Grady (to Wolves), September 1969.

Leicester City

Filbert Street Ground,
Leicester.
Leicester 57111/2

Shirts: Royal Blue
Shorts: White
Stockings: Royal Blue

About a dozen old boys of Wyggeston School had a collection of ninepence each to buy a football and start a soccer team in 1884. They called themselves Leicester Fosse.

One of the first grounds Fosse played on was the Leicester rugby football pitch and they also had matches in public parks. In 1889 the club moved to Filbert Street, and ten years after formation they were elected to the Second Division.

The name was changed from Fosse to City in 1919. By then they were a well-established Second Division club. They have won the Division Two championship five times—they got their first taste of First Division football in 1925. However, until the sixties, Leicester did not figure often in the football honours list. They have played in the F.A. Cup Final four times—thrice in the sixties—and never won it. In 1964 they did win the League Cup and were its runners-up in the following season. City returned to the First Division in 1971 under the managership of Frank O'Farrell, who left to take over Manchester United and was succeeded by Jimmy Bloomfield.

Two Arthurs have been principal goalscoring heroes of Leicester. Arthur Chandler achieved a total of 262 between 1923 and 1935, and Arthur Rowley scored 44 League goals in the 1956–57 season to help them to the Second Division title.

Division 2 Champions: 1924–25, 1936–37, 1953–54, 1956–57, 1970–71.
League Cup Winners: 1963–64.
Record attendance: 47,298 v. Tottenham (F.A. Cup), February 1928.
Modern Capacity: 42,000.
Entered Football League: 1894—Div. 2 (as Leicester Fosse).
Biggest win: 10–0 v. Portsmouth (Div. 1), October 1928.
Heaviest defeat: 0–12 v. Nottingham F. (Div. 1), April 1909.
Best in F.A. Cup: Runners-up 1948–49, 1960–61, 1962–63, 1968–69.
Pitch measurements: 112 × 75 yd.
Highest League Scorer in Single Season: A. Rowley—44 in 1956–57 (Div. 2).
Transfers—
    Highest fee paid: £150,000—Allan Clarke (from Fulham), June 1968.
    Highest fee received: £165,000—Allan Clarke (to Leeds), June 1969.

Lincoln City

Sincil Bank,
Lincoln.
Lincoln 21912/21298

Shirts: Red, White Sleeves
Shorts: White, Red Seam
Stockings: Red, White Top

Lincoln City have experienced sharply contrasting fortunes since becoming founder members of Division Two in 1892. Twice they were voted out of the section after finishing at the foot of the table—in 1908 and 1911. Three times they have won the Championship of the old Division Three North, and five times they have had to apply for re-election to Division Four.

The achievement of winning the Third Division North title in 1948 was particularly noteworthy since City's team was composed entirely of part-time players.

Andy Graver, who had two spells with the club, scored 144 League goals for Lincoln through the 1950s and another successful centre-forward was Jim Hutchinson whose 32 goals in 1947—48 made him leading marksman in the Third Division that season.

Lincoln's most impressive season of all was in 1951—52, the last time they won honours. As Third North Champions they were the highest-scoring Football League side that season with 121 goals. Graver, later transferred to Leicester and then bought back again—each time at a still-existing record fee for Lincoln—scored 37 of them, including six in the club's biggest ever win of 11—1 against Crewe Alexandra.

Division 3 (North) Champions: 1931—32, 1947—48, 1951—52.
Record attendance: 23,196 v. Derby County (League Cup), November 1967.
Modern Capacity: 25,000.
Entered Football League: 1892—Div. 2.
Biggest win: 11—1 v. Crewe Alexandra (Div. 3 North), September 1951.
Heaviest defeat: 3—11 v. Manchester City (Div. 2), March 1895.
Best in F.A. Cup: 4th Round 1953—54, 1960—61.
Best in Football League Cup: 4th Round 1967—68.
Pitch measurements: 110 × 75 yd.
Highest League Scorer in Single Season: A. Hall—42 in 1931—32 (Div. 3 North).
Transfers—
   Highest fee paid: £15,000—Andy Graver (from Leicester), June 1955.
   Highest fee received: £29,500—Andy Graver (to Leicester), December 1954.

Liverpool

Anfield Road,
Liverpool, 4.
051–263–2361

Shirts: Red
Shorts: Red
Stockings: Red

For football fanaticism there is no place quite like Merseyside, where the game is almost a religion, with Anfield the worshipping shrine for half the city's soccer devotees. It is hard to realize that as recently as 1962 Liverpool were in the Second Division.

Twice in three seasons (1963–66) they were crowned League Champions, and in the year between they won the F.A. Cup for the first time. What's more, for the past eight seasons the Kop has witnessed European football, in which Bill Shankly's team went closest to honours in 1966, when they were beaten by Borussia Dortmund in the Cup-Winners' Cup Final.

Liverpool's start in League football augured well for a success-ful future. They took the Second Division title in their first season (1893–94), and altogether have won eleven Championships (seven in the First Division, four in the Second). Yet if it had not been for Everton, Liverpool might never have graced the football world. Everton had been playing at Anfield when, around 1892, the owner decided to put up the rent. Rather than pay the extra money, Everton moved to Goodison Park, but a few of their members stayed behind at Anfield, formed a new club and called it Liverpool.

League Champions: 1900–01, 1905–06, 1921–22, 1922–23, 1946–47, 1963–64, 1965–66.
Division 2 Champions: 1893–94, 1895–96, 1904–05, 1961–62.
F.A. Cup Winners: 1964–65.
Record attendance: 61,905 v. Wolves (F.A. Cup), February 1952.
Modern Capacity: 54,000.
Entered Football League: 1893—Div. 2.
Biggest win: 10–0 v. Dundalk (Fairs Cup), September 1969.
Heaviest defeat: 1–9 v. Birmingham (Div. 2), December 1954.
Best in Football League Cup: 4th Round 1968–69, 1971–72.
Pitch measurements: 110 × 75 yd.
Highest League Scorer in Single Season: R. Hunt—41 in 1961–62 (Div. 2).
Transfers—
   Highest fee paid: £110,000—John Toshack (from Cardiff), November 1970.
   Highest fee received: £80,000—Tony Hateley (to Coventry), September 1968.

60

Luton Town

70–72 Kenilworth Road,
Luton, LU1 1OH.
0582–23151

Shirts: White
Shorts: Black
Stockings: White

Luton Town established more than a club record with the sale of centre-forward Malcolm Macdonald to Newcastle United for £185,000 in May 1971. That fee made him the highest-priced player to leave the Second Division, and Macdonald's personal contribution in two seasons at Luton had been 58 goals.

Thirty-four years before the Macdonald era, Luton had another headline-making centre-forward in Joe Payne, their top scorer, with 55 goals, when they gained promotion to Division Two in 1937. The previous season Payne, who later joined Chelsea, scored *ten* goals as emergency centre-forward in Luton's 12–0 win over Bristol Rovers. It is an individual scoring record that has never been equalled in League or F.A. Cup football.

In 1955 Luton moved up to Division One after a triple tie on points, their superior goal average allowing them, and not Rotherham, to be promoted with Birmingham. Four years later they reached the F.A. Cup Final for the first time, losing 2–1 to Nottingham Forest. But in 1960 Luton were relegated (with Leeds) and continued to drop—to Division Three in 1963 and to the Fourth in 1965. The way back began with promotion to the Third Division in 1968 and two years later Luton were welcomed back to Division Two.

Division 3 (South) Champions: 1936–37.
Division 4 Champions: 1967–68.
Record attendance: 30,069 v. Blackpool (F.A. Cup), March 1959.
Modern Capacity: 31,000.
Entered Football League: 1897—Div. 2.
Biggest win: 12–0 v. Bristol Rovers (Div. 3 South), April 1936.
Heaviest defeat: 1–9 v. Swindon Town (Div. 3 South), August 1921.
Best in F.A. Cup: Runners-up 1958–59.
Best in Football League Cup: 4th Round 1962–63.
Pitch measurements: 112 × 72 yd.
Highest League Scorer in Single Season: J. Payne—55 in 1936–37 (Div. 3 South).
Transfers—
   Highest fee paid: £35,000—David Court (from Arsenal), July 1970.
   Highest fee received: £185,000—Malcolm Macdonald (to Newcastle), May 1971.

Manchester City

Maine Road,
Moss Side,
Manchester, MI4 7WM.
061—226—1191/2

Shirts: Sky Blue, White Trimmings
Shorts: White
Stockings: Sky Blue, Maroon and White Ringed Tops

Since their return from the Second Division as recently as 1966, Manchester City have become one of Britain's most formidable sides under the dual influence of Joe Mercer (now club manager) and Malcolm Allison, promoted from assistant-manager and coach to team manager in autumn 1971.

During the previous four seasons City captain, that ageless full-back Tony Book, collected four of the game's top prizes—the League Championship trophy in 1968, the F.A. Cup in 1969 and, in 1970, the League Cup and Cup-Winners' Cup.

In the 1930s City overshadowed United in Manchester's battle for soccer prestige, but after the war the success pendulum swung Old Trafford way, until City made Mercer their manager at the age of 50, in July 1965.

Formed as Ardwick, in 1887, they became original members of Div. 2 in 1892, changing their name two years later.

Space permits mention of only a few of the club's great-name players of the past such as Billy Meredith, Jimmy McMullan, Eric Brook, Sam Cowan, Jackie Bray, Peter Doherty, Matt Busby, and two of the finest goalkeepers the game has seen, Frank Swift and German-born Bert Trautmann.

League Champions: 1936—37, 1967—68.
Division 2 Champions: 1898—99, 1902—03, 1909—10, 1927—28, 1946—47, 1965—66.
F.A. Cup Winners: 1903—04, 1933—34, 1955—56, 1968—69.
League Cup Winners: 1969—70.
Winners of European Cup-Winners' Cup: 1969—70.
Record attendance: 84,569 v. Stoke (F.A. Cup), March 1934.
Modern Capacity: 65,000.
Entered Football League: 1892—Div. 2 (as Ardwick).
Biggest win: 11—3 v. Lincoln City (Div. 2), March 1895.
Heaviest defeat: 1—9 v. Everton (Div. 1), September 1906.
Pitch measurements: 117×79 yd.
Highest League Scorer in Single Season: T. Johnson—38 in 1928—29 (Div. 1).
Transfers—
    Highest fee paid: £200,000—Rodney Marsh (from Q.P.R.), March 1972.
    Highest fee received: £100,000—Denis Law (to Torino, Italy), June 1961.

Manchester United

Old Trafford,
Manchester, MI6 0RA.
061-872-1661/2

Shirts: Red, White Trimmings
Shorts: White
Stockings: Black, Red Top and
White Band.

Manchester United's is a history of two clubs, not one. The first
died on 6 February 1958, when the aircraft bringing them home
from a European Cup-tie crashed in snow on take-off from
Munich. Among 23 who lost their lives in the worst ever disaster
to hit a British club were eight players—Geoff Bent, Roger Byrne,
Eddie Colman, Mark Jones, David Pegg, Tommy Taylor, Bill
Whelan and Duncan Edwards, who died 15 days later.

The life of manager Matt Busby was also in the balance, and by
the time he was able to return to Old Trafford, a new Manchester
United team had been born. Less than three months later they
played Bolton in the most emotion-charged F.A. Cup Final of all.
In 1963 they returned to Wembley and won the Cup for the
third time; they became League Champions again in 1965 and
1967 and, a year later, on 29 May 1968, achieved a Wembley
triumph exceeded in drama only by England's 1966 World Cup
victory. That night they defeated Benfica 4—1, after extra time, to
become England's first holders of the European Cup.

League Champions: 1907—08, 1910—11, 1951—52, 1955—56,
   1956—57, 1964—65, 1966—67.
Division 2 Champions: 1935—36.
F.A. Cup Winners: 1908—09, 1947—48, 1962—63.
European Cup Winners: 1967—68.
Record attendance:* 76,962—Wolves v. Grimsby (F.A. Cup
   Semi-final), March 1939.
Modern Capacity: 63,500.
Entered Football League: 1892—Div. 1 (as Newton Heath).
Biggest win: 10—0 v. Anderlecht, Belgium (European Cup),
   September 1956.
Heaviest defeat: 0—7 v. Aston Villa (Div. 1), December 1930.
Best in Football League Cup: Semi-final 1969—70, 1970—71.
Pitch measurements: 116 × 76 yd.
Highest League Scorer in Single Season: D. Viollet—32 in
   1959—60 (Div. 1).
Transfers—Highest fee paid: £200,000—Ian Moore (from
   Nott'm Forest), March 1972. **Highest fee received:**
   £40,000—John Connelly (to Blackburn), September 1966.

* The record crowd for a League match in England is 82,950 for
Manchester United v. Arsenal on 17 January 1948—played at
Manchester City's ground at Maine Road, which United were
sharing while Old Trafford was under repair after War damage.

Mansfield Town

Field Mill Ground,
Quarry Lane,
Mansfield.
Mansfield 23567

Shirts: White, Blue and
    Amber Neck and Cuffs
Shorts: Royal Blue, Amber
    Seam
Stockings: White, Blue
    and Amber Ring
    (ankle)

The name of Mansfield Town was on many people's lips one February night in 1969—and no wonder. The Third Division club had just astounded the football world by beating West Ham United—who included three World Cup players, Bobby Moore, Geoff Hurst and Martin Peters—by 3–0 in the fifth round of the F.A. Cup, and it took prodigious efforts by the eventual Finalists, Leicester City, to beat Mansfield 1–0 in the next round.

Such days of spectacular deeds help to compensate followers of smaller clubs for seasons of comparatively unexciting activity. Since winning the Midland League in 1924, 1925 and 1929, Mansfield have rarely attracted national acclaim.

Entering the League (Division Three South) in 1931, they have never reached the Second Division, missing it by one place in 1951 and 1965.

Roy Goodall, Freddie Steele, Charlie Mitten, Sam Weaver, Raich Carter and Tommy Cummings are among illustrious names who as managers of Mansfield have tried, with varying degrees of success since the last war, to bring a higher standard of football to Field Mill. The attempt continues.

Record attendance: 24,467 v. Nott'm F. (F.A. Cup), Jan. 1953.
Modern Capacity: 22,000.
Entered Football League: 1931—Div. 3 (South).
Biggest win: 9–2 v. Rotherham (Div. 3 North), December 1934; 9–2 v. Hounslow Town (F.A. Cup), November 1962.
Heaviest defeat: 1–8 v. Walsall (Div. 3 North), January 1933.
Highest final League position: Runners-up Div. 3 (North) 1950–51.
Best in F.A. Cup: 6th Round 1968–69.
Best in Football League Cup: 3rd Round 1964–65, 1965–66.
Pitch measurements: 115 × 72 yd.
Highest League Scorer in Single Season: E. Harston—55 in 1936–37 (Div. 3 North).
Transfers—
    Highest fee paid: £10,000—Bill Williams (from W.B.A.), January 1966; £10,000—Sam Ellis (from Sheffield Wed.), March 1972.
    Highest fee received: £50,000—Malcolm Partridge (to Leicester), September 1970; £50,000—Stuart Boam (to Middlesbrough), May 1971.

Middlesbrough

Ayresome Park,
Middlesbrough,
Teesside, TS1 4PB.
Middlesbrough 89659/85996

Shirts: Red
Shorts: Red, White Seam
Stockings: Red

Middlesbrough, the only League club to have won the F.A. Amateur Cup under their present title, were formed following a tripe supper at a local hotel in 1876. They turned professional in 1892. But for seven years, from 1892—99, they reverted to their original status and during that time twice won the Amateur Cup.

As a professional club again, Middlesbrough gained admission to Division Two and in their third term (1901—02) they were promoted. Their second season in the First Division was marked by the opening of the club's present ground at Ayresome Park.

They caused a sensation in 1905, when they paid Sunderland the game's first transfer fee of £1000 for Alf Common, and not long afterwards Steve Bloomer, another famous name in soccer history, joined 'Boro' from Derby.

During their earlier years, Middlesbrough set several records. Two came in 1926—27 when, after the change in the offside law, they scored what is still the Division Two record of 122 goals, of which local-born centre-forward George Camsell contributed 59, another unbeaten record for the same division. In 1927—28, Middlesbrough and Tottenham obtained a less enviable record— the highest points totals (37 and 38) for teams relegated from the First Division.

Division 2 Champions: 1926—27, 1928—29.
F.A. Amateur Cup Winners: 1894—95, 1897—98.
Record attendance: 53,596 v. Newcastle Utd (League), December 1949.
Modern Capacity: 42,500.
Entered Football League: 1899—Div. 2.
Biggest win: 10—3 v. Sheffield Utd (Div. 1), November 1933.
Heaviest defeat: 0—9 v. Blackburn (Div. 2), November 1954.
Best in F.A. Cup: 6th Round 1935—36, 1946—47, 1969—70.
Best in Football League Cup: 3rd Round 1961—62, 1965—66, 1967—68, 1970—71.
Pitch measurements: 115 × 75 yd.
Highest League Scorer in Single Season: G. Camsell—59 in 1926—27 (Div. 2).
Transfers—
  Highest fee paid: £60,000—John Craggs (from Newcastle), August 1971.
  Highest fee received: £57,000—Geoff Butler (to Chelsea), September 1967.

Millwall

The Den, Coldblow Lane,
New Cross,
London, SE14 5RH.
01–639–3143/4

Shirts: White
Shorts: White
Stockings: White

Between 1964 and 1967 Millwall established a League record that will not easily be beaten. They played 59 consecutive home matches without defeat, a sequence that started in the Fourth Division on 24 August 1964 and ended in a Second Division match against Plymouth Argyle on 14 January 1967. A much earlier Millwall record was their aggregate of 127 goals in the winning of the Third Division (South) Championship of 1927–28.

The club was formed in 1885 as Millwall Rovers and was among the original members of the Third Division in 1920. In 1937 they became the first Third Division club to reach the F.A. Cup semi-finals, beating First Division opponents Chelsea, Derby County and Manchester City at The Den, before falling 2–1 to Sunderland at the last hurdle before Wembley.

A year later Millwall were back in Division Two, but after the war their fortunes slumped and they dropped from Second Division to Third and then through the trapdoor to the Fourth.

In May 1970 Millwall received their highest fee when they transferred forward Keith Weller to Chelsea for £100,000. A year later, Millwall made a bold bid to achieve a First Division place, their ambition for half a century since they entered the Football League.

Division 3 (South) Champions: 1927–28, 1937–38.
Division 4 Champions: 1961–62.
Record attendance: 48,672 v. Derby County (F.A. Cup), February 1937.
Modern Capacity: 40,000.
Entered Football League: 1920—Div. 3.
Biggest win: 9–1 v. Torquay Utd (Div. 3 South), August 1927; 9–1 v. Coventry City (Div. 3 South), November 1927.
Heaviest defeat: 1–9 v. Aston Villa (F.A. Cup), January 1946.
Best in F.A. Cup: Semi-final 1899–1900, 1902–03, 1936–37.
Best in Football League Cup: 4th Round 1965–66, 1967–68, 1969–70.
Pitch measurements: 110 × 72½ yd.
Highest League Scorer in Single Season: R. Parker—37 in 1926–27 (Div. 3 South).
Transfers—
    Highest fee paid: £40,000—Barry Bridges (from Q.P.R.), September 1970.
    Highest fee received: £100,000—Keith Weller (to Chelsea), May 1970.

Newcastle United

St. James' Park
Newcastle-upon-Tyne
NE1 4ST.
0632—28361/2

Shirts: Black and White Stripes
Shorts: Black
Stockings: Black, White Tops

Blaydon Races, the Geordie folk song, rang out in the unlikely surroundings of Budapest in June 1969. The occasion: Newcastle's 3—2 second-leg victory over the Hungarian side Ujpest Dozsa giving them the Fairs' Cup 6—2 on aggregate at their first attempt in Europe.

Tyneside fans also sang with great gusto at Wembley, in 1951 and 1952, when their club became the first this century to take the F.A. Cup in successive seasons. And in 1955 they won it again, for the sixth time.

Newcastle's most renowned player appeared in the 1920s. Hughie Gallacher helped them to their fourth League Championship in 1926—27, when he set up the club record with 36 goals.

After the Second World War Tyneside roared to the sharp-shooting of 'Wor Jackie' Milburn, who scored 178 League goals (the club aggregate record) from 1946—57. Together with full-back Bob Cowell and left-winger Bobby Mitchell, he played in the Cup-winning teams of 1951, 1952 and 1955, but Newcastle fans did not see the goalscoring like of Milburn again until the start of season 1971—72, with the £185,000 signing of Malcolm Macdonald from Luton.

League Champions: 1904—05, 1906—07, 1908—09, 1926—27.
Division 2 Champions: 1964—65.
F.A. Cup Winners: 1909—10, 1923—24, 1931—32, 1950—51, 1951—52, 1954—55.
European Fairs Cup Winners: 1968—69.
Record attendance: 68,386 v. Chelsea (League). Sept. 1930.
Modern Capacity: 60,000.
Entered Football League: 1893—Div. 2.
Biggest win: 13—0 v. Newport County (Div. 2), October 1946.
Heaviest defeat: 0—9 v. Burton Wanderers (Div. 2), April 1895.
Best in Football League Cup: 3rd Round 1963—64, 1968—69, 1971—72.
Pitch measurements: 110×75 yd.
Highest League Scorer in Single Season: H. Gallacher—36 in 1926—27 (Div. 1).
Transfers—
   Highest fee paid: £185,000—Malcolm Macdonald (from Luton), May 1971.
   Highest fee received: £120,000—Bryan Robson (to West Ham), February 1971.

Newport County

Somerton Park,
Newport, Mon.
Newport 71543/71271

Shirts: Tangerine
Shorts: Black
Stockings: Tangerine

Older supporters of Newport County still wonder what the club might have achieved but for the outbreak of the Second World War. Their speculation is understandable for in 1938–39, the last full League season before hostilities, Newport won the Division Three South Championship in confident style.

But when, after a seven-year wait, League football resumed in 1946–47, they faced the Second Division with a reshaped team and were promptly relegated. They finished bottom with only 23 points from the 42 fixtures, and conceded 133 goals. At Newcastle, on 5 October 1946, County crashed 13–0, which equalled what is still the heaviest Football League defeat (Stockport County 13, Halifax Town 0 in Div. 3 North on 6 January 1934).

These statistics gave Newport all the wrong reasons by which to remember their only season in the Second Division, and since then life for them has been an almost continuous struggle for survival in a Rugby Union stronghold.

For clubs such as Newport who are constantly beset by financial problems, a run in the F.A. Cup can be a boon. Unfortunately, such occasions have been rare, though in 1949 Newport reached the fifth round before losing, a little unluckily, 3–2 at Portsmouth. On the way they overcame Leeds United and Huddersfield Town, and that remains their farthest progress in the F.A. Cup.

Division 3 (South) Champions: 1938–39.
Record attendance: 24,268 v. Cardiff City (League), October 1937.
Modern Capacity: 20,000.
Entered Football League: 1920—Div. 3.
Biggest win: 10–0 v. Merthyr Town (Div. 3 South), April 1930.
Heaviest defeat: 0–13 v. Newcastle Utd (Div. 2), October 1946.
Best in F.A. Cup: 5th Round 1948–49.
Best in Football League Cup: 3rd Round 1962–63.
Pitch measurements: 110 × 75 yd.
Highest League Scorer in Single Season: T. Martin—34 in 1929–30 (Div. 3 South).
Transfers—
  Highest fee paid: £4000—Graham Coldrick (from Cardiff), March 1970.
  Highest fee received: £10,000—Ollie Burton (to Norwich), February 1961.

Northampton Town

County Ground,
Abington Avenue,
Northampton, NN1 4PS.
Northampton 31553

Shirts: Claret, White
   Sleeves
Shorts: Claret, White Trim
Stockings: White

Northampton Town are always assured of one significant entry in the history of the Football League. In 1965 they became the first club to rise from the Fourth to the First Division, a feat they achieved in five remarkable seasons. The tragedy was that their return to the lowest reaches of the League should be even swifter. They lasted only one season in Division One and, almost unbelievably, by 1969 were back in Division Four.

The club first tasted success as Southern League champions in 1909 and the man who guided them to that triumph was Herbert Chapman, later to win much wider managerial fame with Huddersfield Town and Arsenal. Strangely, that was Northampton's only notable football prize until they took the Division Three title in 1962–63.

Dave Bowen, the former Wales and Arsenal wing-half, who managed the club through most of the vicissitudes to the 1970s. Cliff Holton, another previously with Arsenal, Ron Flowers and Jack English are just a few of the experienced players who have starred for the 'Cobblers'.

Division 3 Champions: 1962–63.
Record attendance: 24,523 v. Fulham (League), April 1966.
Modern Capacity: 25,000.
Entered Football League: 1920—Div. 3.
Biggest win: 10–0 v. Walsall (Div. 3 South), November 1927.
Heaviest defeat: 0–8 v. Walsall (Div. 3 South), October 1946.
Best in F.A. Cup: 5th Round 1933–34, 1949–50, 1969–70.
Best in Football League Cup: 5th Round 1964–65, 1966–67.
Pitch measurements: 110×76 yd.
Highest League Scorer in Single Season: C. Holton—36 in 1961–62 (Div. 3).
Transfers—
  Highest fee paid: £27,000—Joe Broadfoot (from Ipswich), November 1965.
  Highest fee received: £45,000—John Roberts (to Arsenal), April 1969.

Norwich City

Carrow Road,
Norwich, Nor 22T.
Norwich 21514

Shirts: Yellow, Green
    Collar and Cuffs
Shorts: Green
Stockings: Yellow

Norwich City won the Football League Cup in only its second season (1961–62), and it is as cup fighters that the East Anglian club are best known. Founded in 1905, they waited only four years before establishing their reputation by knocking out Liverpool at Anfield. Sunderland in 1910–11, Tottenham in 1914–15, Leeds in 1934–35, Liverpool again in 1950–51, and Arsenal at Highbury in 1953–54 were five more of their notable cup 'scalps'.

Their greatest F.A. Cup run came in 1959 when, as a Third Division side, they knocked out Manchester United, Cardiff, Tottenham and Sheffield United before losing 1–0 to Luton after a 1–1 draw in the semi-final.

Norwich, who gained the nickname 'Canaries' when they adopted their green and yellow colours, and moved to a ground called 'The Nest' in 1908, were founder-members of Division Three (South) in 1920. They won promotion to Division Two in 1934, but were relegated five years later and stayed there until 1960. Ron Ashman, later to become City's manager, was captain and he set up the club record of 662 League and F.A. Cup appearances between 1947 and 1964.

In 1971–72, managed by Ron Saunders, Norwich won promotion to the First Division for the first time in their history.

Division 2 Champions: 1971–72.
Division 3 (South) Champions: 1933–34.
League Cup Winners: 1961–62.
Record attendance: 43,984 v. Leicester City (F.A. Cup), March 1963.
Modern Capacity: 42,000.
Entered Football League: 1920—Div. 3.
Biggest win: 10–2 v. Coventry (Div. 3 South), March 1930.
Heaviest defeat: 2–10 v. Swindon Town (S. League), September 1908.
Best in F.A. Cup: Semi-final 1958–59.
Pitch measurements: 114 × 74 yd.
Highest League Scorer in Single Season: R. Hunt—31 in 1955–56 (Div. 3 South).
Transfers—
    Highest fee paid: £40,000—David Cross (from Rochdale), October 1971.
    Highest fee received: £60,000—Hugh Curran (to Wolves), January 1969.

Nottingham Forest

City Ground,
Nottingham, NG2 5FJ.
0602—88236/7/8

Shirts: Red, White Neck
and Cuffs
Shorts: White, Red Seam
Stockings: Red with
White-banded Top

In the strictest sense of the word, Nottingham Forest are the only *true* club in the Football League, run as they are by an elected committee. The other 91 are all limited companies, each with a board of directors. Another oddity is that Forest play outside the city of Nottingham and Notts County play inside the boundary, on the opposite bank of the River Trent.

Forest were founded in 1865, and are the third oldest League club after Notts County and Stoke City. In various ways, Forest helped shape the game's early history. For instance, their England International Sam Widdowson was the first player to wear shinguards, in 1874. It was in a Forest game four years later that a referee used a whistle for the first time—previously signals were given by handkerchief—and in 1891 the crossbar and nets made their first appearance in soccer, at the Forest ground.

The club's first F.A. Cup success came in 1898, but although they won the trophy again in 1959, the Championship has continued to elude Forest.

Yet they have seldom lacked players of International standing, their more recent caps including Terry Hennessey, Joe Baker, Alan Hinton, Jim Baxter and Ian Moore. Bob McKinlay, former centre-half and captain, set the remarkable club record of 614 League appearances between 1951 and 1969.

Division 2 Champions: 1906—07, 1921—22.
Division 3 (South) Champions: 1950—51.
F.A. Cup Winners: 1897—98, 1958—59.
Record attendance: 49,945 v. Manchester Utd (League) October 1967.
Modern Capacity: 49,500.
Entered Football League: 1892—Div. 1.
Biggest win: 14—0 v. Clapton (F.A. Cup), 1890—91.
Heaviest defeat: 1—9 v. Blackburn Rovers (Div. 2), April 1937.
Best in Football League Cup: 4th Round 1960—61, 1969—70.
Pitch measurements: 115 × 78 yd.
Highest League Scorer in Single Season: W. Ardron—36 in 1950—51 (Div. 3 South).
Transfers—
    Highest fee paid: £100,000—Jim Baxter (from Sunderland), December 1967.
    Highest fee received: £200,000—Ian Moore (to Man. Utd.), March 1972.

Notts County

Meadow Lane Ground,
Nottingham, NG2 3HJ.
Nottingham 84152

Shirts: Black and White Stripes
Shorts: Black
Stockings: White

Notts County is the oldest club in the Football League, formed in 1862 and founder member of the League in 1888. Twice in the next six years they reached the final of the F.A. Cup. They lost 3–1 to Blackburn Rovers at Kennington Oval in 1891, but in 1894 they won the trophy by beating Bolton Wanderers 4–1 at Everton. They spent three separate periods in Division One between 1897 and 1926, but their highest final position was third in 1901.

Few events in County's chequered history have caused greater comment than the sensational signing of centre forward Tommy Lawton from Chelsea in November 1947 for £20,000, a figure which few clubs, let alone a Third Division side, could afford in those days. Yet the deal paid off for club and player. County soon won promotion and Lawton gained further caps for England.

Jackie Sewell went from Meadow Lane to Sheffield Wednesday in March 1951, for the then record fee of £34,500, after scoring nearly 100 League goals.

Another remarkable County character was the 6 ft 5 in Albert Iremonger, rated by some as the finest goalkeeper ever to play for England. He made 564 League appearances for the club from 1904–26.

Division 2 Champions: 1896–97, 1913–14, 1922–23.
Division 3 (South) Champions: 1930–31, 1949–50.
Division 4 Champions: 1970–71.
F.A. Cup Winners: 1893–94.
Record attendance: 47,301 v. York (F.A. Cup), March 1955.
Modern Capacity: 45,000.
Entered Football League: 1888 — Div. 1.
Biggest win: 11–1 v. Newport County (Div. 3 South), January 1949.
Heaviest defeat: 1–9 v. Aston Villa (Div. 1), September 1888; 1–9 v. Blackburn Rovers (Div. 1), November 1889; 1–9 v. Portsmouth (Div. 2), April 1927.
Best in Football League Cup: 5th Round 1963–64.
Pitch measurements: $117\frac{1}{2} \times 76$ yd.
Highest League Scorer in Single Season: T. Keetley — 39 in 1930–31 (Div. 3 South).
Transfers—
    Highest fee paid: £25,000 — Leon Leuty (from Bradford), September 1950.
    Highest fee received: £34,500 — Jackie Sewell (to Sheffield Wed.), March 1951.

Oldham Athletic

Boundary Park,
Oldham.
061–624–4972

Shirts: Tangerine, Blue and
White Collar and Cuffs
Shorts: Blue
Stockings: Blue

Although most of Oldham's modern existence has been spent in the Third and Fourth Divisions, they were in the Championship section half a century ago. Indeed, they narrowly failed to carry off the League title in 1914–15, finishing a point behind Everton.

Eric Gemmell performed a notable goalscoring feat for Oldham in season 1951–52. Playing in a Third Division North match against Chester, he scored seven times in an 11–2 win. An even more remarkable feat was achieved by Sam Wynne while playing left-back against Manchester United in October 1923. He scored from a penalty and a free-kick, and also put the ball twice into his own goal!

In addition to developing goalscorers, Oldham have found a number of International goalkeepers, notably Jack Hacking, Ted Taylor, Albert Gray and Frank Moss, who was one of seven Arsenal players capped against Italy in 1934.

Season 1970–71 was notable in two ways for Oldham. They earned promotion to Division Three and their players also won the one-season Ford Sporting League, bringing the club total prize money of £80,000 for the improvement of spectator facilities.

Division 3 (North) Champions: 1952–53.
Record attendance: 47,671 v. Sheffield Wed. (F.A. Cup), January 1930.
Modern Capacity: 36,500.
Entered Football League: 1907 —Div. 2.
Biggest win: 11–0 v. Southport (Div. 4), December 1962.
Heaviest defeat: 4–13 v. Tranmere (Div. 3 North), December 1935.
Best in F.A. Cup: Semi-final 1912–13.
Best in Football League Cup: 2nd Round 1960–61, 1962–63, 1964–65, 1965–66, 1970–71, 1971–72.
Pitch measurements: 110 × 74 yd.
Highest League Scorer in Single Season: T. Davis —33 in 1936–37 (Div. 3 North).
Transfers—
    Highest fee paid: £20,000 —Dennis Stevens (from Everton), December 1965; £20,000 —Ian Towers (from Burnley), December 1965.
    Highest fee received: £35,000 —Ken Knighton (to Preston), December 1967.

Orient

Leyton Stadium,
Brisbane Road, Leyton,
London, E10.
01–539–1368/6800

Shirts: Red
Shorts: Red
Stockings: Red

When Orient sold brilliant young half-back Tommy Taylor to West Ham for £80,000 in October 1970, it was a move of considerable financial significance to a club which three years earlier almost foundered. Orient called a Sunday morning public meeting after disclosing accumulated debts of £100,000. The response was immediate and generous. By 1970 the deficit had been halved, and the sale of Taylor completed an economic recovery.

The club owe their name to the Orient Shipping Company. They were formed in 1881 as Clapton Orient; they became Leyton Orient in 1946 and dropped the prefix 'Leyton' in 1967. Orient made their home at Brisbane Road in 1937, having previously shared Clapton greyhound stadium, the Essex cricket ground at Leyton and the old Lea Bridge speedway stadium. In 1930 they played two home games at Wembley Stadium because their own ground was unavailable.

The club's struggle for survival began early. They were bottom of Division Two in their first League season (1905–06) and again in 1929. But after the lean thirties, manager Alec Stock, who had three spells in charge, took them to second place in Division Three South in 1955 and up into Division Two as Champions 12 months later. Six years later they gained promotion with Liverpool to Div. One, but survived only one season.

Division 3 (South) Champions: 1955–56.
Division 3 Champions: 1969–70.
Record attendance: 34,345 v. West Ham United (F.A. Cup), January 1964.
Modern Capacity: 35,000.
Entered Football League: 1905—Div. 2 (as Clapton Orient).
Biggest win: 9–2 v. Aldershot (Div. 3 South), February 1934; 9–2 v. Chester (League Cup), October 1962.
Heaviest defeat: 0–8 v. Aston Villa (F.A. Cup), January 1929.
Best in F.A. Cup: 6th Round 1925–26, 1953–54, 1971–72.
Best in Football League Cup: 5th Round 1962–63.
Pitch measurements: 110 × 80 yd.
Highest League Scorer in Single Season: T. Johnston—35 in 1957–58 (Div. 2).
Transfers—
    Highest fee paid: £30,000—Phil Hoadley (from Crystal Palace), October 1971.
    Highest fee received: £80,000—Tommy Taylor (to West Ham), October 1970.

Oxford United

Manor Ground,
Beech Road,
Headington, Oxford.
0865—61503

Shirts: Old Gold
Shorts: Black
Stockings: Old Gold

One of the oldest established clubs to stay outside the Football League, Oxford United, were formed in 1896 as Headington United but did not turn professional until 1949. They took their present name in 1961 and, after Accrington Stanley withdrew from Division Four in March 1962, Oxford got the chance of Football League status, quickly proving themselves worthy of it. In 1964 they became the first Fourth Division side to reach the sixth round of the F.A. Cup, and in only six seasons of League membership they climbed two divisions into the Second.

Several of the players who were with the club in their non-League days quickly adapted themselves to higher grade football. Among them were Ron Atkinson, Cyril Beavon, Pat Quartermain and Maurice Kyle. Oxford found Second Division competition fierce for a time, but moved up the table in the 1970—71 season, actually topping it on 26 September, though ultimately finishing in 14th position.

When United gained promotion from the Fourth Division in 1964—65 with 61 points, they scored 87 goals. Their results that season included a record 7—0 success against Barrow.

Division 3 Champions: 1967—68.
Record attendance: 22,730 v. Preston N.E. (F.A. Cup), February 1964.
Modern Capacity: 19,000.
Entered Football League: 1962—Div. 4.
Biggest win: 7—0 v. Barrow (Div. 4), December 1964.
Heaviest defeat: 0—5 v. Cardiff (Div. 2), February 1969.
Best in F.A. Cup: 6th Round 1963—64.
Best in Football League Cup: 5th Round 1969—70.
Pitch measurements: 112 × 78 yd.
Highest League Scorer in Single Season: C. Booth—23 in 1964—65 (Div. 4).
Transfers—
  Highest fee paid: £22,000—Nigel Cassidy (from Scunthorpe), November 1970.
  Highest fee received: £25,000—Jim Barron (to Nottingham Forest), July 1970.

Peterborough United

London Road Ground,
Peterborough, PE2 8AL.
Peterborough 3623

Shirts: Royal Blue
Shorts: White
Stockings: Royal Blue

When Peterborough United, an ambitious Southern League club
with a splendidly appointed ground, won admission to the Football League in 1960–61, the cynics wondered whether they
were really equipped to bridge the gap between the two grades
of football. The 'Posh', as they are familiarly known, gave the best
possible answer: they won the Fourth Division Championship at
the first attempt.

The following season they threatened to go straight into the
Second Division. Finally, however, they had to be content with
fifth place, though they scored more goals, 107, than either of the
promoted teams.

Terry Bly was the player who helped tear defences apart in
Peterborough's first season in League football. His tally of 52
goals remains the highest for the division, just as the 134 goals
obtained by Peterborough is a scoring record for any division of
the Football League.

The years since have been less happy and, at the end of the
1967–68 season, the club were demoted to the Fourth Division
because of alleged irregularities in their books. In 1965, however, they reached the sixth round of the F.A. Cup, beating Salisbury,
Q.P.R., Chesterfield, Arsenal and Swansea before losing to
Chelsea.

Division 4 Champions: 1960–61.
Record attendance: 30,096 v. Swansea (F.A. Cup), February
1965.
Modern Capacity: 30,000.
Entered Football League: 1960—Div. 4.
Biggest win: 8–1 v. Oldham Athletic (Div. 4), November
1969.
Heaviest defeat: 1–8 v. Northampton (F.A. Cup), December
1946.
Best in F.A. Cup: 6th Round 1964–65.
Best in Football League Cup: Semi-final 1965–66.
Pitch measurements: 113 × 76 yd.
Highest League Scorer in Single Season: T. Bly—52 in
1960–61 (Div. 4).
Transfers—
    Highest fee paid: £21,000—Derek Dougan (from Aston
    Villa), June 1963.
    Highest fee received: £30,000—John Wile (to W.B.A.),
    December 1970.

Plymouth Argyle

Home Park,
Plymouth,
Devon.
Plymouth 52561/2/3

Shirts: Green, White Collar and Sleeves
Shorts: White, Green Seam
Stockings: White, Green and Black Tops

Plymouth Argyle achieved some extraordinary feats in their early years in the old Southern Section of the Third Division. For six consecutive years between 1921 and 1927 they finished runners-up, twice missing promotion by a point and once on goal average; in 1920—21 they drew 21 of their 42 matches and the following season their defence conceded only 24 League goals.

The reward for consistency was finally earned in 1930 when the Devon club took the title with unmistakable authority. They finished seven points clear of the second club, Brentford, and lost only four matches.

Probably no League club has travelled more miles *in England* during their history than Argyle. Yet for all the strain which long journeys inevitably impose on players, the club have gone close to winning First Division status on several occasions. They finished fourth in Division Two in 1932 and 1953, and fifth in seasons 1937 and 1962.

Jack Cock led the Third Division South scoring list in 1925—26 with 32 goals, which is still the most obtained in a League season by an Argyle player. Moses Russell played 23 times for Wales in the 1920s and David Jack, later to gain fame with Bolton, Arsenal and England, was another star associated with the club.

Division 3 (South) Champions: 1929—30, 1951—52.
Division 3 Champions: 1958—59.
Record attendance: 43,596 v. Aston Villa (League), October 1936.
Modern Capacity: 40,000.
Entered Football League: 1920—Div. 3.
Biggest win: 8—1 v. Millwall (Div. 2), January 1932.
Heaviest defeat: 0—9 v. Stoke City (Div. 2), December 1960.
Best in F.A. Cup: 5th Round 1952—53.
Best in Football League Cup: Semi-final 1964—65.
Pitch measurements: 112 × 75 yd.
Highest League Scorer in Single Season: J. Cock—32 in 1925—26 (Div. 3 South).
Transfers—
  Highest fee paid: £45,000—Barrie Jones (from Swansea), September 1964.
  Highest fee received: £40,000—Norman Piper (to Portsmouth), May 1970.

Portsmouth

Fratton Park,
Frogmore Road,
Portsmouth, PO4 8RA.
Portsmouth 31204/5

Shirts: Royal Blue, Red,
White and Blue Trimmings
Shorts: Royal Blue
Stockings: Royal Blue, Red
White and Blue Tops

Portsmouth spent 25 consecutive seasons in Division One after gaining promotion in 1927 on the strength of a goal average that was 1/250th of a goal better than Manchester City's. Elevation to football's top flight was to be the launching pad for a catalogue of League and Cup successes. Portsmouth were defeated in the 1929 and 1934 F.A. Cup Finals, but beat hot favourites Wolves 4–1 in the 1939 Final.

The famous 'Pompey Chimes' rang out across Fratton Park as the League title was won in 1949, and Portsmouth successfully defended it the following season, becoming only the eighth club in the history of the game to complete such a double.

Thus Portsmouth were the first former Third Division club to win the Championship, but their star waned dramatically and they dropped to Division Three in 1959, after which they scrapped their reserve and youth sides. Currently they have been in the Second Division since 1962.

Portsmouth's half-back line in those early post-war years was a formidable one—Jimmy Scoular (Scotland), Reg Flewin and Jimmy Dickinson (England), who went on to play a record 764 League games for the club. He is now the club secretary.

League Champions: 1948–49, 1949–50.
Division 3 (South) Champions: 1923–24.
Division 3 Champions: 1961–62.
F.A. Cup Winners: 1938–39.
Record attendance: 51,385 v. Derby County (F.A. Cup), February 1949.
Modern Capacity: 46,000.
Entered Football League: 1920—Div. 3.
Biggest win: 9–1 v. Notts County (Div. 2), April 1927.
Heaviest defeat: 0–10 v. Leicester City (Div. 1), October 1928.
Best in Football League Cup: 5th Round 1960–61.
Pitch measurements: 116 × 72 yd.
Highest League Scorer in Single Season: W. Haines—40 in 1926–27 (Div. 2).
Transfers—
    Highest fee paid: £40,000—Mike Trebilcock (from Everton), January 1968; £40,000—Norman Piper (from Plymouth), May 1970.
    Highest fee received: £50,000—George Smith (to Middlesbrough), January 1969.

Port Vale

Vale Park, Burslem,
Stoke-on-Trent, ST6 1AW.
Stoke-on-Trent 87626/85524

Shirts: White, Black Edging
Shorts: White
Stockings: White, Black
Hooped Turnover

Port Vale nearly wrote a fresh page in the history of the F.A. Cup in 1954. No Third Division club has reached the final of the competition, but that year Vale looked as though they might be the first to do so. Caught up on a wave of enthusiasm which spread far beyond the Potteries, they beat Q.P.R. away (1–0), Cardiff away (2–0), Blackpool at home (2–0) and Leyton Orient away (1–0) on their way to the semi-finals. Before a crowd of 68,221 at Villa Park, they faced their Black Country neighbours and famed Cup fighters, West Bromwich Albion and, incredibly, led them until the second half through a goal by Albert Leake. In the end, however, the First Division side triumphed 2–1, but as consolation Port Vale won the Third North title that season by a margin of eleven points.

A number of players have given the 'Valiants' fine service, but none more so than local-born Roy Sproson who made 760 League appearances between 1950 and 1971. He was a member of the sides which won the Third Division (North) in 1953–54, the Fourth Division title in 1958–59 and was still ever present in the team which again won promotion to the Third Division by finishing fourth in 1970.

Division 3 (North) Champions: 1929–30, 1953–54.
Division 4 Champions: 1958–59.
Record attendance: 50,000 v. Aston Villa (F.A. Cup), February 1960.
Modern Capacity: 50,000.
Entered Football League: 1892—Div. 2.
Biggest win: 9–1 v. Chesterfield (Div. 2), September 1932.
Heaviest defeat: 0–10 v. Sheffield Utd (Div. 2), December 1892; 0–10 v. Notts County (Div. 2), February 1895.
Best in F.A. Cup: Semi-final 1953–54.
Best in Football League Cup: 2nd Round 1960–61, 1962–63, 1963–64, 1967–68.
Pitch measurements: 116×76 yd.
Highest League Scorer in Single Season: W. Kirkham—38 in 1926–27 (Div. 2).
Transfers—
Highest fee paid: £15,000—Albert Cheesebrough (from Leicester), July 1962; £15,000—Billy Bingham (from Everton), August 1963.
Highest fee received: £30,000—Terry Alcock (to Blackpool), August 1967.

Preston North End

Deepdale,
Preston, PR1 6RU.
Preston 53818/9

Shirts: White
Shorts: Dark Blue
Stockings: White

Preston North End won the first League Championship of all in 1888–89 without losing a match, and the F.A. Cup the same season without conceding a goal—a 'double' without parallel.

Founder members of the League, Preston justified their title 'Invincibles' until they were relegated in 1901. They returned in 1904, continuing to move ten times up and down between the divisions until, for the first time in their history, in 1970, they found themselves in Division Three. A year later they were Champions of that section.

After being beaten by Sunderland in the 1937 F.A. Cup Final, Preston carried off the trophy in 1938 when George Mutch gave them a 1–0 victory over Huddersfield from the penalty spot with the last kick of Wembley's first extra-time Final. Scots have always been prominent in Preston sides and Bill Shankly, now manager of Liverpool, was at wing-half in both those Finals.

Alex James was another of Preston's famous Scots; so were Tommy Docherty and Willie Cunningham.

Tom Finney, who made 433 League appearances (187 goals) and won 76 England caps, was the outstanding figure in Preston football from 1946–60.

League Champions: 1888–89, 1889–90.
Division 2 Champions: 1903–04, 1912–13, 1950–51.
Division 3 Champions: 1970–71.
F.A. Cup Winners: 1888–89, 1937–38.
The Double (League and F.A. Cup Winners): 1888–89.
Record attendance: 42,684 v. Arsenal (League), April 1938.
Modern Capacity: 39,500.
Entered Football League: 1888—Div. 1.
Biggest win: 26–0 v. Hyde (F.A. Cup), October 1887.
Heaviest defeat: 0–7 v. Blackpool (Div. 1), May 1948.
Best in Football League Cup: 4th Round 1962–63, 1965–66, 1971–72.
Pitch measurements: 112 × 78 yd.
Highest League Scorer in Single Season: E. Harper—37 in 1932–33 (Div. 2).
Transfers—
    Highest fee paid: £45,000—Willie Irvine (from Burnley), March 1968; £45,000—David Connor (from Manchester City), January 1972.
    Highest fee received: £80,000—Howard Kendall (to Everton), March 1967.

Queen's Park Rangers

Ellerslie Road,
Shepherd's Bush,
London, W12.
01-743-2618

Shirts: Blue and White
Hoops
Shorts: White
Stockings: White

The season of 1966—67 will always be recalled as a vintage one by supporters of Queen's Park Rangers. The club not only took the Third Division title by a margin of twelve points, but became the first outside the first two divisions to win the Football League Cup. In a thrilling decider at Wembley—the first time that venue was used for the League Cup—Rangers beat First Division opponents West Bromich Albion 3—2 after being two down.

The magic continued under Alec Stock's managership and the following year Rangers completed the greatest period in their history by going up into Division One—thus emulating Charlton's feat (1935 and 1936) of moving from Third to First Division in consecutive years. But Rangers immediately found the highest class too much, and were relegated at the end of the 1968—69 season with only 18 points.

Since their formation in 1885 as an amalgam of Christchurch Rangers and St Jude's Institute, Rangers have had twelve different homes, including two stays at White City.

Among Rangers' best-known post-war players have been Reg Allen, Ivor Powell, George Smith, Jimmy Langley, Tony Ingham, Les Allen, Terry Venables and Rodney Marsh.

Division 3 (South) Champions: 1947—48.
Division 3 Champions: 1966—67.
League Cup Winners: 1966—67.
Record attendance: 33,572 v. Chelsea (F.A. Cup), Feb. 1970.
Modern Capacity: 35,000.
Entered Football League: 1920—Div. 3.
Biggest win: 9—2 v. Tranmere Rov. (Div. 3), December 1960.
Heaviest defeat: 1—8 v. Mansfield Town (Div. 3), March 1965; 1—8 v. Manchester Utd (Div. 1), March 1969.
Best in F.A. Cup: 6th Round 1947—48, 1969—70 (also reached last eight—old 4th Round—in 1909—10, 1913—14, 1922—23).
Pitch measurements: 112 × 72 yd.
Highest League Scorer in Single Season: G. Goddard—37 in 1929—30 (Div. 3 South).
Transfers—
   Highest fee paid: £70,000—Terry Venables (from Tottenham), June 1969.
   Highest fee received: £200,000—Rodney Marsh (to Manchester City), March 1972.

Reading

Elm Park, Norfolk Road,
Reading, RG3 2EF.
Reading 57878/9

Shirts: Blue and White
    Hoops
Shorts: White
Stockings: White, Two
    Blue Rings

The Berkshire club were 100 years old in 1971, but far from celebrating their centenary in style, they were relegated to Division
Four for the first time. In the last eight seasons before the war they
never finished lower than sixth in Division Three (South) and
twice were runners-up. When the Football League resumed in
1946 they twice more occupied second place, in 1949 and 1952.
They were particularly unlucky not to gain promotion in season
1951–52 because they obtained their highest points total, 61,
and their second record 112 goals.

Between the wars Reading won the Third Division (South)
Championship in 1925–26 and lasted in the Second Division for
five seasons. During that period the 'Biscuitmen' fielded what
many people believe was their finest half-back line of William
Inglis, Alf Messer and David Evans.

Many other splendid players have served the club, among
them Jack Palethorpe, who later scored in Sheffield Wednesday's Cup-winning side at Wembley in 1935; W. H. McConnell,
an Ireland cap; Tony McPhee, a clever, goalscoring leader;
George Marks, later Arsenal's goalkeeper; Pat McConnell,
another Irish international; Maurice Edelston, an England
Amateur international; and Ronnie Blackman, whose 156 League
goals between 1947–54 stand as a record for the club.

Division 3 (South) Champions: 1925–26.
Record attendance: 33,042 v. Brentford (F.A. Cup), February
    1927.
Modern Capacity: 33,000.
Entered Football League: 1920—Div. 3.
Biggest win: 10–2 v. Crystal Palace (Div. 3 South), September
    1946.
Heaviest defeat: 0–18 v. Preston N.E. (F.A. Cup), 1893–94.
Best in F.A. Cup: Semi-final 1926–27.
Best in Football League Cup: 4th Round 1964–65, 1965–66.
Pitch measurements: 112 × 75 yd.
Highest League Scorer in Single Season: R. Blackman—39
    in 1951–52 (Div. 3 South).
Transfers—
    Highest fee paid: £20,000—Steve Death (from West Ham),
        August 1970.
    Highest fee received: £60,000—Tom Jenkins (to
        Southampton), December 1969.

Rochdale

Willbutts Lane,
Spotland, Rochdale.
Rochdale 44648/9

Shirts: Royal Blue, White
Trimming
Shorts: White, Royal Blue
Seam
Stockings: White, Two
Royal Blue Hoops

With limited financial and playing resources, Rochdale have never succeeded in winning a divisional title. Indeed, often their efforts have been directed at keeping football alive in the face of competition from more successful League rivals in Lancashire. In season 1931–32 they failed to win a single Division Three (North) match after 7 November. During that period they played 26 matches, lost 25 and drew one.

It says much for the resolution and perseverance of those associated with the club that Rochdale have remained in continuous membership of the Football League since being elected to the Northern Section in 1921. Twice they were runners-up, in 1924 and again in 1927 when, with 105 goals, they were the third highest scorers in the Football League.

They gained promotion from the Fourth Division in 1969 by taking third place, and earned themselves a place in the history of the Football League Cup by finishing runners-up to Norwich City in 1962, which makes them still the only Division 4 side to have reached the Final of this tournament. Rochdale also provided a managerial grounding for Harry Catterick, who moved on via Sheffield Wednesday to success with Everton.

Record attendance: 24,231 v. Notts County (F.A. Cup), December 1949.
Modern Capacity: 28,000.
Entered Football League: 1921—Div. 3 (North).
Biggest win: 8–1 v. Chesterfield (Div. 3 North), December 1926.
Heaviest defeat: 0–8 v. Wrexham (Div. 3 North), December 1929.
Highest final League position: Runners-up Div. 3 (North) 1923–24, 1926–27.
Best in F.A. Cup: 4th Round 1970–71.
Best in Football League Cup: Runners-up 1961–62.
Pitch measurements: 110 × 72 yd.
Highest League Scorer in Single Season: A. Whitehurst—44 in 1926–27 (Div. 3 North).
Transfers—
   Highest fee paid: £15,000—Malcolm Darling (from Norwich), October 1971.
   Highest fee received: £40,000—David Cross (to Norwich), October 1971.

83

Rotherham United

Millmoor Ground,
Rotherham.
Rotherham 2434

Shirts: Red
Shorts: Red
Stockings: Red

Fortune has certainly played some unkind tricks on Rotherham United during more than 50 years' membership of the Football League. None more so than in 1955, when, by winning eight of the last nine games and finally slamming Liverpool 6–1, they finished level on points at the top of Division Two with Birmingham City and Luton Town. Yet, despite scoring more goals than their rivals, they missed a First Division place on goal average.

In the three seasons directly after the Second World War they were runners-up in Division Three North (only the Champions gained promotion). Their points totals were 64, 59 and 62, all enough to have won the divisional title in many another season. After such close attempts to take the title, Rotherham slipped to sixth the following season (1949–50), but a year later their perseverance paid off in the grand manner. They became Champions by seven points with this playing record: P 46; W 31; D 9; L 6; Goals for 103; Goals against 41. Pts 71.

Rotherham, in company with other small clubs, rely heavily on finding their own players. Among the best known are: Danny Williams, a stalwart defender who made 459 League appearances between 1946–60; Wally Ardron, whose 38 League goals in 1946–47 are still a Rotherham record; and Colin Grainger, who went on to England honours with Sheffield United and Sunderland in the middle fifties.

Division 3 (North) Champions: 1950–51.
Record attendance: 25,000 v. Sheffield United (League), December 1952.
Modern Capacity: 24,000.
Entered Football League: 1893—Div. 2.
Biggest win: 8–0 v. Oldham Athletic (Div. 3 North), May 1947.
Heaviest defeat: 1–11 v. Bradford City (Div. 3 North), August 1928.
Best in F.A. Cup: 5th Round 1952–53, 1967–68.
Best in Football League Cup: Runners-up 1960–61.
Pitch measurements: 116 × 76 yd.
Highest League Scorer in Single Season: W. Ardron—38 in 1946–47 (Division 3 North).
Transfers—
    Highest fee paid: £27,000—John Quinn (from Sheffield Wed.), November 1967.
    Highest fee received: £100,000—David Watson (to Sunderland), December 1970.

Scunthorpe United

Old Show Ground,
Scunthorpe, Lincs.
Scunthorpe 2954

Shirts: Red
Shorts: Red
Stockings: Red

Officials of Scunthorpe and Lindsey United were among many surprised by the manner in which the club was elected in 1950 at the time the Football League was extending both Northern and Southern Sections of the Third Division by two clubs. When the 'North' vote was taken Scunthorpe were not even placed second. Workington and Wigan tied and so there was a fresh vote. At the new count Scunthorpe and Wigan tied, so there was another poll. This time Scunthorpe and Wigan tied, and it needed a third vote before the Lincolnshire club finally won election. A few years later the name Lindsey was dropped from their title.

Scunthorpe arrived with the reputation of having been Midland League Champions. They were not long in justifying their place in higher company. After finishing third in 1954, and again in 1955, they won the Northern Section Championship in 1958 —the year, in fact, the Football League created the Third and Fourth Divisions.

Scunthorpe came close to providing First Division football at their picturesquely-named Old Show Ground in 1961—62, when finishing fourth, but the promise was not sustained. Two seasons later the 'Irons' lost their Second Division status and four years later were relegated again.

The best known of their players was Jack Brownsword, who made 657 League and Cup appearances between 1950—65, and was the game's first full-back to score 50 League goals.

Division 3 (North) Champions: 1957—58.
Record attendance: 23,935 v. Portsmouth (F.A. Cup), January 1954.
Modern Capacity: 23,000.
Entered Football League: 1950—Div. 3 (North).
Biggest win: 9–0 v. Boston U. (F.A. Cup), Nov. 1953.
Heaviest defeat: 0–8 v. Carlisle United (Div. 3 North), December, 1952.
Best in F.A. Cup: 5th Round 1957—58, 1969—70.
Best in Football League Cup: 3rd Round 1962—63, 1968—69.
Pitch measurements: 112 × 78 yd.
Highest League Scorer in Single Season: B. Thomas—31 in 1961—62 (Div. 2).
Transfers—
    Highest fee paid: £20,000—Barrie Thomas (from Newcastle), November 1964.
    Highest fee received: £42,500—John Kaye (to W.B.A.), May 1963.

Sheffield United

Bramall Lane Ground,
Sheffield, S2 4SU.
0742—25585

Shirts: Red and White Stripes
Shorts: Black
Stockings: White, Two Red
Bands at Top

For all their long Football League history, Sheffield United achieved their greatest feats in the F.A. Cup, by winning the trophy four times by 1925.

In 1925—26 they headed the First Division scorers with 102 goals, beating Cardiff 11—2 and Manchester City 8—3. But after brief moments of glory in the 1920s, 'The Blades' lost their cutting edge and were relegated from the First Division in 1934. Five years later they just beat their neighbours, Wednesday, for second place in the Second Division, but had to wait seven years before actually returning to the First Division, owing to the outbreak of the Second World War.

On three occasions since the war football at Bramall Lane has lost the First Division label. Each time United fought their way back, and manager John Harris's team started season 1971—72 in style, suggesting their latest stay would be a lasting one.

Centre-half Joe Shaw made 690 first-team appearances in 18 seasons from 1948—66. He was one of countless fine players United have produced. In the transfer market they have bought modestly and sold spectacularly—as when they collected £200,000 from the combined sale of Mick Jones to Leeds and Alan Birchenall to Chelsea in two months, late in 1967.

League Champions: 1897—98.
Division 2 Champions: 1952—53.
F.A. Cup Winners: 1898—99, 1901—02, 1914—15, 1924—25.
Record attendance: 68,287 v. Leeds (F.A. Cup), Feb. 1936.
Modern Capacity: 55,000.
Entered Football League: 1892—Div. 2.
Biggest win: 11—2 v. Cardiff City (Div. 1), January 1926.
Heaviest defeat: 0—13 v. Bolton W. (F.A. Cup), February 1890.
Best in Football League Cup: 5th Round 1961—62, 1966—67, 1971—72.
Pitch measurements: 115 × 73 yd.
Highest League Scorer in Single Season: J. Dunne —41 in 1930—31 (Div. 1).
Transfers—
    Highest fee paid: £65,000—John Tudor (from Coventry), November 1968.
    Highest fee received: £100,000—Mick Jones (to Leeds), Sept. 1967; £100,000—Alan Birchenall (to Chelsea) Nov. 1967.

Sheffield Wednesday

Hillsborough,
Sheffield, S6 1SW.
0742–343122

Shirts: Royal Blue, White
    Sleeves and Collar
Shorts: White
Stockings: Royal Blue

Sheffield Wednesday reached a success peak between 1929 and 1935, winning the F.A. Cup and two League Championships, and finishing third in the First Division on four other occasions. Those two League title triumphs, inspired by the veteran inside-forward Jimmy Seed, were in 1929 and 1930. It was a repetition of a similar Championship double by them in 1903 and 1904.

Wednesday, whose lavish ground, with seating for 23,500, was used for World Cup matches in 1966 and is a regular F.A. Cup semi-final venue, have returned to the First Division four times at the first attempt after relegation.

Their most celebrated player in recent years was Derek Dooley, who scored 46 goals in season 1951–52 in 30 Division Two matches. A broken leg, which had to be amputated, ended his playing career the following season, and in January 1971 Dooley was appointed team manager of the club for which he had starred so briefly, so spectacularly.

But until Wednesday return to the First Division, Hillsborough will be something of a white elephant—a stately home of soccer in search of a team capable of filling it with football style and football fans as in days gone by.

League Champions: 1902–03, 1903–04, 1928–29, 1929–30.
Division 2 Champions: 1899–1900, 1925–26, 1951–52, 1955–56, 1958–59.
F.A. Cup Winners: 1895–96, 1906–07, 1934–35.
Record attendance: 72,841 v. Manchester City (F.A. Cup), February 1934.
Modern Capacity: 55,000.
Entered Football League: 1892—Div. 1.
Biggest win: 12–0 v. Halliwell (F.A. Cup), January 1891.
Heaviest defeat: 0–10 v. Aston Villa (Div. 1), October 1912.
Best in Football League Cup: 4th Round 1967–68.
Pitch measurements: 115 × 75 yd.
Highest League Scorer in Single Season: D. Dooley—46 in 1951–52 (Div. 2).
Transfers—
    Highest fee paid: £100,000—Tommy Craig (from Aberdeen), May 1969.
    Highest fee received: £100,000—Wilf Smith (to Coventry), August 1970.

Shrewsbury Town

Gay Meadow,
Shrewsbury.
Shrewsbury 6068

Shirts: Royal Blue, Amber
Collar and Cuffs
Shorts: Royal Blue, Amber
Seam
Stockings: Royal Blue,
Amber Rings

For 65 years Shrewsbury had run a football club, but it was not until 1950 that they were elected to membership of the Football League. They spent the first season in Division Three (North) but then switched to the Southern section, where they remained until the League was extended in season 1958—59. Shrewsbury moved into Division Four and immediately won promotion by finishing fourth. Twice since then the club has missed going up into the Second Division by one place, being third in 1960 and 1968.

Arthur Rowley's League scoring record of 434 goals included 183 for Shrewsbury and he also holds the club's single-season record with 38 in Division Four during 1958—59.

When the Football League Cup was launched in season 1960—61, Shrewsbury reached the semi-final before losing to Rotherham United 4—3 on aggregate.

Shrewsbury have enjoyed years of comparative success, too, in the F.A. Cup, progressing to the fifth rounds in 1965 and 1966. In January 1968, record receipts of £4962 were paid when Arsenal were held to a 1—1 draw at Gay Meadow in a third round tie. Shrewsbury lost the replay 2—0.

Record attendance: 18,917 v. Walsall (League), April 1961.
Modern Capacity: 20,000.
Entered Football League: 1950—Div. 3 (North).
Biggest win: 7—0 v. Swindon Town (Div. 3 South), May, 1955.
Heaviest defeat: 1—8 v. Norwich City (Div. 3 South), September 1952; 1—8 v. Coventry City (Div. 3), October 1963.
Highest final League position: 3rd in Div. 3 1959—60, 1967—68.
Best in F.A. Cup: 5th Round 1964—65, 1965—66.
Best in Football League Cup: Semi-final 1960—61.
Pitch measurements: 116 × 74 yd.
Highest League Scorer in Single Season: A. Rowley—38 in 1958—59 (Div. 4).
Transfers—
  Highest fee paid: £20,000—John Manning (from Tranmere), October 1966.
  Highest fee received: £34,000—Frank Clarke (to Q.P.R.), February 1968.

Southampton

The Dell,
Milton Road,
Southampton, SO9 4XX
Southampton 23408/28108

Shirts: Red and White
  Stripes
Shorts: Black
Stockings: Red with White
  Hooped Ankle

Southampton finally achieved First Division status in 1966 after missing promotion in extraordinary circumstances soon after the Second World War. In April 1949 they led the Second Division by eight points. The title seemed theirs for the taking. But an injury to centre-forward Charlie Wayman changed their luck and, incredibly, they finally finished third behind Fulham and West Bromwich.

The 'Saints' were F.A. Cup runners-up in 1900 and 1902, and became founder-members of the Third Division in 1920. They won the Third Division (South) title two years later and stayed in the Second Division until 1953.

Ted Bates, who played for the club as an inside-forward just before and after the Second World War, returned as manager in 1956 and was largely responsible for Southampton's recent rise to the heights. He made some shrewd buys and discovered local talent in Terry Paine, Martin Chivers and Mike Channon. Paine holds the League appearances record for the club—more than 600 since his début in 1956.

Many International defenders have also represented Southampton, among them Tom Parker, Fred Titmuss, Mike Keeping, Bill Ellerington, Stuart Williams, and Alf Ramsey.

Division 3 (South) Champions: 1921–22.
Division 3 Champions: 1959–60.
Record attendance: 31,044 v. Manchester Utd. (League), October 1969.
Modern Capacity: 31,000.
Entered Football League: 1920—Div. 3.
Biggest win: 11–0 v. Northampton (Southern League), December 1901.
Heaviest defeat: 0–8 v. Tottenham (Div. 2), March 1936; 0–8 v. Everton (Div. 1), November 1971.
Best in F.A. Cup: Runners-up 1899–1900, 1901–02
Best in Football League Cup: 5th Round 1960–61, 1968–69.
Pitch measurements: 110 x 72 yd.
Highest League Scorer in Single Season: D. Reeves—39 in 1959–60 (Div. 3).
Transfers—
  Highest fee paid: £80,000—Jim Steele (from Dundee), January 1972.
  Highest fee received: £125,000—Martin Chivers (to Tottenham), January 1968.

Southend United

Roots Hall Ground,
Victoria Avenue,
Southend-on-Sea.
Southend 40707

Shirts: Royal Blue
Shorts: Royal Blue, Two
    Thin White Stripes
Stockings: White

A succession of ambitious and dedicated Southend United officials have done their best to bring a higher standard of football to London's nearest seaside resort. In 1955 the club moved from Southend Stadium to a new ground at Roots Hall, Prittlewell, and three years later it looked as though Southend United were heading for the Second Division. But though they gained 54 points, their best to date, they were still six points behind Brighton, the promoted club. Sammy McCrory, who won Northern Ireland honours, scored 31 of their 90 League goals that season, but by 1966 Southend had dropped to the Fourth Division.

Twice in their formative years the club finished runners-up in the Second Division of the Southern League, but there have been too few years of glory to satisfy devotees of 'The Shrimpers'. The F.A. Cup competition of 1951–52 produced three months of excitement when, drawn at home five times out of five, Southend fought their way into the last 16 before losing 2–1 to Sheffield United.

Record attendance: 28,059 v. Birmingham City (F.A. Cup), January 1957.
Modern Capacity: 35,000.
Entered Football League: 1920—Div. 3.
Biggest win: 10–1 v. Golders Green (F.A. Cup), November 1934; 10–1 v. Brentwood (F.A. Cup), December 1968.
Heaviest defeat: 1–11 v. Northampton Town (Southern League), December 1909.
Highest final League position: 3rd in Div. 3 (South) 1931–32, 1949–50.
Best in F.A. Cup: 5th Round 1925–26, 1951–52.
Best in Football League Cup: 3rd Round 1963–64, 1964–65, 1969–70.
Pitch measurements: 110×74 yd.
Highest League Scorer in Single Season: J. Shankly—31 in 1928–29 (Div. 3 South); S. McCrory—31 in 1957–58 (Div. 3 South).
Transfers
    Highest fee paid: £11,000—Phil Chisnall (from Liverpool), August 1967.
    Highest fee received: £40,000—Ian Hamilton (to Aston Villa), June 1969.

Southport

Haig Avenue,
Southport.
Southport 5353/5726

Shirts: Old Gold
Shorts: Old Gold
Stockings: Old Gold

Formed in 1881 as Southport Central, the club took their present
name in 1919, two years before joining the Northern section of
the old Third Division.

Twice they finished in fourth place before the Second World
War—in 1924–25 and again in 1938–39. In 1958, Southport
transferred to the Fourth Division and after a number of in-
different seasons they gave a much-needed fillip to football
interest in the area by gaining promotion in 1967, winning 23 and
drawing 13 of their 46 matches, but they were relegated three
seasons later.

In 1971–72 there were signs of another revival for a club which
has always had to compete with more illustrious Lancashire
neighbours.

Older supporters will recall Southport's splendid run in the
1931 F.A. Cup tournament. Millwall, Blackpool and Bradford
were all beaten at Southport. Then the quaintly nicknamed
'Sandgrounders' were drawn to meet Everton at Goodison Park
in the sixth round . . . and crashed to a 9–1 defeat. It was a
calamitous end to what remains to this day Southport's longest
run in the competition.

Record attendance: 20,010 v. Newcastle (F.A. Cup), January
1932.
Modern Capacity: 21,000.
Entered Football League: 1921—Div. 3 (North).
Biggest win: 8–1 v. Nelson (Div. 3 North), January 1931.
Heaviest defeat: 0–11 v. Oldham Athletic (Div. 4), December
1962.
Highest final League position: Runners-up Div. 4 1966–67.
Best in F.A. Cup: 6th Round 1930–31.
Best in Football League Cup: 2nd Round 1962–63, 1963–
64, 1968–69, 1969–70, 1971–72.
Pitch measurements: 113 × 77 yd.
Highest League Scorer in Single Season: A. Waterston—31
in 1930–31 (Div. 3 North).
Transfers—
    Highest fee paid: £6000—Malcolm Russell (from Halifax),
      September 1968.
    Highest fee received: £20,000—Tony Field (to Black-
      burn), October 1971.

Stockport County

Edgeley Park,
Stockport,
Cheshire, SK3 9DD.
061—480—8888/9

Shirts: Blue, Thin White Stripes
Shorts: White
Stockings: White, Blue Rings

Only 13 people paid to watch a Football League match at Old Trafford in May, 1921. This stranger-than-fiction event came about because Stockport's own ground was under suspension and the club used the Manchester United venue for their 'home' Division Two match against Leicester City.

Nearly 13 years later, on 6 January 1934, Stockport scored 13 times without reply against Halifax Town in a Division Three (North) match. This and Newcastle's 13—0 victory over Newport County on 5 October 1946 are the biggest wins in Football League history.

Alex Herd, who played in Manchester City's 1933 and 1934 Cup Final teams, gave Stockport splendid service. He and his son, David, provided a rare instance of father and son playing together in the same League side. They were inside-right and inside-left respectively against Hartlepools at Edgeley Park on 5 May 1951, the last day of the season. It was a proud day for 39-year-old Alex, especially as 17-year-old David scored one of the goals in a 2—0 win.

Division 3 (North) Champions: 1921—22, 1936—37.
Division 4 Champions: 1966—67.
Record attendance: 27,833 v. Liverpool (F.A. Cup), February 1950.
Modern Capacity: 24,000.
Entered Football League: 1900—Div. 2.
Biggest win: 13—0 v. Halifax Town (Div. 3 North), January 1934.
Heaviest defeat: 1—8 v. Chesterfield (Division 2), April 1902.
Best in F.A. Cup: 5th Round 1934—35, 1949—50.
Best in Football League Cup: 2nd Round 1960—61, 1967—68, 1968—69, 1971—72.
Pitch measurements: 111 × 73 yd.
Highest League Scorer in Single Season: A. Lythgoe—46 in 1933—34 (Div. 3 North).
Transfers—
    Highest fee paid: £14,000—Alex Young (from Glentoran), November 1968.
    Highest fee received: £20,000—Ken Mulhearn (to Manchester City), September 1967.

Stoke City

Victoria Ground,
Stoke-on-Trent, ST4 4EG.
0782—44660

Shirts: Red and White Stripes
Shorts: White
Stockings: White, Red Hoops

Until 1972, what success Stoke have achieved in a long tradition of football had been linked with the name of Stanley Matthews. In 1933, the young Matthews was a promising winger in the Stoke side that brought back First Division football to the Potteries after an absence of ten years.

When all seemed set for Stoke to take top honours in the game, the Second World War broke out. In the first post-war season, Stoke had a great chance to pull off the League Championship with the mature Matthews and players such as Freddie Steele and Neil Franklin in their team. But Matthews dropped out with an injury and the title chance was lost. At the end of that season he moved to Blackpool.

After relegation in 1953, Stoke spent another ten-year spell in the Second Division. In 1960 Tony Waddington took over as manager and he recruited several veterans including Matthews, then 46. Matthews and company—their average age was the highest in the four divisions—took the club back into the First Division in 1963, and Stoke have remained there.

One of the League's original twelve in 1888, they are the second oldest League club—formed in 1863, the year after Notts County. Into the seventies they had still to reach the F.A. Cup Final or win a trophy, but Wembley 1972 brought them their long-awaited first prize, for in the League Cup Final they beat Chelsea 2—1.

Football League Cup Winners: 1971—72.
Division 2 Champions: 1932—33, 1962—63.
Division 3 (North) Champions: 1926—27.
Record attendance: 51,380 v. Arsenal (League), March 1937.
Modern Capacity: 49,500.
Entered Football League: 1888—Div. 1.
Biggest win: 10—3 v. W.B.A. (Div. 1), February 1937.
Heaviest defeat: 0—10 v. Preston N.E. (Div. 1), September 1889.
Best in F.A. Cup: Semi-final 1898—99, 1970—71, 1971—72.
Pitch measurements: $116\frac{1}{2} \times 75$ yd.
Highest League Scorer in Single Season: F. Steele—33 in 1936—37 (Div. 1).
Transfers—
　Highest fee paid: £100,000—Jimmy Greenhoff (from Birmingham), August 1969.
　Highest fee received: £140,000—Mike Barnard (to Everton), May 1972.

Sunderland

Roker Park Ground,
Sunderland.
Sunderland 72077/58638

Shirts: Red and White Stripes
Shorts: White
Stockings: Red, White Tops

A record run of 57 seasons in the First Division ended for
Sunderland in 1958. Although the club regained First Division
status six years later, a second drop took them down the soccer
scale for the start of the seventies. Ever since gaining election to
the Football League in 1890, Sunderland had built up a tradition
as one of the great clubs of football. In their first season they
reached the semi-final of the F.A. Cup. They did so again the
following year and at the same time won the League Championship—the first of six.

One of Sunderland's finest seasons came in 1912–13. They not
only won the Championship but also reached the F.A. Cup Final
for the first time, losing 1–0 to Aston Villa.

By then Charlie Buchan had emerged as one of their great
players. After the club's steady progress through the 1920s,
Raich Carter appeared on the scene to score 31 goals in their
next Championship season, 1935–36.

In 1937, Sunderland won the Cup for the first, and still only,
time. They were trailing at half-time at Wembley, but fought back
to beat Preston 3–1, and fittingly it was Carter, born and bred in
Sunderland, who put them ahead and later received the trophy.
The highly creative Len Shackleton, Willie Watson, who represented England at football and cricket, Welsh International
centre-forward Trevor Ford and Billy Bingham, capped 54 times
by Ireland, are among the club's distinguished post-war players.

League Champions: 1891–92, 1892–93, 1894–95, 1901–02,
1912–13, 1935–36.
F.A. Cup Winners: 1936–37.
Record attendance: 75,118 v. Derby County (F.A. Cup),
March 1933.
Modern Capacity: 57,500.
Entered Football League: 1890—Div. 1.
Biggest win: 11–1 v. Fairfield (F.A. Cup), 1894–95.
Heaviest defeat: 0–8 v. West Ham (Div. 1), October 1968.
Best in Football League Cup: Semi-final 1962–63.
Pitch measurements: 112 × 72 yd.
Highest League Scorer in Single Season: D. Halliday—43
in 1928–29 (Div. 1).
Transfers—
    Highest fee paid: £100,000—David Watson (from Rother-
ham), December 1970.
    Highest fee received: £170,000—Colin Todd (to Derby),
February 1971.

Swansea City

Vetch Field,
Swansea, SA1 3SU.
Swansea 42855

Shirts: White
Shorts: White
Stockings: White, Black-
hooped Turnover

When Swansea won the Third Division (South) Championship in 1949 by seven points, they fielded seven Internationals in their side. They were Paul, Richards and Lucas (Wales), Feeney, McCrory, Keane and O'Driscoll (Ireland). This title enabled Irish manager Billy McCandless to complete a remarkable 'hat trick' of successes with Welsh clubs. He had previously guided Newport (1938–39) and Cardiff City (1946–47) into the Second Division.

Swansea has always been a reservoir of great soccer talent. Roy John, Trevor Ford, Ivor and Len Allchurch, Cliff Jones and Barrie Jones are just a few of many fine players whom the club have developed.

In season 1963–64, Swansea only just avoided relegation from Division Two, yet almost reached the F.A. Cup Final. They won their way through to the last four with victories over such formidable First Division opponents as Sheffield United, Stoke City and Liverpool (League Champions that season) before going down 2–1 to Preston in the semi-final.

Swansea's only other semi-final appearance was in 1926, when they lost 3–0 to Bolton at Tottenham.

The 'Swans' changed their title from Town to City in 1970.

Division 3 (South) Champions: 1924–25, 1948–49.
Record attendance: 32,700 v. Arsenal (F.A. Cup), February 1968.
Modern Capacity: 35,000.
Entered Football League: 1920—Div. 3.
Biggest win: 8–1 v. Bristol Rovers (Div. 3 South), April 1922, 8–1 v. Bradford City (Div. 2), February 1926.
Heaviest defeat: 1–8 v. Fulham (Div. 2), January 1938.
Best in F.A. Cup: Semi-final 1925–26, 1963–64.
Best in Football League Cup: 4th Round 1964–65.
Pitch measurements: 110 x 70 yd.
Highest League Scorer in Single Season: C. Pearce—35 in 1931–32 (Div. 2).
Transfers—
    Highest fee paid: £26,000—Ronnie Rees (from Nottingham Forest), January 1972.
    Highest fee received: £45,000—Barrie Jones (to Plymouth), September 1964.

Swindon Town

County Ground,
Swindon.
Swindon 22118

Shirts: Red, White Edging
Shorts: White
Stockings: Red

Enthusiasm reached unprecedented heights in the West Country on 6 March 1969, when Swindon Town became League Cup holders by beating Arsenal 3–1 in extra time at Wembley—and at the end of the season also gained promotion to Division Two.

A clergyman formed the club in 1881 and it became the top amateur side in Wiltshire, turning professional and entering the Southern League in 1894.

After 43 years as a Third Division club, Swindon gained promotion as runners-up in 1963. They started off well in Second Division football, being undefeated for their first nine games, but eventually finished the season well down the table, and the following year they were back in the Third Division.

One of the club's earliest stars was Harold Fleming, an inside-forward capped nine times for England. His skills played a major part in Swindon's two F.A. Cup semi-final appearances in 1910 and 1912. Others of renown have included Grenville Morris, who scored 47 League goals in 1926–27 and a total of 216 in eight seasons; Maurice Owen, another with goalscoring flair and 554 League appearances for the club (1946–63); Norman Uprichard, Ireland's goalkeeper in the 1950s; England International Mike Summerbee and Under-23 caps Ernie Hunt and Don Rogers; and Dave Mackay (ex-Tottenham and Scotland), who joined Swindon in the summer of 1971.

League Cup Winners: 1968–69.
Record attendance: 32,000 v. Arsenal (F.A. Cup), January 1972.
Modern Capacity: 32,000.
Entered Football League: 1920—Div. 3.
Biggest win: 10–1 v. Farnham Utd. Breweries (F.A. Cup), November 1925.
Heaviest defeat: 1–10 v. Manchester City (F.A. Cup), January 1930.
Highest final League position: Runners-up Div. 3 1962–63, 1968–69.
Best in F.A. Cup: Semi-final 1909–10, 1911–12.
Pitch measurements: 117 × 78 yd.
Highest League Scorer in Single Season: D. Morris—47 in 1926–27 (Div. 3 South).
Transfers—
    Highest fee paid: £17,000—Arthur Horsfield (from Newcastle), May 1969.
    Highest fee received: £40,000—Ernie Hunt (to Wolves), September 1965.

Torquay United

Plainmoor Ground,
Torquay, Devon.
Torquay 38666/7

Shirts: Gold, Royal Blue Neck
and Cuffs
Shorts: Gold, Royal Blue Seam
Stockings: Gold, Royal Blue
Ringed Tops

Two local amateur clubs, Torquay Town and Babbacombe, joined forces to form the present club which became professional in 1922. In season 1927–28 the Football League clubs recognized Torquay's promise by electing them to the Southern Section of the old Division Three. Their first season ended disastrously—in bottom place—and in the years before and immediately after the Second World War they rarely rose above half-way in the table.

This applied until 1956, when they finished fifth. The following year they were runners-up, missing promotion to the Second Division only on goal average, but by the time the League was extended in 1958 they found themselves in Division Four.

Since then Torquay have alternated between Third and Fourth Divisions without achieving a title. With little money available, and situated in an area of the country where League football has seldom attracted national attention, Torquay United struggle along on small attendances. In 1970–71, for instance, although they finished tenth in Division Three, home gates averaged only 5616.

Record attendance: 21,736 v. Huddersfield Town (F.A. Cup), January 1955.
Modern Capacity: 22,000.
Entered Football League: 1927—Div. 3 (South).
Biggest win: 9–0 v. Swindon Town (Div. 3 South), March 1952.
Heaviest defeat: 2–10 v. Fulham (Div. 3 South), September 1931; 2–10 v. Luton Town (Div. 3 South), September 1933.
Highest final League position: Runners-up Div. 3 (South) 1956–57.
Best in F.A. Cup: 4th Round 1948–49, 1954–55, 1970–71.
Best in Football League Cup: 3rd Round 1967–68, 1971–72.
Pitch measurements: 112 × 74 yd.
Highest League Scorer in Single Season: R. Collins—40 in 1955–56 (Div. 3 South).
Transfers—
  Highest fee paid: £15,000—David Tearse (from Leicester), November 1971.
  Highest fee received: £21,000—Tommy Mitchinson (to Bournemouth), December 1971.

Tottenham Hotspur

748 High Road,
Tottenham,
London, NI7 0AP
01—808—1020

Shirts: White
Shorts: Navy Blue
Stockings: White

Since the war there have been two truly great Spurs eras—
Arthur Rowe's 'push and run' team, which won the Second and
First Division titles in successive years (1950 and 1951) and Bill
Nicholson's Tottenham, which achieved the Championship and
F.A. Cup double a decade later and continued the club's success
story into the seventies.

In the ten years after the 1960—61 'double', Nicholson became
soccer's biggest spender, splashing more than a million pounds
on Greaves (£99,999 from AC Milan, November 1961—Spurs
refused to make him Britain's first £100,000 player!); Mullery
(£72,000 from Fulham, March 1964); Knowles (£45,000 from
Middlesbrough, July 1964); Gilzean (£72,500 from Dundee,
December 1964); Venables (£80,000 from Chelsea, April 1966);
England (£95,000 from Blackburn, August 1966); Chivers
(£125,000 from Southampton, January 1968); Morgan
(£110,000 from Q.P.R., February 1969); Peters (Britain's first
£200,000-valued signing, from West Ham, March 1970) and
Coates (£180,000 from Burnley, May 1971).

League Champions: 1950—51, 1960—61.
Division 2 Champions: 1919—20, 1949—50.
F.A. Cup Winners: 1900—01, 1920—21, 1960—61, 1961—62,
1966—67.
Winners of European Cup-Winners' Cup: 1962—63.
League Cup Winners: 1970—71.
The Double (League and F.A. Cup Winners): 1960—61.
Record attendance: 75,038 v. Sunderland (F.A. Cup),
March 1938.
Modern Capacity: 57,000.
Entered Football League: 1908—Div. 2.
Biggest win: 13—2 v. Crewe (F.A. Cup), February 1960.
Heaviest defeat: 2—7 v. Liverpool (Div. 1), October 1914;
2—7 v. Newcastle Utd. (Div. 1), January 1951; 2—7 v. Black-
burn Rovers (Div. 1), September 1963.
Pitch measurements: 111 x 73 yd.
Highest League Scorer in Single Season: J. Greaves—37
in 1962—63 (Div. 1).
Transfers—
  Highest fee paid: £200,000 equivalent—Martin Peters
  (from West Ham), March 1970—(£146,000 plus Jimmy
  Greaves).
  Highest fee received: £70,000—Terry Venables (to
  Q.P.R.), June 1969.

Tranmere Rovers

Prenton Park,
Prenton Road West,
Birkenhead.
051—608—3677/4194

Shirts: White, Blue Edging
Shorts: Royal Blue
Stockings: White, Blue Band

Living in the shadows of those two giant Merseyside clubs, Everton and Liverpool, has meant a continual battle for players and supporters for Tranmere Rovers. Yet the Rovers, formed in 1883 and League members since 1921, have certainly had their moments. They won the Northern Section of the Third Division in fine style in 1937—38, only to suffer an astonishing reversal of form the following season. They lost 31 of their 42 matches and were promptly relegated.

Devotees of the Birkenhead club fondly recall the nine goals by 'Bunny' Bell in a 13—4 Third Division (North) victory over Oldham Athletic on Boxing Day, 1935, the only time 17 goals have been scored in a Football League match. 'Pongo' Waring scored seven in Tranmere's 11—1 win against Durham City in another Division Three (North) fixture in January 1928. Waring and the legendary 'Dixie' Dean both gained their early experience of League football with Rovers.

While 'Bunny' Bell is remembered for his goalscoring feats, centre-half *Harold* Bell also earned a distinguished place in the records for Tranmere. He was ever present for nine seasons between 1946 and 1955, playing 401 consecutive matches—the League record—and altogether made 595 League appearances for the club, the last of them in 1964.

Division 3 (North) Champions: 1937—38.
Record attendance: 24,424 v. Stoke City (F.A. Cup), February 1972.
Modern Capacity: 29,000.
Entered Football League: 1921—Div. 3 (North).
Biggest win: 13—4 v. Oldham Athletic (Div. 3 North), December 1935.
Heaviest defeat: 1—9 v. Tottenham Hotspur (F.A. Cup), January 1953.
Best in F.A. Cup: 5th Round 1967—68.
Best in Football League Cup: 4th Round 1960—61.
Pitch measurements: 112 × 72 yd.
Highest League Scorer in Single Season: R. Bell—35 in 1933—34 (Div. 3 North).
Transfers—
　　Highest fee paid: £15,000—George Hudson (from Northampton), January 1967.
　　Highest fee received: £35,000—Jim Cumbes (to W.B.A.), August 1969.

Walsall

Fellows Park,
Walsall, WS2 9DB.
Walsall 22791

Shirts: White, Red Trimming
Shorts: Red
Stockings: White

Whenever the name of Walsall is mentioned someone is almost certain to remark: 'Do you recall the day they knocked Arsenal out of the F.A. Cup?' Few football events between the two World Wars caused a greater stir than Walsall's famous 2–0 win over Arsenal in the third round on 14 January 1933. The 'Gunners' team, then the most powerful in the land, was packed with internationals; Walsall were a Third Division North side of no special skills. Yet they won that afternoon on their merits. Gilbert Alsop, a centre-forward who gave the club wonderful service, getting one of the goals.

The story and the legends of this game will continue to be told until Walsall achieve something more extraordinary. As it is, the rest of their history recounts few achievements, though they won the Division Four title in 1960 convincingly enough with 65 points, five more than their nearest challengers. A year later Walsall again won promotion to the Second Division, but survived there only two seasons.

Perhaps the best known of their 'home produced' players has been Allan Clarke, who was in England's 1970 World Cup side in Mexico. Walsall transferred him to Fulham for £35,000 in March 1966, and by the time Clarke joined Leeds United via Leicester City, his transfer deals had involved £350,000.

Division 4 Champions: 1959–60.
Record attendance: 25,453 v. Newcastle Utd. (League), August 1961.
Modern Capacity: 25,000.
Entered Football League: 1892—Div. 2.
Biggest win: 10–0 v. Darwen (Div. 2), March 1899.
Heaviest defeat: 0–12 v. Small Heath (Div. 2), December 1892; 0–12 v. Darwen (Div. 2), December 1896.
Best in F.A. Cup: 5th Round 1938–39.
Best in Football League Cup: 4th Round 1966–67.
Pitch measurements: 113 × 73 yd.
Highest League Scorer in Single Season: G. Alsop—40 in 1933–34 and 40 in 1934–35 (both in Div. 3 North).
Transfers—
    Highest fee paid: £17,000—Trevor Smith (from Birmingham), October 1964.
    Highest fee received: £35,000—Allan Clarke (to Fulham), March 1966.

Watford

Vicarage Road Ground,
Watford, WD1 8ER.
Watford 21759

Shirts: Gold
Shorts: Black
Stockings: Gold

After spending 49 years in lower grade League football, Watford came out of comparative obscurity in 1969 to win better promotion to the Second Division and earn a name as F.A. Cup fighters. They became Third Division champions on goal average over Swindon and held Manchester United to a fourth round draw at Old Trafford in the F.A. Cup.

The following season, Watford enjoyed an even better Cup run, beating Bolton, Stoke and Liverpool before losing 5—1 to Chelsea in the semi-final. But Second Division life was hard.

Watford were formed in 1889 and turned professional eight years later. They played at Cassio Road until 1919, when the club moved to their present ground at Vicarage Road. The following year they became founder members of the Third Division. Apart from two seasons (1958—60) in the newly-formed Fourth Division, Watford spent the whole of their League career up to 1969 in the Third Division.

Before the Second World War, Tommy Barnett made 445 League appearances for the club in 12 seasons (1928—39) and scored 164 goals. Cliff Holton broke Watford's scoring record for a single season with 42 goals in 1959—60. The club's two outstanding discoveries since the war were Northern Ireland goalkeeper Pat Jennings, sold to Tottenham in June 1964, and forward Stewart Scullion, who moved to Sheffield United in June 1971.

Division 3 Champions: 1968—69.
Record attendance: 34,099 v. Manchester Utd. (F.A. Cup), February 1969.
Modern Capacity: 36,500.
Entered Football League: 1920—Div. 3.
Biggest win: 10—1 v. Lowestoft Town (F.A. Cup), November 1926.
Heaviest defeat: 0—10 v. Wolves (F.A. Cup), January 1912.
Best in F.A. Cup: Semi-final 1969—70.
Best in Football League Cup: 3rd Round 1961—62, 1971—72.
Pitch measurements: 112×74 yd.
Highest League Scorer in Single Season: C. Holton—42 in 1959—60 (Div. 4).
Transfers—
    Highest fee paid: £20,000—Jimmy Lindsay (from West Ham), May 1971.
    Highest fee received: £30,000—Stewart Scullion (to Sheffield United), May 1971.

West Bromwich Albion

The Hawthorns,
West Bromwich.
021–553–0095

Shirts: Navy Blue and
White Stripes
Shorts: White
Stockings: White

As F.A. Cup winners five times, West Bromwich Albion have a proud record, but League honours have usually eluded them. In the post-war years they have mostly been 'middle men' of the First Division. Up to 1971, the club appeared in ten F.A. Cup Finals—a record shared with Newcastle—and in 17 semi-finals (which equalled Aston Villa's record). In 1965–66, West Bromwich made a belated entry into the League Cup and won it; they were also Finalists in 1967 and 1970. In the summer of 1971 they appointed as manager their former full-back Don Howe, under whose coaching Arsenal did the 'double' the previous season.

One of the highlights in Albion's history was their 1931 F.A. Cup Final triumph (as a Second Division team) over Birmingham, which earned them the distinction of being the only club to win the Cup and promotion in the same season.

West Bromwich were among the original 12 members of the Football League in 1888, but have won the Championship only once—in 1920—despite long spells in the First Division. England full-back Jesse Pennington was one of their earliest star players. In their Championship season of 1919–20 they often fielded seven Internationals.

League Champions: 1919–20.
Division 2 Champions: 1901–02, 1910–11.
F.A. Cup Winners: 1887–88, 1891–92, 1930–31, 1953–54, 1967–68.
League Cup Winners: 1965–66.
Record attendance: 64,815 v. Arsenal (F.A. Cup), March 1937.
Modern Capacity: 50,000.
Entered Football League: 1888—Div. 1.
Biggest win: 12–0 v. Darwen (Div. 1), March 1892.
Heaviest defeat: 3–10 v. Stoke City (Div. 1), February 1937.
Pitch measurements: 115 × 75 yd.
Highest League Scorer in Single Season: W. G. Richardson —39 in 1935–36 (Div. 1).
Transfers—
  Highest fee paid: £100,000—Colin Suggett (from Sunderland), June 1969.
  Highest fee received: £60,000—Ronnie Rees (to Nottingham F.), February 1969; £60,000—Ian Collard (to Ipswich T.), May 1969.

102

West Ham United

Boleyn Ground,
Green Street,
Upton Park,
London, E13
01–472–0704

Shirts: Claret, Blue
    Sleeves
Shorts: White
Stockings: White

When England won the World Cup in 1966, West Ham provided the captain, Bobby Moore, and two other members of that great team—Geoff Hurst and Martin Peters. The East London club has also produced an 'academy' of players who have become distinguished managers, among them Frank O'Farrell, Malcolm Allison, Dave Sexton, Noel Cantwell, Jimmy Bloomfield and John Bond. So perhaps it is surprising that Hammers' own honours list has not been greater.

In 1923, four years after being elected to the Football League, they gained promotion to the First Division and also reached the first Wembley Cup Final, which they lost 2–0 to Bolton. They were relegated in 1932, and it was 1958 before they returned to the top division under the managership of Ted Fenton.

During manager Ron Greenwood's reign, West Ham have been among the most attractive sides in Britain, especially during the sixties, when they won the F.A. Cup (1964) and the European Cup-Winners' Cup (1965).

F.A. Cup Winners: 1963–64.
Winners of European Cup-Winners' Cup: 1964–65.
Division 2 Champions: 1957–58.
Record attendance: 42,322 v. Tottenham Hotspur (League), October 1970.
Modern Capacity: 42,500.
Entered Football League: 1919—Div. 2.
Biggest win: 8–0 v. Rotherham United (Div. 2), March 1958; 8–0 v. Sunderland (Div. 1), October 1968.
Heaviest defeat: 0–10 v. Tottenham Hotspur (Southern League), 1904—05.
Best in Football League Cup: Runners-up 1965—66.
Pitch measurements: 110 × 72 yd.
Highest League Scorer in Single Season: V. Watson—42 in 1929–30 (Div. 1).
Transfers—
    Highest fee paid: £120,000—Bryan Robson (from Newcastle), February 1971.
    Highest fee received: £200,000 equivalent—Martin Peters (to Tottenham—£146,000 plus Jimmy Greaves in part exchange), March 1970.

Wolverhampton Wanderers

Molineux Grounds,
Wolverhampton, WV1 4QR.
0902—24053

Shirts: Old Gold, Black
  Collar and Cuffs
Shorts: Black
Stockings: Old Gold

Football fame came back to the Wolves in the fifties. Not only did they challenge for the title of Britain's top club, but they also shone in prestige matches against the best of that era in Europe.

Behind their amazing record of success was the genius of manager Stan Cullis, the captaincy of Billy Wright and the playing ability of such stars as Johnny Hancocks, Jimmy Mullen, Jesse Pye, Bert Williams, Ron Flowers and Peter Broadbent.

Wolves began the most glamorous period in their history with a 3—1 Wembley win over Leicester City in the 1949 F.A. Cup Final. They went on to become League Champions in 1954, 1958 and 1959, and won the Cup again in 1960.

Formed in 1877, Wolves were among the League's founder clubs in 1888. They are the only club to have won the Championships of the First, Second and Third (North) Divisions.

Billy Wright, England's second most-capped footballer with 105 appearances, played more League and Cup games—535 between 1946 and 1959—than anyone in Wolves' history.

League Champions: 1953—54, 1957—58, 1958—59.
Division 2 Champions: 1931—32.
Division 3 (North) Champions: 1923—24.
F.A. Cup Winners: 1892—93, 1907—08, 1948—49, 1959—60.
Record attendance: 61,315 v. Liverpool (F.A. Cup), February 1939.
Modern Capacity: 53,500.
Entered Football League: 1888—Div. 1.
Biggest win: 14—0 v. Crosswell's Brewery (F.A. Cup), 1886—87.
Heaviest defeat: 1—10 v. Newton Heath (Div. 1), October 1892.
Best in Football League Cup: 4th Round 1968—69, 1969—70.
Pitch measurements: 115 × 72 yd.
Highest League Scorer in Single Season: D. Westcott—37 in 1946—47 (Div. 1).
Transfers—
  Highest fee paid: £80,000—Derek Parkin (from Huddersfield), February 1968; £80,000—Mike O'Grady (from Leeds), September 1969.
  Highest fee received: £100,000—Alun Evans (to Liverpool), September 1968.

Workington

Borough Park,
Workington.
Workington 2871

Shirts: Red
Shorts: White
Stockings: Red and White

A continual struggle for existence has failed to daunt the hard core of enthusiasts devoted to the cause of Workington F.C. They have poured money, time and creative ideas into sustaining League football in this outpost of the game on the coast of Cumberland.

Such zeal deserves to succeed and in 1971—72 there were signs that a brighter future does lie ahead for the club. They were originally founded in 1884, reformed in 1921 and won election to the Third Division (North) of the Football League in 1951.

Excitement ran high in the area during season 1963—64 when they came third, only a point behind their local rivals, Carlisle. Two seasons later they were among the leading clubs in Division Three, finishing fifth, but this rich promise was not fulfilled the following year when they occupied bottom place.

Several well known personalities have gained valuable managerial experience with Workington, among them Bill Shankly, Joe Harvey and Ken Furphy.

Record attendance: 21,500 v. Manchester Utd. (F.A. Cup), January 1958.
Modern Capacity: 21,000.
Entered Football League: 1951—Div. 3 (North).
Biggest win: 9—1 v. Barrow (League Cup), September 1964.
Heaviest defeat: 0—8 v. Wrexham (Div. 3 North), October 1953.
Highest final League position: 3rd in Div. 4 1963—64.
Best in F.A. Cup: 4th Round 1933—34.
Best in Football League Cup: 5th Round 1963—64, 1964—65.
Pitch measurements: 112 × 76 yd.
Highest League Scorer in Single Season: J. Dailey—26 in 1956—57 (Div. 3 North).
Transfers—
  Highest fee paid: £6000—Ted Purdon (from Sunderland), March 1957.
  Highest fee received: £18,000—Kit Napier (to Newcastle), November 1965.

Wrexham

Racecourse Ground,
8 Mold Road,
Wrexham.
Wrexham 2414

Shirts: Red, White Trim-
mings
Shorts: White, Red Seam
Stockings: Red

Wrexham hold the distinction of being the oldest Association
football club in Wales. They were founded in 1873 and have
provided a steady flow of players to the International team.
Wrexham have also won the Welsh Cup many times, yet they are
unable to point to a single Championship during their Football
League membership which began in 1921.

The two highlights of their League existence are widely
separated. In 1932–33 they finished second to Hull in the old
Northern Section of Division Three, and 37 years later, in 1970,
they were runners-up in Division Four. They did finish third in
1961–62, but returned to Division Four two seasons later.

The most League goals obtained in a season for Wrexham were
44 by Tommy Bamford during the 1933–34 campaign.

Wales staged most of their early matches at the Racecourse
Ground, which can hold 36,000, and is still an occasional International venue. A record crowd of 34,445 attended the F.A. Cup
fourth round tie on 26 January 1957, when Manchester United
beat Wrexham 5–0.

Record attendance: 34,445 v. Manchester Utd. (F.A. Cup),
January 1957.
Modern Capacity: 36,000.
Entered Football League: 1921—Div. 3 (North).
Biggest win: 10–1 v. Hartlepools Utd. (Div. 4), March 1962.
Heaviest defeat: 0–9 v. Brentford (Div. 3), October 1963.
Highest final League position: Runners-up Div. 3 (North),
1932–33; runners-up Div. 4 1969–70.
Best in F.A. Cup: 4th Round 1927–28, 1929–30, 1956–57,
1969–70.
Best in Football League Cup: 5th Round 1960–61.
Pitch measurements: 117 × 75 yd.
Highest League Scorer in Single Season: T. Bamford—44
in 1933–34 (Div. 3 North).
Transfers—
    Highest fee paid: £13,000—Brian Tinnion (from Working-
ton), January 1969.
    Highest fee received: £28,000—David Powell (to Sheffield
Utd.), September 1968.

York City

Bootham Crescent,
York, YO3 7AQ.
York 24447

Shirts: Maroon
Shorts: White
Stockings: Maroon

York City are one of only four Third Division clubs who have reached the semi-final round of the F.A. Cup. Millwall (1937), Port Vale (1954) and Norwich City (1959) are the others. City startled the football world in 1955 with an extraordinary Cup run which actually carried them further than any other Third Division side in history; they took Newcastle United to a replay before losing the semi-final. This is how they progressed that season (from the time the big clubs joined the tournament): Third round: Blackpool 0, York 2; fourth round: Bishop Auckland 1, York 3; fifth round: Tottenham 1, York 3; sixth round: Notts County 0, York 1; Semi-final (at Hillsborough): Newcastle 1, York 1; replay (at Sunderland): Newcastle 2, York 0.

York had reached the last eight in 1938 when their team, said to have cost only £50, defeated teams from all four divisions. Some of the club's best performances have been achieved more recently. Three times since the League was extended in 1958 they have won promotion to the Third Division—in 1959, 1965 and 1971.

The club was formed in 1903 and reconstituted in 1922, when many local workers purchased shares in the company. Their practical interest helped York City to be elected to the Third Division (North) in 1929.

Record attendance: 28,123 v. Huddersfield Town (F.A. Cup), March 1938.
Modern Capacity: 23,500.
Entered Football League: 1929—Div. 3 (North).
Biggest win: 9–1 v. Southport (Div. 3 North), February 1957.
Heaviest defeat: 0–12 v. Chester (Div. 3 North), Feb. 1936.
Highest final League position: 3rd in Div. 4 1958—59, 1964—65.
Best in F.A. Cup: Semi-final 1954—55.
Best in Football League Cup: 5th Round 1961—62.
Pitch measurements: 115 × 75 yd.
Highest League Scorer in Single Season: W. Fenton—31 in 1951—52 (Div. 3 North); A. Bottom—31 in 1954—55 (Div. 3 North).
Transfers—
    Highest fee paid: £10,000—Paul Aimson (from Huddersfield), March 1968.
    Highest fee received: £20,000—Phil Boyer (to Bournemouth), December 1970.

The Scottish League

(First Division members 1971–72)

Aberdeen, the principal club in the north-east of Scotland, were founded in 1903 and from the early years they built a reputation for playing attractive football although rarely achieving top honours.

In 1905 they left the North-east Alliance to enter the Scottish League, and although they stayed in the First Division, it took them half a century to become League Champions. After being runners-up in 1911 and 1937, they at last took the title in 1955. They were runners-up the following year and again in 1971.

By 1967 Aberdeen had reached the Scottish Cup Final six times but won the trophy only once—when defeating Hibernian 2–1 in 1947. Their second F.A. Cup triumph came in 1970, when they beat Celtic 3–1 in the Final. They took the League Cup in its inaugural season (1945–46) and won it again ten years later.

Airdrieonians climbed their highest peaks in the early 1920s when they challenged the supremacy of Rangers and Celtic. They were First Division runners-up in four successive seasons (1923–26) and won the Scottish Cup for the only time in 1924, beating Hibernian 2–0 in the Final.

In the League during that era, Airdrie were unbeaten on their own Bloomfield Park pitch for more than three years. They fielded six Scottish Internationals, the greatest of them Hughie Gallacher.

Airdrie dropped into the Second Division in 1936 and did not get back into the top class until 1947, since when they have fought an almost constant battle to stay up—or go up.

Ayr United have enjoyed steady support since they entered the Scottish First Division in 1913. But they have always struggled on the fringe of the First Division. Between 1925 and 1969, they had to win promotion six times and that gives some indication of their up-and-down existence.

In the early 1920s Ayr had four Scottish Internationals in their side and that was the most colourful period in their history.

Celtic, arch rivals of Rangers as the top club in Scottish football, were formed in 1888 by Irish Catholics living in Glasgow, the first object being to raise money for the poor of the city's East End.

Under former captain Jock Stein (appointed manager in 1965) they have reached astonishing heights, with 1966–67 their greatest season. In an historic clean sweep, they became the first British club to win the European Cup, defeating Inter-Milan 2–1 in the Final; they won the League Championship (scoring 111 goals and losing only one game out of 34); they took the Scottish Cup; and the Scottish League Cup also went to Parkhead.

Celtic's famous green and white strip has long been an emblem of attacking football. Season 1971–72 brought them their 27th League Championship—the last seven in succession—the Scottish Cup for the 22nd time, and the Double for the fourth time in six years. They have also won the League Cup on seven occasions.

Clyde were formed in 1877 and took their name from the river and dockyards of Glasgow. Their home, Shawfield Park, is in the East End and they have constantly struggled to keep up with their big city rivals.

Although they have slipped out of the First Division on five occasions, they have always made a rapid return to the top bracket.

Clyde have never been Champions of Scotland, nor have they won the League Cup, but they have triumphed three times in the F.A. Cup.

After defeats in the 1910 and 1912 Finals, they at last won the trophy in 1939, when they beat Motherwell 4–0. They were also Cup winners in 1955, defeating Celtic 1–0 in a replay, and in 1958 another single goal gave them victory over Hibernian.

Dundee, a First Division club for most of their history, did not win the League Championship until 1962—after four times being runners-up. That is still their only League title to date, but they were F.A. Cup winners in 1910, and their two League Cup successes were gained in 1952 and 1953.

In 1963 Dundee were close to becoming the first British club to win the European Cup, losing in the semi-finals to AC Milan, who went on to win the competition. They have a good record in European football, having beaten such celebrated clubs as Sporting Lisbon, Anderlecht, Standard Liège and Zürich.

Dundee United, founded in 1910, have constantly struggled to emulate the deeds of their next-door neighbours, Dundee —and are still trying to win their first major prize. Originally known as Dundee Hibernian, they changed their name in 1923 on gaining election to the Second Division of the Scottish League. Two years later they won promotion but they led an up-and-down existence (relegated three times) until stability was brought to the side at the start of the 1960s. A noticeable feature at Tannadice Park in recent years has been the presence of International players signed from Norway, Sweden and Denmark.

Dunfermline Athletic did not 'arrive' as a top club in Scotland until the sixties, although they were formed as long ago as 1907. Their real rise began in 1960, when Jock Stein was appointed manager. The following year they reached the Scottish Cup Final for the first time, and after a goalless draw beat Celtic 2–0 in a replay. Their second F.A. Cup victory came in 1968 when they defeated Hearts 3–1 in the Final.

Although Stein left, Dunfermline remained strong and were only two points from putting their name on the First Division title in 1964—65, when finishing third (49 pts) to champions Kilmarnock and runners-up Hearts (each with 50 pts).

In 1969, Dunfermline reached the semi-finals of the European Cup-Winners' Cup, eventually losing 1–2 on aggregate to Slovan Bratislava.

East Fife are unique in having won the Scottish Cup while members of the Second Division. That highest peak came in 1938, when they beat Kilmarnock 4–2 in a Final replay after a 1–1 draw.

As a Second Division side, East Fife had sprung a surprise in 1927 by reaching the Final, but were beaten 3–1 by Celtic. In their only other F.A. Cup Final they lost 3–0 to Rangers in 1950.

Third has been their highest final position in the Championship (in 1952 and 1953), and the League Cup has been East Fife's most successful tournament with three triumphs—in 1948, 1950 and 1954.

Falkirk's closest bid for the Scottish League Championship was made at the start of the century, when they finished runners-up to Celtic in 1908 and 1910. Since the last war they have three times been relegated to the Second Division.

In the Scottish F.A. Cup they have had two successes, beating Raith 2–0 in the 1913 Final and then, after a break of 44 years, taking the trophy again in 1957 with a replay victory by 2–1 against Kilmarnock.

Falkirk have produced many fine players—for English as well as bigger Scottish clubs—and none better than Scottish International inside-forward John White, who moved to Tottenham for £20,000 in October 1959.

Heart of Midlothian were among the founder-members of the Scottish League in 1890 and have never been out of the First Division—a wonderful record, even if it is more than a decade since they won the last of their four Championships in 1960.

Hearts' Scottish Cup triumphs number five (1891, 1896, 1901, 1906 and 1956) and the League Cup has been won by the famous Maroons of Tynecastle Park, Edinburgh, on four occasions—1955, 1959, 1960 and 1963. The 1960 success gave them a double, because they were League Champions as well that season.

Among more than 50 Scottish Internationals to represent the club, there has been no greater artist than Tommy Walker, ace inside-forward of the 1930s and beyond. After a spell with Chelsea just after the war, he returned to Tynecastle and managed Hearts through one of the most spectacular phases in their history.

Hibernian form with Hearts the football strength in the city of Edinburgh, and although their combined records do not begin to measure up to those of the Glasgow 'big two', they have nevertheless made an invaluable contribution to the Scottish soccer scene. Hibs' two Scottish F.A. Cup victories were achieved long ago, in 1887 and 1902. The first time they took the League title was in 1903.

Apart from two seasons at the start of the thirties, they have spent the whole of this century as members of the First Division, with the Championship won in 1948, 1951 and 1952. They became the first British club to take part in the European Cup when it was launched in 1955.

In recent times Hibernian, like many Scottish clubs, have

been forced for financial reasons to sell star players. Forward 'exports' have been their speciality—Colin Stein was sold to Rangers for £100,000 in October 1968, Peter Marinello went to Arsenal at the same fee in January 1970, and two months later the transfer of Peter Cormack to Nottingham Forest fetched £85,000.

No one could say that **Kilmarnock** were winning out of turn when they took the Scottish League title in 1965; they had been runners-up in four of the previous five seasons.

That remains the only League honour to go so far to Rugby Park, and the League Cup has still to be won, but Kilmarnock have had two successes in the Scottish Cup, in 1920 and 1929.

Over the years they have become almost the champion runners-up of Scottish football; besides those four 'seconds' in the League in the early 1960s, they have been beaten F.A. Cup Finalists five times and three times losers of the League Cup Final.

The only major honour to come to Greenock **Morton** was the Scottish Cup in 1922 by a shock 1–0 win over Rangers in the Final. But they are very much part of the fabric of Scottish football with their home at Cappielow Park close to the ship-yards and sugar refineries of Clydeside.

In 1964, Morton became the first Scottish club to recruit Scandinavian players by taking on goalkeeper Eric Sorenson, a Dane. The idea came from director-manager Hal Stewart, who took over in 1962 when they were a dying club—the last but one in the Second Division with only two signed players on the staff.

Under his magical guidance, they won the Scottish Second Division in 1964 by a margin of 14 points and reached the final of the League Cup.

Until season 1931–32, Celtic and Rangers had monopolized Scottish League football for 27 years, but then **Motherwell** came upon the scene as new champions—a reward for the attractive football they had played for many years without winning any major honours.

The previous season, Motherwell reached the Scottish Cup Final for the first time and would have won it but for a

Plate 1 They Did the 'Double' (1) Since the Football League was formed in 1888, four clubs have performed the League Championship & F.A. Cup double by winning both competitions in the same season. First were **Preston North End** in the League's inaugural year (1888–89). They won the Championship undefeated and the Cup without conceding a goal. *Standing:* R. Holmes, N. Ross, D. Russell, R. Howarth, J. Graham, Dr R. H. Mills-Roberts. *Seated:* J. Gordon, J. Ross, J. Goodall, F. Dewhurst, G. Drummond.

Plate 2 They Did the 'Double' (2) Aston Villa were the second double-event club in 1896–97. *Back row:* R. Chat. H. Spencer. A. Evans. T. Wilkes. J. Campbell *Middle row:* C. Athersmith. J. Devey. F. Wheldon. S. Smith. *Front:* J. Crabtree. J. Cowan.

Plate 3 They Did the 'Double' (3)
Tottenham Hotspur.
1960—61
Standing: Bill Brown,
Peter Baker, Ron Henry,
Danny Blanchflower,
Maurice Norman,
Dave Mackay.
Seated: Cliff Jones,
John White, Bobby
Smith, Les Allen,
Terry Dyson.

Plate 4 They Did the 'Double' (4) Arsenal 1970–71 *Standing:* Fred Street (physiotherapist), Pat Rice, Peter Marinello. Sammy Nelson, Bob Wilson, Geoff Barnett, Charlie George, Eddie Kelly, George Armstrong, Steve Burtenshaw (coach). *Seated:* John Roberts, Bob McNab, Peter Storey, Frank McLintock, Bertie Mee (manager), Peter Simpson, George Graham. Ray Kennedy, John Radford **Trophies** (*l. to r.*) League Championship, Footballer of the Year (Frank McLintock) Manager of the Year (Bertie Mee), F.A. Cup. (Street and Burtenshaw were appointed physiotherapist and coach respectively after the double was completed Don Howe was coach to the 1970–71 team, then left Arsenal to manage West Bromwich.)

Plate 5 Historic Moments (1) The first Wembley Final

This was the scene on 28 April 1923 at the time Bolton Wanderers and West Ham United should have kicked off, with a crowd estimated at nearly 200,000 invading the stadium. Eventually, the match was cleared, the match started 40 minutes late, and Bolton won 2–0. How many attended the 'first Wembley' could only be guessed. The official crowd figure given as 126,047 (still the biggest for a match in England), but the railway companies said that 241,000 passengers booked to the ground from London stations. Cup Finals at Wembley have been all-ticket ever since.

Plate 6 Historic Moments (2) Wembley's most dramatic penalty With the 1938 F.A. Cup Final into the last seconds of extra time, there was still no score between Preston North End and Huddersfield Town. Then Preston forward George Mutch was brought down in the penalty-area. He took the spot-kick himself and beat goalkeeper Hesford with a shot that went off the underside of the crossbar to win the Cup for Preston.

Plate 7 Historic Moments (3)

29 June 1950 was the day the football world turned upside down. In the World Cup at Belo Horizonte, Brazil, England were beaten 1–0 by the United States of America. The goal was scored by centre-forward Gaetjens, and at the end he was carried shoulder-high from the pitch by jubilant fans. More than 20 years after football's most unbelievable result, the game has still not become established in the USA.

Plate 8 Historic Moments (4) Bobby Charlton, with 106 full
International appearances, is England's most-capped footballer. He
reached his century on 21 April 1970 in the match against Ireland at
Wembley, and on behalf of the Football Association Dr Andrew Stephen
(chairman) marked the occasion by presenting a silver salver to
Charlton. England completed the night, on which he was captain, by
winning 3–1.

Plate 9 England's World Cup (1)
Wembley, 30 July 1966. With almost the last kick of extra time, Geoff Hurst shoots the final goal against West Germany at Wembley, and England have triumphed 4–2 to win the World Cup for the first time.

Plate 10
England's World Cup (2)
West Germany, the match officials and England line up before the 1966 World Cup Final at Wembley, (England, dark shirts). *From right:*
Jack Charlton,
Martin Peters,
Geoff Hurst
(partly hidden),
Bobby Charlton,
Nobby Stiles,
Ray Wilson,
Roger Hunt,
Gordon Banks,
Alan Ball,
George Cohen,
Bobby Moore.

**Plate 11
England's
World Cup (3)**
England
manager
Alf Ramsey,
subsequently
knighted, joins
the 1966
World Cup-
winning
celebrations
with his captain
Bobby Moore,
Nobby Stiles
and reserve
Jimmy Armfield

**Plate 12
Britain's First
European Cup**
In May 1967,
Celtic became
the first British
club to win the
European Cup,
beating Inter-
Milan 2–1 in
Lisbon. This
was the scene
when they
returned to
Glasgow, to
the acclaim of
thousands of
supporters
waiting to
greet them
at their
Parkhead home.

Plate 13 A Dream Comes True for Matt Busby Manchester United win the European Cup for the first time. In the Final at Wembley in May 1968 they beat Benfica 4–1 in extra time, and as he raises the trophy, the smile on the face of United's manager—who became Sir Matt a few months later—reflects the joy that Britain shared at his club's success.

Plate 14 Save of His Life England and Stoke City goalkeeper Gordon Banks beat out a penalty by West Ham's Geoff Hurst in the closing minutes of extra time in the League Cup semi-final second leg at Upton Park in December 1971. If Hurst had scored, West Ham would have gone to Wembley, instead, Banks's save turned the course of Stoke's history, because after a four-match marathon they beat West Ham and then, by defeating Chelsea in the Final at Wembley, won their first trophy in 109 years of trying.

Plate 15 The Big Three

F.A. Cup

Football League
Championship
Trophy

Football League Cup

**Plate 16 Leeds win
F.A. Cup
Centenary Final**
The 1972 F.A. Cup
marked the
Centenary of the
competition, and a
new name went on
the trophy—that of
Leeds United. To a
background of flags
representing all the
previous winners,
manager Don Revie
leads United into
the Wembley arena
alongside Bertie
Mee and his Arsenal
team. Ninety
minutes later Leeds,
having scored the
only goal, added
their name to the
list of winners, and
two nights later
they just missed
completing the
Double.

tragic last-minute own goal allowing Celtic the chance of a replay which they won 4—2.

Motherwell had to wait another 21 years for their F.A. Cup Final victory which came in 1952 (4—0 against Dundee), but the year before they put their name on the League Cup for the first time.

October 23, 1971 was a red-letter day in the history of **Partick Thistle**. They caused the biggest sensation in Scottish football for years by thrashing odds-on favourites Celtic 4—1 in the League Cup Final. With an average age of 22—and just six months after winning back their First Division place following one season in the Second—Thistle astonished a crowd of 62,740 at Hampden Park by scoring four goals in a 30-minute spell. It was their first major success in 50 years.

Skipper Alex Rae started the goal-rush, left-winger Bobby Lawrie scored the second, right-winger Denis McQuade made it three, and centre-forward Jimmy Bone shot the fourth . . . and mighty Celtic, playing in their eighth successive League Cup Final, were humbled. They made a mere token response through a 70th-minute goal by Ken Dalglish.

Thistle's only other triumph since being formed in the north-west of Glasgow in 1876 was a Cup Final victory in 1921, when they beat Rangers 1—0.

Although their great rivals Celtic have dominated Scotland's honours list in modern times, **Rangers** are still well ahead in the overall Championship-winners' table with 34 titles. The Scottish F.A. Cup has gone to Ibrox 19 times, and the 'Gers' have won seven League Cups, giving them a grand total of 60 prizes in the three tournaments.

Rangers' richest phase came just after the first war with the appointment of Willie Struth as manager in 1920. In 33 years under his command—until at 79 he went on the board— Rangers won the League 18 times, the Cup ten times and the League Cup twice. Some record!

Under Struth's successor, Scot Symon, Rangers continued triumphantly until, in 1967, Celtic became predominant. Davie White followed him, lasted two years and was succeeded in the managerial chair by Willie Waddell, whose first success was of double value in that it came against Celtic in the 1970–71 League Cup Final.

In European campaigns, Rangers are one of Britain's most experienced clubs, failing to qualify only twice in the past 16 seasons. They have come closest to honours in the Cup-Winners' Cup, reaching the Finals of 1961, 1967 and 1972.

St Johnstone, one of the sturdy provincials of Scottish football, were formed in 1884 but, apart from twice winning the Second Division championship, they took 85 years to make their mark. Then in season 1969–70, they reached the Final of the League Cup and football fever gripped the usually quiet town of Perth. At Hampden Park, however, the mighty Celtic beat them, though only by the lone goal of a fiercely fought game.

Scottish League—Division 2
(Members as in season 1971–72)

Albion Rovers	Hamilton Academicals
Alloa Athletic	Montrose
Arbroath	Queen of the South
Berwick Rangers	Queen's Park
Brechin City	Raith Rovers
Clydebank	St Mirren
Cowdenbeath	Stenhousemuir
Dumbarton	Stirling Albion
East Stirling	Stranraer
Forfar Athletic	

Prominent European Clubs

(Details as at 1 January, 1972)

Ajax Amsterdam: Formed in 1900 and came to prominence only after professionalism introduced in 1953. Have a tiny ground of their own (22,000) but play their big matches at the Olympic Stadium (capacity 65,000). Dutch Champions 14 times (a record) including a hat-trick between 1966 and 1968, and also F.A. Cup winners 1969–70 (when they completed the double) and 1970–71. Have won the Cup six times altogether. Finalists in the European Cup in 1969, their open attacking play foundered against the *cattenacio* defence of AC Milan. After crashing 1–4, they were more cautious when they reached the Final again in 1971 and won the trophy 2–0 against Panathinaikos at Wembley. Managed through most of their triumphs by former player Rinus Michels (now with CF Barcelona). Stars: centre-forward Johan Cruyff and inside-left Piet Keizer.

RSC Anderlecht: Formed in 1908, the Royal Sporting Club Anderlecht play at their own Parc Astrid in Brussels (capacity 28,000) with the 60,000 Stade de Heysel reserved for big games. Champions of Belgium 14 times (a record) and F.A. Cup winners once—in 1964–65. Recorded a spectacular success in the sixties when they won the championship five times in a row (another record) between 1964 and 1968. Crashed 0–10 to Manchester United in their first venture into the European Cup (1956–57), but improved later to become one of the few teams to have the distinction of eliminating Real Madrid in Di Stefano's time. Fairs Cup Finalists 1970. Best known players: Jeff Mermans (56 caps) in the fifties; Joseph Jurion (64 caps) in the sixties; today, Paul Van Himst.

Atletico Madrid: Founded in 1923 and adopted by the Spanish forces in the thirties, when known as Aviaciones Atletico. Champions of Spain six times and F.A. Cup winners four times. Most recent success—champions in 1969–70. Built the futuristic Estadio Manzanares in the sixties, intended to rival Real's Chamartin, but still incomplete, with a capacity of 70,000. Won the European Cup-Winners' Cup in 1962 and were Finalists again in 1963. Perhaps their most meritorious achievement came in 1959 when, with international stars Vava (centre-forward in Brazil's 1958 World Cup-winning team) and Portuguese schemer Jorge Mendonca in the side, they took Real Madrid, then at their peak, to a third game in the European Cup semi-final and lost 3—4 overall. Current star: centre-forward Garate.

CF Barcelona: Formed in 1899 and today the wealthiest club in Spain with their Nou Camp Stadium (completed in 1968) accommodating 90,000. Spanish champions eight times and F.A. Cup winners 17 times. Most recent successes in the Spanish Cup were in 1968 and 1971. Also Latin Cup winners in 1949 and 1951. European Cup Finalists in 1961; Cup-Winners' Cup Finalists in 1969 and the only club to win the Fairs Cup three times—in 1958, 1960 and 1966. Their most successful phase was 1959—61 when, under the guidance of Helenio Herrera, they won the championship two years in succession. Best known stars of the sixties: Luis Suarez, Sandor Kocsis (Hungary), Ladislav Kubala (Hungary).

FC Bayern München: The outstanding West German team of recent years but omitted from the Bundesliga when it was formed in 1963, preference being given to neighbours München 1860, who were subsequently relegated. Bayern were promoted in 1965 and quickly established themselves by winning the F.A. Cup in 1966. A year later they added the European Cup-Winners' Cup to their trophies and also retained the F.A. Cup. Champions of West Germany twice, the most recent success being in 1968—69, and Cup winners on five occasions (a record), four of those times since 1966. Yugoslav coach Zlatko Cajkowski led the club to promotion and their early triumphs but resigned in 1969. Current stars: Gerd Muller and Franz Beckenbauer.

Benfica: Champions of Portugal 18 times and F.A. Cup winners 17 times—both records. Also Latin Cup winners 1950. Formed in 1904 and play at the 75,000-capacity Estadio de Luz. Their most successful period was in the sixties when champions eight times in ten seasons. Most recent successes: champions 1970—71 and Cup-winners 1969—70. Rose to international eminence soon after professionalism was introduced and under guidance of Hungarian-born manager Bela Guttman twice won the European Cup—1961 and 1962. Also reached the Final in 1963, 1965 and 1968. Beaten in the World Club Championship by Penarol (1961) and Santos (1962). Mario Coluna (captain) and Jose Aguas best-known stars of their triumphs, with Eusebio and Graca their current aces. Now managed by former England international Jimmy Hagan.

Borussia Monchengladbach: Like their West German rivals Bayern, they failed to gain a Bundesliga place on its inception in 1963 but won promotion in 1965. Steadily developed since then and at their best are today one of the Continent's strongest teams. Champions of West Germany twice—1969–70 and 1970–71 and F.A. Cup winners once. Thrashed Internazionale-Milan 7–1 in a European Cup-tie in 1971 only to have U.E.F.A. demand a replay in Berlin because of crowd trouble. Star players: full-back Berti Vogts (1971 Footballer of the Year in West Germany), forward Josef Heynckes and Gunter Netzer, a midfield general and free-kick expert.

C.S.K.A. Sofia: Formed in 1948 as the team of the Bulgarian Army and immediately successful. Champions 14 times (a record) and Cup winners seven times. Pulled off an incredible run of success when winning the championship nine times in a row between 1954 and 1962. Most recent success—Bulgarian champions 1970–71. Took part ten times in European Cup, reaching the semi-finals in 1967 and taking Inter-Milan to a third game. Inside-left Ivan Kolev was the big star of the sixties with a record 76 caps. Currently the club's best-known players are centre-forward Petar Jekov and inside-left Dimiter Yakimov, each capped more than 50 times and together forming an effective combination of creative skill and finishing power.

Dukla Prague: The Sports Club of the Czechoslovak Army, formerly known as U.D.A. and later A.T.K. Prague. Champions eight times (a post-war record) under manager Jaroslav Vejvoda, and Cup winners four times (the competition started only in 1961). Most recent successes, champions in 1965–66 and Cup winners 1968–69, but they slumped when Vejvoda left to take over Legia (Poland). Seven times in European Cup but never progressed beyond the quarter-finals; twice (1961 and 1962) won the International Cup staged in New York. Best-known players of the sixties: wing-halves Josef Masopust and Svatoplik Pluskal, and left-back

Ladislav Novak. Fortunes have improved since 1971, when Vejvoda returned with Masopust as his assistant.

Dynamo Kiev: Achieved a unique double in being the first provincial club to break the Moscow clubs' stranglehold on the major Russian honours—winning the F.A. Cup for the first time in 1954 and taking the league title in 1961. They have gone on to win five league championships and the F.A. Cup three times. Most recent honours: champions three times in a row (1966 to 1968) and again in 1971. The current team includes many top Russian players often strangely ignored by the national team chief and including goalkeeper Jevgueni Rudakov, star spearhead Anatoli Bychevetz and an exceptionally skilful midfield trio—Josif Szabo (Hungarian-born), Viktor Serebrianikov and Vladimir Muntjan.

Dynamo Moscow: Formed in 1887 and today the team of the Electrical Trades Union in Moscow. League champions ten times (a Russian record) and F.A. Cup winners four times. Most recent successes—four times champions in the fifties, champions again in 1963 and Cup winners in 1967 and 1970. Gained world-wide fame when in November 1945, they toured briefly and very successfully in Britain, but 12 years of isolation followed for Russian football. Made their bow in international competition in 1971–72 Cup-Winners' Cup. Most famous player Alexei 'Tiger' Khomich, goalkeeper in the fifties, and they provided another world-class goalkeeper, Lev Yashin, and right-winger Igor Chislenko for the 1966 World Cup. Best current players: forwards Kozlov and Jevruchkin.

Dynamo Zagreb: Known before the last war as Gradjanska SK and re-organized in 1945. Champions of Yugoslavia eight times and F.A. Cup winners on four occasions. Most recent success: F.A. Cup winners 1969. Won the Fairs Cup in 1967 and did it the hard way, eliminating Dunfermline, Dynamo Bucharest, Juventus, Eintracht Frankfurt and Leeds United in the Final 2–0 and 0–0. Stars of the sixties: Skoric, Perusic, Brncic and Zambata, who all moved to West European clubs. Rudolf Belin, Yugoslavia's Footballer of the Year in 1964, was transferred to Olimpija. Since Branko Zebec left to manage Bayern München, Dynamo have struggled to regain their stature.

Ferencvaros: Formed in 1899 as an athletics and gymnastic club. Champions of Hungary 21 times (a record) and winners of the F.A. Cup once (the Cup is still not accepted by the fans in Hungary as important). Also Mitropa Cup winners in 1928 and 1937. Most recent successes: champions in 1967 and 1968. The first East European club to win a modern international tournament when they won the Fairs Cup in 1965—beating AS Roma, Bilbao, Manchester United and Juventus (in the Final). Finalists again in 1968. Best known stars: Florian Albert (centre-forward); Mate Fenyvesi (left wing) and Sandor Matrai (stopper), who all gained more than 70 caps. Only Albert is still playing.

Feyenoord: Founded 1908 and established as top club in Holland during the thirties, they built a superb 64,000-capacity stadium in Rotterdam in 1938. Champions nine times and F.A. Cup winners four times (the Cup was abandoned in the fifties because of lack of public interest). Most recent successes: a double in 1968–69 and champions 1970–71. Surprised everyone by winning the European Cup in 1970, beating Celtic 2–1 in the Final in Milan after extra time. Star of that team, Swedish centre-forward Ove Kindvall. Pre-war, Puck Van Heel was their big name, winning a record 64 caps. Current stars: Rinus Israel, Wim Van Hanegem, Franz Hasil (Austria) and Coen Moulijn. Manager: Ernst Happel (Austria).

Fiorentina: Formed relatively late in 1926 and champions of Italy three times. Also Cup winners three times. Most recent successes: F.A. Cup winners 1965–66 and champions in 1968–69. Won the European Cup-Winners' Cup in 1961 and were Finalists in 1962. Their most distinguished performances came when they ran away with the 1955–56 Italian championship—they were unbeaten until the last day of the season—and the following year (1956–57) when they reached the European Cup Final, only to meet Real Madrid playing on their home ground and lost 0–2. Best known stars: Julinho (Brazil) and Michelangelo Montuori (Argentina), who played in the fifties. Current star: Giancarlo De Sisti, who played for Italy in 1970 World Cup Final v. Brazil.

Gornik Zabrze: Gornik, meaning 'Miners', have established themselves as the leading club in Poland since the war and built something of an international reputation, too. Champions eight times and Cup winners five times, they have been consistently successful in recent years, winning the league five times in a row (1963–67) and four consecutive F.A. Cups (1968–71). In the European Cup reached the quarter-final in 1968, falling to Manchester United (1–2 on aggregate) directly after their three-month winter lay-off. Responded better to this challenge in 1970 and reached the 1970 Cup-Winners' Cup Final, losing 1–2 to Manchester City. In the sixties their stars were Ernst Pohl (inside-forward) and Stanislas Oslizlo (stopper), who both earned 60 caps. Current star: Wlodzimierz Lubanski.

Grasshoppers FC: Based in Zürich and one of the old-established Swiss clubs, they have been champions 16 times (a record) and F.A. Cup winners 13 times (another record). In 1937 won an F.A. Cup Final 10–0 against Lausanne and went on to take the Cup six times in seven seasons between 1937 and 1943 under Austrian-born manager Karl Rappan, who devised the Swiss 'bolt' defensive system. In 1955–56 they achieved a Cup and League double, with Yugoslav star Vukosaljevic scoring 33 league goals. In 1970–71 beat FC Basle 4–3 in a play-off after extra time to win the league once more. Most capped players: Josef Minelli (79) and Fredy Bickel (71). Current stars: Rainer Ohlhauser (West German international) and centre-forward Kurt Muller.

Internazionale FC: Formed in 1909 as a breakaway from AC Milan and known before the war as Ambrosiana-Inter. Champions of Italy 11 times (including three successes in the sixties) but they have never won the F.A. Cup. Most recent success: champions 1970–71. Reached international prominence under manager Helenio Herrera, winning the European Cup in 1964 and 1965. Also finalists in 1967. Their peak achievement came in 1964, when they won the Italian championship, the European Cup and the World Club Championship—and they retained the World title in 1965 by beating Independiente (Argentina) a second time. Current stars: Sandro Mazzola, Roberto Boninsegna and Giacinto Facchetti, who all appeared for Italy in the 1970 World Cup Final.

Juventus: Founded in 1897 and share the Stadio Communale in Turin (75,000) with AC Torino. Known affectionately throughout Italy as the 'Old Lady', they have been champions of Italy 13 times and F.A. Cup winners five times (both records). Most recent successes: champions in 1966–67 and F.A. Cup winners 1964–65. Fairs Cup Finalists in 1965 and 1971, the last being a frustrating experience when they lost the trophy to Leeds on the away goals rule. Rarely outside the top four in the Italian league, they have imported some of the world's outstanding players over the years; their best period was perhaps in the early sixties, when John Charles (Wales) and Enrico Sivori (Argentina) spearheaded their attack.

AC Milan: Formed in 1899 as Milan Cricket and Football Club, they play at the 90,000-capacity San Siro stadium. Italian champions nine times and F.A. Cup-winners once – they went on to win the European Cup-Winners' Cup the following season (1967–68). Most recent successes: champions 1967–68 and European Cup Winners 1963 and 1969. Also Finalists in 1958. Won the World Club title in 1969 against Estudiantes (Argentina) in Buenos Aires. Also won the now defunct Latin Cup in 1951 and 1956. Best-ever team was probably in 1955. Studded with stars, their line-up included Nils Liedholm and Gunnar Nordahl (Sweden), Eduardo Ricagni (Argentina), Arne Sorensen (Denmark) and Juan Schiaffino (Uruguay). Current star: Gianni Rivera.

Partizan Belgrade: The team of the Yugoslav Army who took over Belgrade S.K. (five times pre-war champions) in 1946. Play at the Partizan Stadium, capacity 60,000. Champions 11 times and F.A. Cup winners on five occasions. Won the league title four times in five seasons in the sixties. Their best side of recent years was probably that of 1965–66 which eliminated Manchester United in the European Cup semi-final with a superb rearguard action. They were then beaten in the Final 1–2 by Real Madrid after leading. Stars of the sixties: goalkeeper Milutin Soskic and full-back Fahrudin Jusufi (both now in Germany) and centre-half Velibor Vasovic, who recently retired after helping Ajax Amsterdam win the European Cup in 1971.

SC Rapid: Vienna's traditional masters of the Austrian game, formed in 1898 and champions 25 times (a record). Also F.A.

Cup winners seven times, though Cup knockout competitions have never been popular in Austria. Champions four times in the sixties, Cup winners in 1969 and did the Cup and League double in 1967–68. Also had the unique distinction of winning the German Championship and Cup during the war when Austria was annexed. Eliminated Real Madrid from the European Cup in 1969. Gerhardt Hanappi, a play-anywhere type, has been their greatest post-war star with 92 caps.

Real Madrid: Founded in 1898 and rose to world eminence under chairmanship of Santiago Bernabeu, who built the 120,000-capacity Chamartin Stadium and signed Alfredo Di Stefano in the fifties. Champions of Spain 14 times (a record) and F.A. Cup winners ten times. Champions five times in succession (1961–65), a record, and again in 1967, 1968 and 1969. Also Cup winners 1969–70, they went on to reach the European Cup-Winners' Cup Final in 1971. Latin Cup Winners 1955 and 1957, but best known for their fabulous team of the fifties which won the first five European Cup tournaments (1956 to 1960) with Di Stefano, Ferenc Puskas and Jose Santamaria the stars. Won the European Cup again in 1966 and Finalists in 1962 and 1964. First World Club Champions in 1960. Current stars: Amancio and Pirri.

Red Star Belgrade: Known pre-war as Jugoslawija FK, they were re-formed in 1945 as the sports club of Belgrade University. Champions of Yugoslavia 11 times (a record) and F.A. Cup winners nine times (all in the post-war period). Most recent successes in seasons 1967–68, 1968–69 and 1969–70, when they achieved a league title hat-trick, adding the F.A. Cup to their honours in 1968 and 1970 to pull off two 'doubles'. Won the Cup again in season 1970–71. Best known players: Vladimir Beara (goalkeeper) and Rajko Mitic (inside-forward) in the fifties; Dragoslav Sekularec (inside-forward) in the sixties and, today, left-winger Dragan Dzajic, who is among the world's most sought-after players.

Reims: Founded in 1931 as Stade de Reims, but only a Division II club until they developed during the 1939–45 war. Elected to First Division in 1946 and quite the most successful French club post-war. Champions six times between 1949 and 1962, they produced football to match the champagne district they represent. Also won the French Cup in 1950 and

1958 (completing a double that year). With former inside-forward Albert Batteux as coach, they twice reached the European Cup Final (1956 and 1959) only to lose to Real Madrid on each occasion. At their peak, around 1958, they provided seven players plus coach Batteux when France won third place in the World Cup in Sweden. Reims post-war stars: Raymond Kopa, Just Fontaine, Roger Piantoni.

St Etienne: Share with Reims the record number of French championship successes (6) and have been F.A. Cup winners three times. Between 1966–67 and 1969–70 took the league title four times in succession, adding the F.A. Cup to make 'doubles' in 1968 and 1970. Linking the Saints with Reims is coach Albert Batteux, who joined them from Reims after a brief spell with Division II Grenoble. League leaders in 1970–71, they were shattered when two key men, goalkeeper Carnus and stopper Bosquier, revealed they had signed to join chief rivals Marseille at the end of the season and were dropped for the remainder of the campaign while Marseille overtook them. Star player: Salif Keita, a gifted inside-forward from Mali.

Slovan Bratislava: They have shone in Czechoslovakian football when the Prague clubs have failed. Champions five times (all post-war) including a hat-trick of league successes in the fifties and Cup winners three times. Most recent success: champions 1969–70 and F.A. Cup winners 1968. Became the first East European Club to win one of the two senior international club tournaments when winning the Cup-Winners' Cup in 1969, beating FC Porto, AC Torino on the way and CF Barcelona in the Final by 3–2. Stars in that success: Alexander Vencel (goal), Vladimir Hrivnak, Ludwig Cvetler and Jan Capkovic. Current manager Jan Hucko has steered the club back to the top, with the Capkovic twins, Jan and Josef, and Karol Jokl the stars.

Spartak Moscow: Founded in 1922 and over the years one of the most consistent Russian clubs. Champions nine times and F.A. Cup-winners on ten occasions. Most recent honours: Cup winners 1965, champions in 1969 and Cup winners again in 1971. Took the championship four times in the fifties (and the Cup three times) with star centre-forward

Nikita Simonian the key man. His career record of 156 league goals for Spartak seems unassailable in the defence-dominated game played in Russia today. Manager of his old club for the last five years, Simonian insists on quality first, which means attacking football. Current stars: Anzor Kavazashvili (goal) defenders Gennadij Logofet and Jevgueni Lovchev and centre-forward Nikolaj Osjanin.

Sporting Lisbon: Eternal rivals of Benfica, they play at the 45,000 Estadio Jose Alvalade. Champions of Portugal 13 times and F.A. Cup winners on 12 occasions. Most recent successes: champions in 1969–70 and, after Benfica had overshadowed them in the 1970–71 title race, they had the satisfaction of crushing their neighbours 4–1 in the 1971 Cup Final. In the international arena their best performance was to win the European Cup-Winners' Cup in 1964, beating Atalanta (Italy), Manchester United, Lyon (France) and, in the Final, MTK (Hungary). After losing 1–4 at Old Trafford that year, they produced an astonishing 5–0 victory over Manchester United in Lisbon. Provided seven men for Portugal's 1966 World Cup squad. Current stars: Vitor Goncalves and Jaime Mosquera (from Peru).

Standard Liège: Playing at the Stade de Sclessin (capacity 40,000), they have been pace-makers in the Belgian game since professionalism came into the open. Champions six times and F.A. Cup winners three times. In recent years have won the Cup in 1967, and the championship in successive seasons 1969, 1970 and 1971. The only Belgian club to reach the European Cup semi-finals, they did so in 1962, beating Real Madrid 2–0 in their home leg but losing 0–4 in Madrid. Best-known players of the sixties were Paul Bonga Bonga (Congo), Johnny Crossan (N. Ireland) and Istvan Sztani (Hungary). The current team includes six of Belgium's 1970 World Cup side, with Wilfried Van Moer, Ludwig Cvelter (a Czech) and Sylvestre Takac (Yugoslavia) the stars.

Ujpest Dozsa: Founded in 1899 and now the team of the Hungarian Ministry of the Interior. The Dozsa stadium, which holds 40,000, is probably the best-equipped club ground in Budapest. Champions 12 times and F.A. Cup winners twice (the knockout competition began only in the last decade).

Most recent successes: 1969—Cup and League double;
1970—Cup and League double, 1970–71 (changeover
season)—champions. Also winners of the Mitropa Cup in
1929 and 1939. Ujpest reached the Fairs Cup Final in 1969,
losing 2–6 on aggregate to Newcastle United. Star players:
Ferenc Bene (centre-forward) and Antal Dunai (inside-left).

Valencia: Founded in 1902, their Estadio Mestalla holds
70,000 and their reserves (Mestalla CF) play in Spanish
Division II. Champions of Spain four times and F.A. Cup
winners on four occasions. Most recent successes—champions in 1970–71 and F.A. Cup Finalists—beaten by
Barcelona after extra time. Twice winners of the Fairs Cup
(1962 and 1963) and beaten Finalists in 1964. Best-known
players of the sixties: Waldo, a free-scoring centre-forward
from Brazil; Didi, who had a brief spell with them, and another
Brazilian inside-forward, Walter, who was tragically killed in
a road accident. Present manager: Alfredo Di Stefano, who
guided the club to the championship in his first season.

Prominent South American Clubs

(Details as at 1 January 1972)

BRAZIL

Botafogo: Formed in 1904 and champions of Rio de
Janeiro on 13 occasions, the most recent successes being in
1961, 1962 and 1968. Also winners of the Taca de Prata
(Gold Cup) four times in the 1960s. Their own little ground
beside the 'Sugar Loaf' holds only 23,000 spectators and is
largely reserved for training, with league matches staged at
the 200,000-capacity Maracana Stadium. Perhaps the most
youth-conscious club in Rio, they have produced swarms of
stars, providing Garrincha, Didi, Nilton Santos and Zagalo for
the 1958 World Cup-winning team; the same four and
Amarildo (deputy for Pele) in 1962. In Mexico 1970 they had
Jairzinho on full-time World Cup duty with two reserves,
Paulo Cesar and Roberto.

Corinthians: Currently the biggest crowd-pulling team
in São Paulo and champions 15 times—including three
occasions when they took the title three years in a row.

Winners of the Taca de Prata in 1953, 1954 and 1966 (shared because the proximity of the World Cup prevented a play-off) Play most of their home league matches at the giant Estadio Morumbi in São Paulo (capacity 180,000), the world's second-largest ground. Provided three players for the 1966 World Cup—Garrincha, Flavio, Dino Sani (currently the manager), and in the 1970 Mexico World Cup they produced a revelation—Rivelino. Supporting him in the present team are other internationals including Ado (Brazil's reserve goalkeeper for the last World Cup), Paulo Borges, Eduardo, Ditao and Luiz Carlos.

Cruzeiro: Because of Brazil's size—bigger than all Europe—state leagues are organized and Cruzeiro, from the mining area of Belo Horizonte, play in the league of Minas Gerais. Champions 15 times, the most recent success being in 1969, they have great rivals in neighbours Atletico Mineiro. Won the Brazilian F.A. Cup (this competition decides which clubs represent Brazil in the South American Clubs' Cup) in 1966. Honoured by having two players, centre-forward Tostao and half-back Wilson Piazza, chosen as regular members of Brazil's World Cup-winning team in 1970.

Flamengo: Winners of the Rio de Janeiro championship 13 times, including three consecutive titles in the fifties. Last championship success in 1965. Formed in 1895, they are the oldest club in Brazil and the best supported with 70,000 club members. The club publishes its own weekly magazine (circulation 120,000 copies). Winners of the Taca de Prata in 1961 and their fans boast they would prefer Flamengo's attractive football to the more efficient (and successful) modern game played elsewhere in Brazil. It seems to pay, too, for they regularly pull crowds of 100,000 and their two highest league attendances are world club records: Flamengo v. Fluminense (1963) 177,656 and (at the same fixture in 1969) 171,599.

Fluminense: Champions of Rio de Janeiro 17 times (a record), the most recent successes coming in 1964 and 1969. Also winners of the Taca de Prata three times, including the 1970 series. Formed in 1897 by an Englishman named Oscar Cox, they are now probably the most wealthy club in Brazil.

They hold one unassailable record, having won all 16 league matches in the 1911 campaign. This was the first senior club of Didi (played in 1954 World Cup with goalkeeper Castilho) and for the 1950 World Cup they provided Brazil with the fabulous Ademir and Jair. In the Mexico World Cup they were represented by goalkeeper Felix and reserve defender Marco Antonio, and in 1971 they pulled off a coup by engaging Brazil's World Cup manager Mario Zagalo.

Palmeiras:: Formed by Italian residents of São Paulo in 1897, and known until 1942 as Palestra Italia. Winners of the São Paulo championship on 14 occasions and winners of the Taca de Prata three times—1951, 1965 and 1967. Also won the Brazilian F.A. Cup in 1960 and 1967 with entry to the South American Champions' Cup and twice reached the Final (1961 and 1968). The successes of 1967–68 coincided with the final fling of right-winger Julinho, who became a superb midfield general in his forties. Their best-known players have been Djalma Santos (98 caps) and Altafini who, like Julinho, spent the greater part of his career in Italy.

Santos: The world's most popular club, with Pele the star attraction. They were champions of São Paulo only once until 1955, but with Pele at his peak they won the title five times in a row between 1958 and 1962. Champions again for the third successive time in 1969, they then took 12 titles in 15 years and 13 overall. Won the Taca de Prata five times and the Brazilian F.A. Cup five times in a row (1961 to 1965). Winners of the South American Champions' Cup in 1962 and 1963, they went on each time to win the World Club title. Provided many of Brazil's World Cup-winning stars: Gylmar, Zito, Pele (1958); Gylmar, Mauro, Zito (1962) and Pele, Clodoaldo and Carlos Alberto (1970).

ARGENTINA

Boca Juniors: Formed in 1905 in the suburb of Boca with an Irishman, boxer-footballer Patrick MacCarthy, as their first president. Seventeen times champions of Argentina, a record, they have a stadium (Bombonera—the 'Chocolate Box') that accommodates 80,000 and most games are a sell-out. Thousands demonstrated when it was known that Di Stefano (manager in 1969) was leaving. Finalists in the

127

South American Clubs' Cup in 1963, they provided the back-bone of the 1966 World Cup team, including Rattin (sent off v. England at Wembley), Marzolini, Roma and Gonzalez. They have specialized in exporting players to Italy; Luis Monti left them in 1931 to win a World Cup-winner's medal in 1934, while more recent exports include Ernesto Grillo (AC Milan) and Valentin Angelillo (Inter).

Estudiantes: The only Argentinian club of renown that does not play in Buenos Aires, they have their home in La Plata 70 miles from the capital in a town of 100,000. Three times champions of South America, they have never won the Argentinian title and qualified for the Taca de los Libertadores first as league runners-up, then as holders of the trophy. Fans boast they do not buy players but make them in the Zubeldia laboratories—a reference to Osvaldo Zubeldia, who has been coach since 1964. Copying the tough, ruthless methods of Racing, they were also World Club Champions in 1968, but more recently they have been forced to break up their team and sell players for financial reasons.

Independiente: Comparative newcomers to the big scene in Argentina, but winners of the league title seven times—the most recent success coming in 1967. With two clubs from each country playing in the South American Club championship, Independiente twice qualified as runners-up and surprised everyone by winning the trophy in 1964 and again in 1965. On both occasions, however, they met the super-defence of Internazionale-Milan in the World Club decider, and were beaten. Their best year was 1964 with a run of 40 games without defeat, including 33 consecutive victories before they lost their final league match to Boca Juniors.

Racing Club: Formed in 1893 and the oldest club in Argentina. Champions 15 times—three times in the fifties—and their most recent success was gained in 1966, when they played 39 consecutive games without defeat. South American champions in 1967, their play-off with Celtic brought them the World Club title and a great deal of criticism for their negative tactics and lack of sportsmanship. The club was formed by French immigrants and named after the Racing Club de Paris. They have exported many famous players in the past, including Ruben Bravo (to France) and Pedro Manfredini and Humberto Maschio (to Italy).

River Plate: The 'established' club of Buenos Aires with 67,000 enrolled supporters. Thirteen times champions, including a hat-trick of successes in the late fifties and often runners-up since. Changing their manager frequently, they still seek the right formula, but Didi (in charge of Peru in the World Cup) has been there since 1970 and, with River Plate close to the 1971 title, he looked to be entrenched. Old supporters claim their best team was that of the forties—the goal-machine that could not be shown off to the world because of the war. Finalists in the South American Clubs' Cup in 1966, they are perhaps best known in Europe for their exports, which have included Alfredo Di Stefano and Enrico Sivori.

URUGUAY

Nacional: Two years younger than Penarol, their great rivals and virtually their only opposition. Champions of Uruguay 28 times, including 1969 and 1970, they went on to win the 1971 South American Championship and the World Club title against Panathinaikos. Previously finalists in the South American Champions' Cup three times—in 1964, 1967 and 1969. Share the 70,000 capacity Estadio Centenario .stadium in Montevideo with Penarol, whom they beat 2–0 on the way to the league title in 1969—their first such victory in eight years. Provided seven of Uruguay's 1970 World Cup semi-final team, with Luis Cubilla the best known.

Penarol: Formed in 1891 by British workers as Railway Cricket and Football Club', and the last South American team to add to its dignity in the World Club Championship when they beat Real Madrid 2–0 and 2–0 in 1966. Thirty times champions of Uruguay, including five in a row and nine times in the last 12 seasons. Remarkably by modern standards, they were champions in 1967 and 1968 without losing a league game. South American champions three times—1960, 1961 and 1966—and finalists in 1962 and 1965. World Club Champions in 1961 and 1966. Provided seven men for Uruguay's 1950 World Cup-winning team and great exporters of players to Europe, the best known being perhaps Schiaffino to AC Milan (at a world record £72,000 fee in 1954) and Santamaria (Real Madrid).

World Stars of 1972–73 *(Career details as at 1 January 1972)*

Artime, *Luis*: Centre-forward of Nacional (Uruguay) and Argentina. A powerful, much-travelled player, consistently successful over the last decade. One of the few Argentinian players to make a good impression in the 1966 World Cup, in which he scored three of his country's four goals. Born Mendoza. His first club was Atlanta but he rose to stardom with River Plate and Independiente, helping both to win the Argentine championship and topping the scorers' list three times. In 1968 he was transferred to Palmeiras (Brazil) and as top scorer helped them qualify for the South American Champions' Cup, before joining Nacional in 1969. In the 1970 Uruguayan season Artime was again top marksman with 22 goals in 14 games, and he scored all three goals in the matches v. Panathinaikos which brought Nacional the World Club title for the first time. 33 years old (20 caps).

Anastasi, *Pietro*: Centre-forward of Juventus and Italy. A native of Sicily which, unlike most of the poorer regions of Europe, produces few top-class players. From the local club Catania he was transferred as a teenager, for a small fee in 1966 to First Division Varese, apparently the only club to recognize his potential. Two years later, with all the wealthy Italian clubs after him, he set a world transfer record when signed by Juventus (Turin) for £440,000. Now, at 24, one of the key men in the talented young Juventus side. Quick, skilful, strong in the air and a regular scorer of spectacular goals, he is the complete spearhead. 15 caps for Italy.

Artime   Anastasi

Banks   **Beckenbauer**

Banks, *Gordon*: Goalkeeper of Stoke City and England. Rated
the game's greatest 'keeper over the last two World Cups ... and
since. Had totalled 69 International appearances by the end of
1971, easily a record for a British goalkeeper. Born at Sheffield, he
began with Chesterfield and moved to Leicester City in 1959.
Played more than 300 first-team games for them and was transferred to Stoke City in April 1967 for £50,000. Has subsequently
hurled his 6 ft 1 in., 13 st 7 lb frame across goalmouths to even
more spectacular effect for club and country, with deep con-
centration and razor-sharp reflexes enabling him to make 'impossible' saves (viz. Pele in the 1970 World Cup in Mexico). Won
the first of his caps against Scotland at Wembley in April 1966
(Sir Alf Ramsey's second match in charge of England), and his
ambition is to play in his third World series in West Germany in
1974, when he will be 36.

Beckenbauer, *Franz*: Centre-half of Bayern München and
West Germany. A complete player of all-round ability said by the
purists to be 'wasted' playing defensively as sweeper for his
club. West Germany use him in a creative midfield role from right-
half, where he is a firm tackler, wins many balls with astute
anticipation and interception, and distributes passes with the
flair and precision of a gifted inside-forward. However, for
Bayern he is not restricted and frequently goes forward to display
his skills and is often among the scorers for club and country.
He is 25 years old, with more than 50 caps, and twice voted West
Germany's Footballer of the Year.

Bene, *Ferenc*: Centre-forward of Ujpest Dozsa and Hungary. Began the climb to fame in the 1964 Olympic Games (which he helped Hungary win) and established himself as top scorer for the series. The previous season he had been Hungary's highest league scorer when only 18 years old. The most consistent Hungarian marksman in the last decade—despite being rather short and frail—he earns most of his goals with craft and guile, hitting swerving shots and dribbling through defences to carve out his own chances. Also creates many openings for colleagues and is almost as useful at inside-forward or on the right wing, where he has often been capped. Collected a triple distinction in 1969—Cup and League honours for Ujpest and was himself Hungary's leading scorer with 27 goals. Age 26, with more than 50 caps.

Best, *George*: Outside-right/left for Manchester United and Northern Ireland. Currently Britain's most gifted player, he joined United from school at 15 and disliked living in Manchester at first, but was persuaded to stay by Sir Matt Busby. Becoming a full-time professional at 17, he soon forgot his homesickness for Belfast and leapt to stardom almost overnight. Equally at home on either wing, this lightly-built genius is particularly difficult to mark because he drops deep and wanders in search of the ball; once in possession his superb skills make him a menace to opponents. Voted 1968 Footballer of the Year in both Europe and England. In season 1971–72 began to play more 'inside', so adding a new dimension to his game. Balance, ball control and sheer enthusiasm are his chief assets. Aged 25 with 28 caps for Northern Ireland.

Bene **Best**

Cruyff   **Cubillas**

Cruyff, *Johan*: Centre-forward of Ajax Amsterdam and Holland. The Dutch club's biggest asset, he signed a seven-year contract in 1971 that guaranteed him a minimum £100,000. Top Dutch scorer with 33 goals in his first full league season when only 18, he played a vital role in Ajax winning the European Cup in 1971. Superbly skilful, fast and with deceptive feints, he is equally at home as midfield schemer or striking spearhead. Twice the Dutch Footballer of the Year, he was awarded the supreme honour in 1971 when voted European Footballer of the Year. Is 24 years old with 20 caps, a total limited because of a dispute which followed his sending-off when making his début for Holland.

Cubillas, *Teofilo*: Inside-left of Allianza (Lima) and Peru. An exciting personality who burst on the world scene during the 1970 World Cup in Mexico. He starred for shock team Peru, who might have gone even further had they not clashed with Brazil in the quarter-finals and lost 2—4. A naturally talented and instinctive player, Cubillas is adept at giving and receiving one-twos, and alternates his game with bewildering feints and dribbles. His close control at high speed and in tight situations enables him to score spectacular goals, and he would do even better in higher company. But although top clubs of Brazil and Argentina pursued him, the Peru F.A. refused to sanction his transfer abroad, labelling him a national asset. 24 years old (35 caps).

133

Dzajic, *Dragan*: Outside-left of Red Star (Belgrade) and Yugoslavia. Perhaps the only world-class natural left-winger in the modern game, a schoolteacher by profession and a supremely elegant player who scores goals himself and creates many more for his colleagues with his speed, dribbling technique and superb passes. Made a big impact in 1968 when, largely as a result of his promptings, Yugoslavia reached the Final of the European Championship and took Italy (the host country) to a replay. Now 26 years old with more than 50 caps, he could choose his club and name his terms if he became available for transfer—as he will do under Yugoslav rules in two years' time.

Facchetti, *Giacinto*: Left-back of Internazionale and Italy, but in reality a half-defender-cum-half-forward. Manages to combine these demanding roles through his tremendous physique and no mean skill. Born at Treviglio in Northern Italy and joined Inter-Milan in 1960 as a teenager. Developed by Helenio Herrera into a revolutionary full-back who swept forward and scored goals—often at critical moments in vital matches. Standing 6 ft 3 in., he is virtually unbeatable in the air and his long raking stride carries him over the ground in near Olympics time—10·5 seconds for 100 metres. Aged 29, he set an all-time Italian record in 1971 when winning his 60th cap. Further testimony to his prowess is the fact that he has scored more than 50 League goals in a country where centre-forwards do well to get ten per season!

Dzajic   **Facchetti**

Jairzinho *(real name Jair Ventura Filho)*: Centre-forward of Botafogo and Brazil. Born in Rio de Janeiro 28 years ago, he has been with Botafogo since he was ten. Strong, quick, courageous and with a fierce shot, he made his début for Brazil in 1964, but with the advent of Tostao was successfully switched from centre to a striking role on the right wing for the Mexico World Cup. His instinct for goals frequently carried him into the middle, where he created many dangerous situations. Brazil's top scorer with seven goals in the 1970 World Cup, he netted in all six matches from qualifying group to Final. 65 caps.

Jairzinho

Jekov

Jekov, *Petar:* Centre-forward of CSKA Sofia and Bulgaria. Came to prominence in 1967, when his goals for unknown Beroe Stara Zagora made him top Bulgarian scorer. Achieved the feat four seasons in succession between 1967 and 1970, changing clubs in 1968, when he joined CSKA, the Bulgarian Army team. By scoring 36 goals in 1968–69 season, he won the trophy awarded to Europe's highest league scorer, and he has continued to be a prolific marksman. Selected regularly for Bulgaria since his Beroe days, he is 26 and recently topped the half century of caps. Played for Bulgaria in the 1968 Olympics Final and also the 1970 World Cup.

Mazzola
Moore

Mazzola, *Sandrino*: Centre-forward of Internazionale and Italy. The son of an outstanding centre-forward who was killed in an air crash in 1948, he has starred in the tough Italian game since he was first capped at 18. Began as an intuitive but skilful goal-scorer of the spearhead type, but as his ability was sharpened and matured by experience he gradually moved back until he operated largely from midfield. In his new role during the 1970 World Cup, he ousted Rivera from the national team and steered Italy to the Final. The complete all-rounder, he needs the closest attention; he can bend a powerful long-range shot swerving at goal, or send through a delightful defence-splitting pass for a colleague. 29 years old, with more than 50 caps.

Moore, *Bobby*: Left-half of West Ham United and England. Sir Alf Ramsey's first lieutenant and captain of the 1966 England World Cup-winning team. Cool and skilful in his distribution, he plays left centre-back and brings a class and craft to the role that few rivals can match. Supremely confident, always seems to be in the right place doing the right thing and like all masters of their craft makes everything appear so simple. The basis of his game is superb covering, anticipation and interception allied to his ability to spot the 'easy' ball and play it quickly and without elaboration. Has often been said to be susceptible when under pressure, but at 30, and with 92 caps to his credit, he is playing as well as ever.

Muller, *Gerd*: Centre-forward of Bayern München and West Germany. Though he confesses freely to having a weight problem, his chunky, muscular frame frequently outjumps all challengers for balls in the air, and on the ground his shooting, particularly left foot, is deadly. He is quick off the mark, strong on the ball and volleys superbly, but above all it is an uncanny instinct for the goal-chance and his aggressive determination that make him king of the scorers in West Germany. With 38 goals in 34 league matches, he was Europe's top scorer in 1969–70, and at 25 he has already scored more goals for West Germany than any other player in history. There are 30 full caps, two championships, four German F.A. Cup Final victories and a European Cup-Winners' Cup success among his battle honours, and he was leading scorer for the 1970 World Cup tournament in Mexico with ten goals.

Pele *(real name Edson Arantes do Nascimento)*: Inside-forward of Santos and Brazil. Fêted throughout the world and without doubt the most talented, exciting and fabulous player of his time, he is 31 years old with 109 caps for Brazil, and more than a 1000 goals in his 14-year career. Burst into prominence during the 1958 World Cup in Sweden, having made his début against Argentina at 16 the previous year, just after joining Santos from his local club Baura. As an 'unknown' he scored a spectacular hat-trick in the semi-final against France and then two goals in the 5–2 Final victory over Sweden, so becoming a world figure within a few days. Plays as a *ponta de lanca* according to the Brazilian system which, translated, means 'striker' or football devil!

Muller

Pele

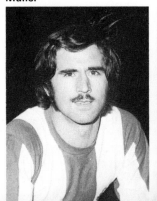

Riva, *Luigi*: Left-winger (nominally) for US Cagliari and Italy, but more often to be found scoring spectacular goals from centre-forward. Predominantly left-footed, he specializes in first-time shooting and diving headers. Three times the top league scorer in Italy, he has also achieved a 'double' in recovering from two broken legs. He was a bargain buy by Cagliari when they signed him for £3000 in 1963 from Division III club Legnano, and his goalscoring took the 1970 Italian championship to Cagliari—and to the Mediterranean island of Sardinia—for the first time. It also brought a world record transfer bid of £660,000 from Juventus, which Cagliari turned down. Riva is 26 years old with 30 caps.

Riva **Rivelino**

Rivelino, *Roberto*: Inside-left of Corinthians (São Paulo) and Brazil. At first he failed to shine for Brazil as an orthodox inside-forward, but in the 1970 World Cup in Mexico he was cast in a dual role. He lined up on the left wing but played a half-and-half game, dropping back to forage but frequently becoming an orthodox spearhead on the wing. The result was devastating, with stamina, left-foot shooting and superb ball control combining to make him a world-class star. Next to Pele he is reputedly the world's best-paid player at £80 a day. 26 years old (40 caps).

Rivera, *Gianni*: Inside-left of AC Milan and Italy. An accountant with extensive business interests outside football and one of the most devastating players in world football. He can destroy the best organized defences with his tantalizing dribbles and pin-point passes. Elegantly skilful, he differs from many ball artists in knowing exactly *when* to release the ball to greatest advantage; uses the long pass superbly and often scores himself. Rivera was the subject of an unusual transfer when only 16; his club Alessandria (Division II) sold a half-interest to AC Milan for £20,000 and a year later the other 'half' cost £60,000! Now 27 years old with more than 40 caps, he is valued at £400,000.

Tostao *(real name Eduardo Goncalves de Andrade)*: Centre-forward of Cruzeiro and Brazil. He was in England for the 1966 World Cup as a fledgling with one cap, but failed to shine. Developed quickly, however, and by 1969 was firmly established, having scored ten goals in Brazil's six World Cup qualifying matches. Six months before the Final series he was almost written off through injury—a displaced retina in the left eye—but he made a superb comeback, regained his place and shone in Mexico as a withdrawn, wandering spearhead. His intelligent running off the ball created havoc, pulling defenders out of position and leaving Pele and Jairzinho to take full advantage. Aged 25 with 30 caps.

Rivera

Tostao

The World Cup

THE ORIGINAL WORLD CUP
Jules Rimet Trophy

THE NEW F.I.F.A. WORLD CUP
At stake in 1974

The greatest football show on earth, the most prized possession in the soccer universe, is the World Cup, staged every four years. For the first 40 years of its existence it was known as the Jules Rimet trophy, after the French lawyer who aired the idea of a world football championship among nations when he became president of F.I.F.A. in 1920.

Ten years later the dream turned to reality with the launching of the World Cup in Montevideo, Uruguay . . . but when the winners of the tenth tournament collect their fabulous prize in West Germany in 1974, it will not be the Jules Rimet Cup they receive but the F.I.F.A. World Cup.

The reason for the change of trophy dates from the time the rules were framed for the very first tournament in 1930. Included was a clause to the effect that if any country won the Jules Rimet Cup three times, it would become theirs permanently—and Brazil's success in Mexico in 1970 was their third world conquest in the last four series. Amid unprecedented scenes of welcome and celebration, they took home to Rio the original World Cup— made of solid gold and weighing nine pounds, though standing only a foot high—to keep for ever.

Next to Brazil's triple triumph, Uruguay and Italy have each won the competition twice, and the only other winners have been Germany and England, the last new name to be added to the haloed list of World Champions in 1966.

In Britain the tournament was not regarded as truly representative of world football until 1950 when, having rejoined F.I.F.A. after lengthy disagreement over amateurism and broken-

140

time payments, the Home Countries became eligible to compete for the first time. The prize remained beyond British reach for another 16 years; then, in 1966, England became the third host country to triumph, the first since 1934. They took it from Brazil with football that was functional, disciplined and supremely efficient. In Mexico four years later Brazil, committed to all-out attack to cover their suspect defence and weakness in goal, won it back with the magic and flair of Pele, Gerson, Jairzinho and Rivelino. No country could more worthily have won the World Cup outright.

The 1930 World Cup: Uruguay staged and won the first World Cup. Only 13 countries took part, and all 17 matches were played in Montevideo. Because of travelling difficulties and the lengthy absence involved in a trip by sea to South America and back, Europe's representatives were restricted to France, Yugoslavia, Rumania and Belgium. Uruguay, who had trained their players in isolation for two months, and Argentina each won their semi-final by 6–1 (against U.S.A. and Yugoslavia respectively), and in the first World Cup Final, played on 30 July 1930, the host country rallied from 2–1 down at half-time to triumph 4–2, to the delight of a 90,000 crowd.

The 1934 World Cup: The holders, Uruguay, refused to go to Italy to defend their title, as so few European countries had participated in the first tournament. Of the 16 nations who qualified from an entry of 29, 12 were from Europe. The 'group qualifying' method up to the semi-finals was replaced by an unsatisfactory knock-out system throughout—defeat at the first attempt meant that Brazil, Argentina and U.S.A. travelled halfway across the world for only one match each. Italy kicked off with the 7–1 thrashing of U.S.A., then beat Spain and Austria, both 1–0, to reach the Final against Czechoslovakia in Rome. There the unfancied Czechs took a surprise lead with 20 minutes left, but Italy scored a late equalizer and in extra time they squeezed home 2–1 to emulate Uruguay's feat as the second successive host nation to take the World Cup.

The 1938 World Cup: Now it was Argentina's turn to stay out, in protest over their request to stage the tournament being rejected. Instead, the series was held in Europe for the second successive series, this time in France, and Italy impressively retained the trophy. Victories over Norway, France and Brazil carried them to the Final, in which Hungary were well beaten by 4–2. Once again Italy, under the managership of Vittorio Pozzo, had done it, and with the Second World War soon to break out, they were to hold the Cup longer than anyone before or after—until 1950.

The 1950 World Cup: After an interval of 12 years, the war having erased two tournaments, the world football championship was resumed in Brazil. The British Associations had rejoined F.I.F.A. in 1946, so were eligible for the first time, but only England entered; Scotland could have done so as runners-up in the Home Championship, but all along they had declared they would take part only if they were British Champions. In their first World Cup, England suffered their greatest-ever humiliation, for after beating Chile 2—0 in their opening match in Rio, they took the same eleven to Belo Horizonte on Sunday, 25 June and ludicrously lost one—nil to the United States' part-timers. America won by a 30th-minute goal by their centre-forward Gaetjens, miraculously surviving a rearguard action that lasted all the second half. England contributed an equal part to their own destruction by missing so many chances. The team was: Williams; Ramsey, Aston, Wright, Hughes, Dickinson, Finney, Mannion, Bentley, Mortensen, Mullen. England's elimination was complete when Spain beat them 1—0 in Rio. This was the only time that the competition was based on four qualifying groups, whose winners went into a final pool which comprised Brazil, Spain, Sweden and Uruguay (participating for the first time since the inaugural tournament). After magnificent wins against Sweden (7—1) and Spain (6—1) in the final pool, Brazil needed only to draw with Uruguay in the grand finale to be crowned World Champions for the first time, and in anticipation the all-time world record attendance of 200,000 filled the Maracana Stadium. Brazil began brilliantly and scored first, directly after half-time, but with a superbly marshalled defence Uruguay gradually wore them down, then hit them with two smoothly taken goals to triumph 2—1 and bring their World Cup record to two conquests in two attempts spanning 20 years.

The 1954 World Cup: The fifth World Championship, in Switzerland, established the tournament format that was to be used until 1974, with four groups each providing two qualifiers to contest the quarter-finals and beyond on a knock-out system. Hungary, with Puskas, Hidegkuti and Kocsis superb in attack, were rated 'unbeatable'. In the previous six months they had shattered England's unbeaten home record against foreign countries with an astonishing 6—3 victory at Wembley and completed the double by 7—1 in Budapest. So England were hardly in better shape to face the world than when they had left Brazil demoralized four years earlier, and after topping their group with little conviction, they went out in the quarter-final 4—2 to Uruguay, who had still to be beaten in the World Cup after 24 years! Scotland's entry meant that Britain was doubly represented for the first time, but theirs was no more than a token appearance. In the qualifying group they failed to register a goal or a point, being humbled 7—0 by Uruguay and losing 1—0 to Austria. Meanwhile, Hungary clinched their group by slamming Korea 9—0 and Germany 8—3, and went through to the Final with 4—2 victories over both Brazil and Uruguay; but Germany countered their mastery with guile off the field and then deprived them of the World Cup on it. In their group match against Hungary, the Germans purposely fielded a weak team and did not mind losing 8—3 because they were confident that they could still qualify for the quarter-finals by beating Turkey in a play-off—and did so 7—2. Thus the easier passage to the Final was open to them, and they took it with wins by 2—0 against Yugoslavia and 6—1 against Austria. Yet, for all their strategy, Germany seemed to be heading for defeat in the Final as Puskas (playing for the first time since being injured in the group match against Germany) and Czibor gave Hungary a 2—0 lead. But skipper Fritz Walter rallied his side magnificently, and goals by Morlock and Rahn (2) earned Germany an extraordinary victory by 3—2, which made them the only country in World Cup history to win the trophy after being beaten during the final series.

The 1958 World Cup: In Sweden, Britain was represented for the only time by all four Home Countries, but England (apart from holding Brazil 0—0) and Scotland made no show. Surprisingly, it was the outsiders, Northern Ireland and Wales, who reached the quarter-finals. There, however, a catalogue of injuries proved insurmountable to Ireland, who lost 4—0 to France, and Brazil's one goal was too much for Wales. Hosts Sweden delighted their supporters by reaching the Final, then sent them almost delirious by scoring the first goal, but Brazil answered with one of the greatest exhibitions ever seen in a World Cup Final, devastatingly using 4—2—4 to stamp their mark on the tournament. Garrincha, Didi, Vava and a 17-year-old named Pele showed the world a new conception of attacking play, which brought them the biggest-ever World Cup victory by 5—2—Vava and Pele each scored twice—and a spectacular first success in the competition.

The 1962 World Cup: In contrast to Sweden, Chile staged the least memorable contest for the Jules Rimet Cup since it became a truly world-wide tournament. There was a saturation of negative, defence-ridden football and England, Britain's lone representatives, went out 3—1 to Brazil in the quarter-finals. Pele was lost to Brazil through injury early in the competition, but, although now an ageing side and far less impressive than four years previously, they retained the trophy, beating Czechoslovakia in the Final 3—1 after being a goal down.

The 1966 World Cup: Four months before they staged and won the World Cup, England literally lost it. For 36 years the solid gold cup had been in existence. While in Italy's possession it had survived the war years hidden under the bed of Italian F.A. vice-president Dr Ottorino Barassi. Since 1958 it had been in the safe keeping of Brazil, and London saw it ceremonially for the first time in January 1966, at the making of the draw for the qualifying rounds of the final series. Two months later, at about midday on Sunday, 20 March, it vanished in a daring daylight theft from a padlocked cabinet while on display at a £3-million stamp exhibition at the Central Hall, Westminster. For seven days the football world was held spellbound with conjecture that the game's greatest trophy—like the F.A. Cup stolen in 1895—might never be seen again. Then a black and white mongrel dog named Pickles sniffed at a parcel lying under a laurel bush in the garden of his home in Upper Norwood, London—and the World Cup had been found intact! The motive for the theft had been a ransom demand for £15,000 to Football Association chairman Joe Mears; one of the accomplices, a London dock labourer, was jailed for two years, while Pickles earned some £6000 in rewards for his owner and a medal for himself. And England, having lost and found the Jules Rimet Cup, won it at Wembley on 30 July in the most sensational World Cup Final of all

The start of their march to glory, a 0–0 draw against Uruguay, could hardly have been less exciting for Wembley's 75,000 crowd. Then came two 2–0 wins to stir the blood a little, against Mexico (scorers Bobby Charlton and Roger Hunt) and France (Hunt 2). Argentina in the quarter-final posed the toughest problem yet, and England's World Cup hopes might have ended there had not Antonio Rattin, captain of the Argentinians, got himself sent off towards half-time for rough play and arguing with West German referee Rudolf Kreitlein. During a seven-minute hold-up before Rattin finally departed, the entire Argentine team threatened to walk off. The ten who eventually decided to stay stepped up their spoiling tactics and England struggled through 1–0 with a 77th-minute header by Geoff Hurst, replacing the injured Jimmy Greaves.

Brazil's hopes of a World Cup hat-trick dived when Pele was injured in the opening game against Bulgaria, and they failed to survive the qualifying stage. While England were playing that nasty quarter-final with Argentina at Wembley, up at Goodison Park, Portugal and rank outsiders North Korea produced a match straight out of the realms of fiction. Having shocked Italy 1–0 at Middlesbrough to qualify, Pak Doo Ik and his happy-go-lucky Korean team-mates went one . . . two . . . three up against Portugal. But they lacked the tactical know-how to hold such an advantage, and Eusebio, striking irresistible form, scored the first four goals (two of them penalties) in Portugal's eventual victory by 5–3. At Hillsborough, Sheffield, West Germany comprehensively beat Uruguay 4—0, and in the other quarter-final at Sunderland Russia defeated Hungary 2—1.

The semi-finals provided an enormous contrast. At Goodison, West Germany scored a laborious 2—1 win against Russia (who were quickly reduced to ten fit men by injury to Sabo, and to nine when Chislenko was sent off for retaliation after a foul that injured him, too). At Wembley the following night the score was also 2—1, but this game between England and Portugal put the seal of world stature back on the competition. In terms of technique it was the finest match of the whole series in England. Bobby Charlton cracked both England goals; late on, brother Jack handled and from the spot Eusebio explosively took his only chance of the game—the first time Banks's net had been stretched in the tournament.

For only the second time, the first since 1934, the Final went to an extra half-hour. Haller shot West Germany ahead after 13 minutes, but Hurst equalized six minutes later with a splendid header from Bobby Moore's free-kick and, with 13 minutes left, victory seemed assured as Martin Peters scored at close range after Hurst's shot had been blocked. But in the last seconds Weber slammed Germany level from a disputed free-kick by Emmerich, and at two-all the match went into extra-time. England found the inspiration they needed to win the game all over again in the ceaseless running of Ball. His was the centre which Hurst hammered in off the crossbar for the third goal—Swiss referee Gottfried Dienst awarded it after what seemed a timeless consultation with his Russian linesman Tofik Bakhramov—and through to the closing seconds Moore and his men clung desperately to their lead. Then, in a last-fling attack, West Germany left themselves uncovered at the back and Hurst pounded away down the left flank from halfway and finished with a lashing left-foot shot past Tilkowski from 20 yards. Moments later, England fans in their thousands swept across the Wembley pitch to acclaim the incongruously unemotional Alf Ramsey, who had promised, predicted and fashioned the triumph with his wingless, 4—3—3 tactics; to mob the three-goal hero Hurst, first man to score a hat-trick in the World Cup Final; and to salute the whole team with chants of 'Eng-land! Eng-land!' that billowed across the vast arena as Bobby Moore collected the world's greatest soccer prize.

The 1970 World Cup: By winning all six matches they were required to play in Mexico, Brazil worthily became the first country to take the World Cup three times and, in doing so, they won the trophy outright. Compared with the lowest-ever aggregate of 89 goals in each of the two previous tournaments, the 32-match programme now produced 95, with Brazil responsible for 19 of them. It mattered not that they had a suspect defence; their game was based on creation in midfield and a flair for all-out attack in which Pele, kicked out of the two previous World Cups, once again touched his spectacular best in this his fourth tournament. England, as indeed most of the European countries did, overcame the problems of altitude and heat better than expected. They were based at Guadalajara, and Hurst began as he had finished in 1966—on the scoresheet. England's three group qualifying matches each produced a 1–0 result, with wins against Rumania (Hurst) and Czechoslovakia (Clarke, penalty) and defeat by Jairzinho's goal against Brazil. It was enough to take them through to the quarter-finals as group runners-up to Brazil. Then, with the venue switching to Leon, they were paired with West Germany. For an hour England played as splendidly as they had done against them in the 1966 Final, and when Martin Peters added to Alan Mullery's first-half goal directly after half-time, a lead of 2–0 looked unassailable. But it was far from over. Beckenbauer put Germany back in the game with a diagonal shot that flashed under Bonetti (Banks was in his bed, the victim of a stomach bug) and England were shaken again as Seeler scored with a back-header when the odds were stacked against an equalizer. So, again as in the Wembley Final, the sides went into extra time at 2–2, and in the second period Muller, right in front of the target, smashed in the goal that gave Germany victory by 3–2 and avenged 1966. There were inevitable question-marks—over the tactical substitution of Bobby Charlton (in his record-breaking 106th International) and Norman Hunter, as well as over two of the German goals—but nothing could alter the fact that the World Champions had been dethroned.

In the other quarter-finals Brazil overcame some difficult moments to beat Peru 4–2 in Guadalajara; Uruguay dismissed Russia 1–0 on a disputed goal in the last minute of extra time in Mexico City; and Italy, having scored only one goal in three matches to head their qualifying group, threw away caution, when a goal down, to the hosts Mexico in Toluca, and won 4–1.

Goals were cheap, in extra time, anyway, in the Mexico City semi-final between Italy and West Germany. Boninsegna gave Italy an early lead, and that was still the only goal as the match went into injury time. Then Schnellinger equalized, and West Germany went ahead with the first of five goals scored in the extra half-hour, which finished with Italy winners of an extra-ordinary match by 4–3. In the other semi-final in Guadalajara, Cubilla gave Uruguay a shock lead, but Brazil, albeit belatedly, turned on the full range of talents and won 3–1, with goals by Clodoaldo, Jairzinho and Rivelino.

The Azteca Stadium, home of Mexican football, did not see Brazil until the Final itself. Their performance in beating Italy 4–1 was well worth the wait. It started with Pele heading in Rivelino's cross after 18 minutes, and although Italy were level by half-time, Boninsegna punishing one of those defensive mistakes to which Brazil were prone, midfield general Gerson restored the lead with a magnificent shot from outside the penalty-area. Gerson and Pele combined to set up the third goal for Jairzinho, and the final scene was stolen by Brazil's captain, Carlos Alberto. He shot a stunning last goal from Pele's perfect pass, and three minutes later he stepped forward to receive the Jules Rimet Cup that was to be Brazil's for ever. Their hat-trick was an incredible achievement for Mario Zagalo, a member of the winning teams in 1958 and 1962, and now triumphant again only a few months after succeeding Joao Saldanha as Brazil's manager.

WORLD CUP SUMMARIES

1930 World Cup—First Tournament—in Uruguay

Winners: Uruguay. **Runners-up:** Argentina. **Third:** U.S.A. **Entries:** 13.
Other countries taking part: Belgium, Bolivia, Brazil, Chile, France, Mexico, Paraguay, Peru, Rumania, Yugoslavia.
All matches played in Montevideo.
Top scorer in tournament: Stabile (Argentina) 8 goals.

Final:
Uruguay 4 (Dorado, Cea, Iriarte, Castro), *Argentina* 2 (Peucelle, Stabile).
Half-time: Uruguay 1, Argentina 2. *Attendance:* 90,000.
Uruguay: Ballesteros; Nasazzi, Mascheroni, Andrade, Fernandez, Gestido, Dorado, Scarone, Castro, Cea, Iriarte.
Argentina: Botasso; Della Torre, Paternoster, Evaristo (J). Monti, Suarez, Eucelle, Varallo, Stabile, Ferreira, Evaristo (M).

1934 World Cup—Second Tournament—in Italy

Winners: Italy. **Runners-up:** Czechoslovakia. **Third:** Germany. **Entries:** 29 (16 qualifiers).
Other countries taking part in final series: Argentina, Austria, Belgium, Brazil, Egypt, France, Holland, Hungary, Rumania, Spain, Sweden, Switzerland, U.S.A.
Venues: Rome, Naples, Milan, Turin, Florence, Bologna, Genoa, Trieste.
Top scorers in tournament: Schiavio (Italy), Nejedly (Czechoslovakia), Conen (Germany) each 4 goals.

Final (Rome):
Italy 2 (Orsi, Schiavio), *Czechoslovakia* 1 (Puc). After extra time.
Half-time: Italy 0, Czechoslovakia 1. *Score after 90 minutes:* 1–1. *Attendance:* 50,000.
Italy: Combi; Monzeglio, Allemandi, Ferraris, Monti, Bertolini, Guaita, Meazza, Schiavio, Ferrari, Orsi.
Czechoslovakia: Planicka; Zenisek, Ctyroky, Kostalek, Cambal, Krcil, Junek, Svoboda, Sobotka, Nejedly, Puc.

1938 World Cup—Third Tournament—in France

Winners: Italy. **Runners-up:** Hungary. **Third:** Brazil. **Entries:** 25 (15 qualifiers).
Other countries taking part in final series: Belgium, Cuba, Czechoslovakia, Dutch East Indies, France, Germany, Holland, Norway, Poland, Rumania, Sweden, Switzerland.
Venues: Paris, Marseilles, Bordeaux, Lille, Antibes, Strasbourg, Le Havre, Reims, Toulouse.
Top scorer in tournament: Leonidas (Brazil) 8 goals.

Final (Paris):
Italy 4 (Colaussi 2, Piola 2), *Hungary* 2 (Titkos, Sarosi).
Half-time: Italy 3; Hungary 1. *Attendance:* 45,000.
Italy: Olivieri; Foni, Rava, Serantoni, Andreolo, Locatelli, Biavati, Meazza, Piola, Ferrari, Colaussi.
Hungary: Szabo; Polgar, Biro, Szalay, Szucs, Lazar, Sas, Vincze, Sarosi, Szengeller, Titkos.

1950 World Cup—Fourth Tournament—in Brazil

Winners: Uruguay. **Runners-up:** Brazil. **Third:** Sweden. **Entries:** 29 (13 qualifiers).
Other countries taking part in final series: Bolivia, Chile, England, Italy, Mexico, Paraguay, Spain, Switzerland, U.S.A., Yugoslavia.
Venues: Rio de Janeiro, São Paulo, Recife, Curitiba, Belo Horizonte, Porto Alegre.
Top scorer in tournament: Ademir (Brazil) 7 goals.

*Deciding Match (Rio de Janeiro):
Uruguay 2 (Schiaffino, Ghiggia), *Brazil* 1 (Friaca).
Half-time: 0–0. *Attendance:* 200,000.
Uruguay: Maspoli; Gonzales, Tejera, Gambetta, Varela, Andrade, Ghiggia, Perez, Miguez, Schiaffino, Moran.
Brazil: Barbosa; Augusto, Juvenal, Bauer, Danilo, Bigode, Friaca, Zizinho, Ademir, Jair, Chico.
* For the only time, the World Cup was decided on a Final Pool system, in which the winners of the four qualifying groups met in a six-match series. So, unlike previous and subsequent tournaments, there was no official Final as such, but Uruguay v. Brazil was the deciding final match in the Final Pool.

1954 World Cup—Fifth Tournament— in Switzerland

Winners: Germany. **Runners-up:** Hungary. **Third:** Austria. **Entries:** 35 (16 qualifiers).
Other countries taking part in final series: Belgium, Brazil, Czechoslovakia, England, France, Italy, Korea, Mexico, Scotland, Switzerland, Turkey, Uruguay, Yugoslavia.

Venues: Berne, Zürich, Lausanne, Basle, Geneva, Lugano.
Top scorer in tournament: Kocsis (Hungary) 11 goals.

Final (Berne):
Germany 3 (Morlock, Rahn 2), *Hungary* 2 (Puskas, Czibor).
Half-time: 2—2. *Attendance:* 60,000.
Germany: Turek; Posipal, Kohlmeyer, Eckel, Liebrich, Mai, Rahn, Morlock, Walter (O), Walter (F), Schaefer.
Hungary: Grosics; Buzansky, Lantos, Boszik, Lorant, Zakarias, Czibor, Kocsis, Hidegkuti, Puskas, Toth.

1958 World Cup—Sixth Tournament—in Sweden

Winners: Brazil. **Runners-up:** Sweden. **Third:** France.
Entries: 47 (16 qualifiers).
Other countries taking part in final series: Argentina, Austria, Czechoslovakia, England, Hungary, Mexico, Northern Ireland, Paraguay, Russia, Scotland, Wales, West Germany, Yugoslavia.
Venues: Stockholm, Gothenburg, Malmö, Norrköping, Borås, Sandviken, Ekilstuna, Cerebro, Västeras, Hälsingborg, Halmstad.
Top scorer in tournament: Fontaine (France) 13 goals.

Final (Stockholm):
Brazil 5 (Vava 2, Pele 2, Zagalo), *Sweden* 2 (Liedholm, Simonsson).
Half-time: Brazil 2, Sweden 1. *Attendance:* 50,000.
Brazil: Gilmar; Santos (D), Santos (N), Zito, Bellini, Orlando, Garrincha, Didi, Vava, Pele, Zagalo.
Sweden: Svensson; Bergmark, Axbom, Boerjesson, Gustavsson, Parling, Hamrin, Gren, Simonsson, Liedholm, Skoglund.

1962 World Cup—Seventh Tournament—in Chile

Winners: Brazil. **Runners-up:** Czechoslovakia. **Third:** Chile.
Entries: 53 (16 qualifiers).
Other countries taking part in final series: Argentina, Bulgaria, Colombia, England, Hungary, Italy, Mexico, Russia, Spain, Switzerland, Uruguay, West Germany, Yugoslavia.
Venues: Santiago, Vina del Mar, Rancagua, Arica.
Top scorers in tournament: Garrincha (Brazil), Vava (Brazil), Sanchez (Chile), Albert (Hungary), Ivanov (Russia), Jerkovic (Yugoslavia) each 4 goals.

Final (Santiago):
Brazil 3 (Amarildo, Zito, Vava), *Czechoslovakia* 1 (Masopust).
Half-time: 1—1. *Attendance:* 69,000.
Brazil: Gilmar; Santos (D), Mauro, Zozimo, Santos (N), Zito, Didi, Garrincha, Vava, Amarildo, Zagalo.
Czechoslovakia: Schroiff; Tichy, Novak, Pluskal, Popluhar, Masopust, Pospichal, Scherer, Kvasniak, Kadraba, Jelinek.

1966 World Cup—Eighth Tournament—in England

Winners: England. **Runners-up:** West Germany. **Third:** Portugal. **Entries:** 53 (16 qualifiers).
Other countries taking part in final series: Argentina, Brazil, Bulgaria, Chile, France, Hungary, Italy, Mexico, North Korea, Russia, Spain, Switzerland, Uruguay.
Venues: London (Wembley and White City), Sheffield (Hillsborough), Liverpool (Goodison Park), Sunderland, Middlesbrough, Manchester (Old Trafford), Birmingham (Villa Park).
Top scorer in tournament: Eusebio (Portugal) 9 goals.

Final (Wembley):
England 4 (Hurst 3, Peters), *West Germany* 2 (Haller, Weber). After extra time.
Half-time: 1–1. *Score after 90 minutes:* 2–2 *Attendance:* 100,000.
England: Banks; Cohen, Wilson, Stiles, Charlton (J), Moore, Ball, Hurst, Hunt, Charlton (R), Peters.
West Germany: Tilkowski; Hottges, Schnellinger, Beckenbauer, Schulz, Weber, Haller, Held, Seeler, Overath, Emmerich.

1970 World Cup—Ninth Tournament—in Mexico

Winners: Brazil. **Runners-up:** Italy. **Third:** West Germany. **Entries:** 68 (16 qualifiers).
Other countries taking part in final series: Belgium, Bulgaria, Czechoslovakia, El Salvador, England, Israel, Mexico, Morocco, Peru, Rumania, Russia, Sweden, Uruguay.
Venues: Mexico City, Guadalajara, Leon, Puebla, Toluca.
Top scorer in tournament: Muller (West Germany) 10 goals.

Final (Mexico City):
Brazil 4 (Pele, Gerson, Jairzinho, Carlos Alberto), *Italy* 1 (Boninsegna).
Half-time: 1–1. *Attendance:* 107,000.
Brazil: Felix; Carlos Alberto, Brito, Piazza, Everaldo, Clodoaldo, Gerson, Jairzinho, Tostao, Pele, Rivelino.
Italy: Albertosi; Burgnich, Facchetti, Cera, Rosato, Bertini (substitute Juliano), Domenghini, De Sisti, Mazzola, Boninsegna (substitute Rivera), Riva.

OTHER WORLD CUP FACTS

The 1970 World Cup in Mexico set a new attendance record for the final series with an aggregate of 1,673,975 spectators attending the 32 matches. The previous record was 1,458,043 present when England staged the tournament in 1966.

Brazil's success in Mexico gave South America the edge against Europe in the balance of World Cup power. It was their fifth triumph (Brazil three wins, Uruguay two) against four by Europe (Italy two wins, West Germany and England one each). But if tradition is maintained, the two Continents will be level again after Munich 1974, because with one exception (Brazil's triumph in Sweden in 1958) the World Cup has always been won by a country from the hemisphere in which the Finals are staged.

The individual goalscoring record for a World Cup final series is 13 by Just Fontaine (France) in the 1958 tournament in Sweden. Two other players have reached a double-figure total: Sandor Kocsis with 11 goals for Hungary (Switzerland, 1954 tournament) and Gerd Muller with 10 for West Germany (Mexico, 1970).

Host countries have won three of the nine World Cup tournaments: Uruguay in 1930, Italy in 1934 and England in 1966. This is how the other host nations have fared: 1938—France, unplaced; 1950—Brazil, runners-up; 1954—Switzerland, unplaced; 1958—Sweden, runners-up; 1962—Chile, third; 1970—Mexico, unplaced.

Hungary set two records that still stand when they were runners-up to West Germany in the 1954 World Cup in Switzerland. Their 9–0 win against Korea was the highest score in any Final series, and their total of 27 goals remains the most ever scored by one country in any series of the World Cup proper.

Highest match aggregates in World Cup Final series: 12—Austria 7, Switzerland 5 (Switzerland, 1954); 11—Brazil 6, Poland 5 (France, 1938) and Hungary 8, Germany 3 (Switzerland, 1954).

Mexican goalkeeper Antonio Carbajal holds a World Cup record that may never be equalled. He represented his country in *five* tournaments: in Brazil 1950, Switzerland 1954, Sweden 1958, Chile 1962 and, finally, at Wembley in 1966.

England did not enter the first three World Cup tournaments (1930, 1934 and 1938). This is how they have fared in the competition:
1950 finished second in qualifying group; 1954 beaten in quarter-final; 1958 beaten in play-off for quarter-final place;

1962 beaten in quarter-final; 1966 Winners; 1970 beaten in quarter-final.

Scotland's record: 1954 bottom in qualifying group; 1958 bottom in qualifying group.

Northern Ireland's record: 1958 beaten in quarter-final.

Wales's record: 1958 beaten in quarter-finals.

Britain has only twice been represented by more than one country in the World Cup Final series—in 1954, when England and Scotland participated in Switzerland, and in 1958, when England, Scotland, Northern Ireland and Wales all qualified for the tournament held in Sweden.

In seven of the nine World Cup Finals the eventual winners have been behind at one stage of the match. The exceptions: Italy 1938 and Brazil 1970.

World Cup Final Results

1930	(Montevideo)	Uruguay	4	Argentina	2
1934	(Rome)	Italy	2	Czechoslovakia	1
				(after extra time)	
1938	(Paris)	Italy	4	Hungary	2
1950	(Rio de Janeiro)	Uruguay	2	Brazil	1
1954	(Berne)	Germany	3	Hungary	2
1958	(Stockholm)	Brazil	5	Sweden	2
1962	(Santiago)	Brazil	3	Czechoslovakia	1
1966	(Wembley)	England	4	West Germany	2
				(after extra time)	
1970	(Mexico City)	Brazil	4	Italy	1

Venues for the three World Cup tournaments *after* West Germany in 1974 have been arranged as follows: 1978 Argentina, 1982 Spain, 1986 Yugoslavia.

THE 1974 WORLD CUP

World Cups take a deal of preparation, and the beginning of the tenth global tournament that will reach its climax with the Final in Munich on 7 July 1974 was made precisely three years earlier —in July 1971, when the draw for the qualifying competition took place in Düsseldorf.

It involved 98 of F.I.F.A.'s 138 affiliated member countries— the biggest-ever World Cup entry, comprising 33 from Europe (including West Germany, the host country), 10 from South America (including reigning World Champions Brazil who, like West Germany, qualify automatically), 17 from the Asian group,

24 from Africa and 14 from the group combining Central and North America, and the Caribbean.

The qualifying round must be completed by 31 December 1973 to produce the 16 countries who will contest the Final series in West Germany from the following June 13–July 7. They will be made up of nine from Europe, three from South America, one from Asia, one from Africa, one from the Central, North American, Caribbean group, and the sixteenth place will be decided in a play-off between the winners of European qualifying group 9 (Russia, France or the Republic of Ireland) and the winners of South American group 3 (Peru, Chile or Venezuela).

The full qualifying round draw was made as follows:

Europe
Group 1   Sweden, Hungary, Austria, Malta.
Group 2   Italy, Switzerland, Turkey, Luxembourg.
Group 3   Belgium, Holland, Norway, Iceland.
Group 4   Rumania, East Germany, Albania, Finland.
Group 5   England, Poland, Wales.
Group 6   Bulgaria, Portugal, Northern Ireland, Cyprus.
Group 7   Yugoslavia, Spain, Greece.
Group 8   Czechoslovakia, Denmark, Scotland.
Group 9   Russia, France, Republic of Ireland.

South America
Group 1   Uruguay, Colombia, Ecuador.
Group 2   Argentina, Paraguay, Bolivia.
Group 3   Peru, Chile, Venezuela.

Asia
Winners of the two groups to play off for place in Finals.
Group 1   Israel, Thailand, Malaysia, Philippines, Hong Kong, Republic of Korea, Japan, South Vietnam.
Group 2   Iran, Iraq, Kuwait, Ceylon, Syria, India, Indonesia, plus winners of Australia v. New Zealand.

Africa
Pairs to play on a knock-out system, with one winner of the section to go forward to the Finals.
Group 1   Morocco and Senegal; Guinea and Algeria; United Arab Republic and Tunisia; Ivory Coast and Sierra Leone.
Group 2   Sudan and Kenya; Mauritius and Madagascar; Ethiopia and Tanzania; Zambia and Lesotho.
Group 3   Nigeria and Congo-Brazzaville; Ghana and Dahomey; Togo and Congo-Kinshasa; Cameroun and Gabon.

Central America, North America & Caribbean
Regional tournament to decide one winner.
Group 1   Canada, U.S.A., Mexico.
Group 2   Guatemala, El Salvador.

Group 3   Honduras, Costa Rica.
Group 4   Jamaica, Netherlands Antilles.
Group 5   Haiti, Puerto Rico.
Group 6   Surinam, Trinidad, Antigua.

The Germans' reputation for meticulous attention to detail is certain to be enhanced when they stage their first World series. By the autumn of 1971 they had drawn up their blueprint for the 1974 F.I.F.A. World Cup.

They announced that ten different centres would be used: Munich, Hamburg, West Berlin, Frankfurt, Dortmund, Hanover, Gelsenkirchen, Düsseldorf, Nuremberg and Stuttgart.

As in the past five World Cups, the 16 qualifiers will be drawn into groups of four, with the hosts West Germany in Group 1 and the holders Brazil in Group 2. There will be a break with tradition in that the holders—not the host nation—will open the tournament. That will be in Frankfurt on June 13, and the dates and venues of the full qualifying programme are scheduled thus:

Group 1   Hamburg and West Berlin (June 14, 18, 22).
Group 2   Frankfurt and Dortmund (June 13, 14, 18, 22).
Group 3   Hanover, Gelsenkirchen and Dusseldorf (June 15, 19, 23).
Group 4   Nuremberg and Munich (June 15, 19, 23).

Then, compared with past tournaments, comes an important change in the schedule. For the first time since 1950 there will be no quarter-finals. Instead, the top two teams from each section (i.e. eight countries) will advance to the semi-finals, and these will also be played on a group system, not on the normal knock-out basis. This will be the semi-final programme:

Group A   Winners of Groups 1 and 3; runners-up of Groups 2 and 4. Venues: Hanover, Gelsenkirchen and Dortmund. Dates: June 26, 30, July 3.
Group B   Winners of Groups 2 and 4; runners-up of Groups 1 and 3. Venues: Düsseldorf, Stuttgart and Frankfurt. Dates: June 26, 30, July 3.

The runners-up from Groups A and B will play off for third place in Munich on July 6, and the Final will be between the winners of those groups in Munich on July 7.

The European Championship

Originally known as the Henri Delaunay Cup, after its French founder, later as the Nations Cup, and now as the European Championship, it was introduced in 1958. The tournament takes two years to complete, with the Final scheduled to take place exactly halfway between one World Cup and the next. The qualifying competition is divided into eight groups, with quarter-final ties decided on a home-and-away basis. The semi-finals and Final are staged in one of the last four surviving countries. Semi-final and Final results:

1958–60: in France
Semi-finals: Yugoslavia 5, France 4 (Paris); Russia 3, Czechoslovakia 0 (Marseilles).
Final (Paris): *Russia* 2, Yugoslavia 1 (after extra time).

1962–64: in Spain
Semi-finals: Russia 3, Denmark 0 (Barcelona); Spain 2, Hungary 1 (Madrid).
Final (Madrid): *Spain* 2, Russia 1.

1966–68: in Italy
Semi-finals: Yugoslavia 1, England 0 (Florence); Italy 0, Russia 0 (Naples) after extra time—Italy won on toss.
Final (Rome): *Italy* 2, Yugoslavia 0 in replay after 1–1 draw.

1970–72: Tournament not completed at time of going to press.

The European Cup

In its 17-year history, the European Cup has presented a standard of international club football that could hardly have been imagined when it was launched in 1955. The idea was conceived by French soccer journalist Gabriel Hanot, a former international player, and developed rapidly after a meeting which he and the proprietors of his newspaper, *L'Equipe*, called in Paris in the spring of 1955 among all the leading European clubs. Six months later the dream became reality, and so began a contest bringing together the champion clubs of all the European countries and now long-established as football's greatest outside the World Cup.

In 1949 Hanot had been a prominent figure in the introduction of the Latin Cup, featuring the champion clubs of France, Spain, Italy and Portugal. As long ago as 1927 a similar competition, the Mitropa Cup, had been started in Central Europe among the principal clubs of Austria, Czechoslovakia, Hungary, Italy and Yugoslavia. By combining those two tournaments, and inviting the champion teams of North and Western Europe to participate, Hanot found the formula for the European Cup.

The champions of 17 countries entered the opening tournament in season 1955–56, but Chelsea subsequently withdrew under pressure from the Football League, who saw the new venture as a threat to their own competition. A year later Manchester United, disregarding the Establishment, both entered and took part. Fittingly, in 1968, they became the first English club to win the trophy—ten years after a European Cup journey had decimated the Old Trafford club with the Munich air disaster.

Ironically, although France was the birthplace of the European Cup and the first final was staged in Paris, no French club has taken the prize.

With bewildering football, Spanish champions Real Madrid made the competition their own 'spectacular', winning it for the first five years (1956–60). In the last of that astonishing sequence of finals, they beat the German champions, Eintracht Frankfurt, by 7–3 at Hampden Park, Glasgow with one of the most dazzling displays in the game's history. Outshining all others in a magnificent team performance were Real's legendary strikers Ferenc Puskas, who scored four goals, and Alfredo di Stefano, who got the other three.

Real Madrid appeared in eight of the first eleven European Cup finals and won the trophy on six of those occasions. Either as its holders or as champions of Spain, they took part in the first 15 seasons of the competition and the following year (1970–71) reached the final of the European Cup-Winners' Cup.

Until the inception of the European Cup, Real Madrid were little known outside Spain. Suddenly they found themselves the centre of world-wide acclaim—and if Real Madrid made the European Cup, it can also be said that the 'European Coupe des Clubs Champions' made Real. Their vast profits from the competition were invested in a permanent monument to their triumphs with the construction of the 120,000-capacity Bernabeu Stadium in the Chamartin suburb of Madrid.

For the first 11 years the European Cup was the 'Latins' Cup', with Spanish, Portuguese and Italian clubs dominating the tournament. During that period its winners came exclusively from three cities: Madrid, Lisbon and Milan.

Britain, through the medium of Glasgow Celtic, finally broke the Latin grip in 1967. Entering the competition for the first time, they had a comfortable passage through the rounds against Zurich, Nantes, Vojvodina and Dukla. The final, in Lisbon, brought them opposition of the strongest calibre in Inter-Milan, and after falling behind to an early penalty, Celtic saved the tie with Gemmell's second-half equalizer and, five minutes from the end, won it with a goal by Chalmers.

Thus Jock Stein's magnificent Celtic put Britain's hand on the European Cup for the first time. At Wembley a year later England took possession of it from Scotland with a wonderful extra-time victory by Manchester United against Benfica. Three times before —in 1957, 1958 and 1966—Matt Busby's men had been foiled at the semi-final stage. Now, in 1968, they beat their bogey, winning the first leg against Real Madrid by Best's only goal at Old Trafford and storming back from 3–1 down with 18 minutes left to draw the return match in Madrid 3–3, so winning the tie 4–3 on aggregate.

The Final, on 29 May 1968, produced at Wembley an emotional occasion which approached England's 1966 World Cup triumph. Remembering how close Manchester United had been to European success in the past, unable to forget how the European Cup had destroyed the famous 'Busby Babes' in the snows of Munich Airport in 1958, everyone, it seemed, was willing them to victory over Benfica, the Eagles of Lisbon.

Charlton's dipping header early in the second half looked to be sufficient when, with 11 minutes left, that was still the only goal. Then Graca smashed Benfica level, and Stepney miraculously held Eusebio's shot to earn extra time. It was a save that lifted the hearts of United and, with fresh wind in their sails, they moved majestically to victory. Aston demoralized Benfica's right defensive flank, and from the moment Best beat one man, then dribbled the 'keeper, to put United back in front, the European Cup was destined for Old Trafford, the margin stretching to 4–1 as Kidd celebrated his 19th birthday by heading in a crossbar rebound and Charlton himself, shooting the final goal.

A year later AC Milan took the European Cup back to Italy, thus sharing four successes in the competition for that country equally with Inter-Milan. In 1970 Celtic were finalists again, and following Arsenal's victory in the Fairs Cup and Manchester City's success in the Cup-Winners' Cup, there was the prospect of a clean sweep by Britain in all three European tournaments.

In anticipation, 25,000 fanatical Celtic supporters travelled to Milan—the biggest following any British team has ever had abroad—for the final against Dutch 'outsiders' Feyenoord. In the semi-final Celtic had twice beaten Leeds United; in Milan full-back Gemmell shot them ahead after half an hour and the Cup seemed to be heading for Glasgow again. But Feyenoord equalized, dominated the second half, and deservedly triumphed with a goal by Swedish international Kindvall four minutes from the end of extra time.

Their success compensated Holland for the defeat of Ajax (Amsterdam) in the previous final, and at Wembley a year later the European Cup stayed in Dutch possession with the victory of Ajax by 2—0 against Panathinaikos, of Athens. Britain's hopes had both been dismissed in the quarter-finals—Everton astonishingly by Panathinaikos on the away goal the Greeks scored in a 1—1 draw at Goodison Park (the second leg was a 0—0 draw) and Celtic sent crashing 3—0 by Ajax in Amsterdam and able to retrieve only one goal in the return.

Results of European Cup Finals

Year	Venue	Winners	Runners-up	Score
1956	Paris	Real Madrid	Reims	4–3
1957	Madrid	Real Madrid	Fiorentina	2–0
1958	Brussels	Real Madrid	AC Milan	3–2
1959	Stuttgart	Real Madrid	Reims	2–0
1960	Glasgow	Real Madrid	Eintracht Frankfurt	7–3
1961	Berne	Benfica	CF Barcelona	3–2
1962	Amsterdam	Benfica	Real Madrid	5–3
1963	Wembley	AC Milan	Benfica	2–1
1964	Vienna	Inter-Milan	Real Madrid	3–1
1965	Milan	Inter-Milan	Benfica	1–0
1966	Brussels	Real Madrid	Partizan Belgrade	2–1
1967	Lisbon	Celtic	Inter-Milan	2–1
1968	Wembley	Manchester United	Benfica	4–1
1969		AC Milan	Ajax Amsterdam	4–1
1970		Feyenoord	Celtic	2–1
1971	Wembley	Ajax Amsterdam	Panathinaikos	2–0

The European Cup-Winners' Cup

Staged for the first time in season 1960–61, the Cup-Winners' Cup is the youngest of the three European club tournaments, but in prestige it stands second to the Champions' Cup and British teams have done much to popularize it. In nine seasons between 1963 and 1971 the Cup of Cups was won by Football League clubs no fewer than four times, with Tottenham, West Ham, Manchester City and Chelsea all using victory in the F.A. Cup one year as the passport to European success the following season, and in three of the first seven finals Britain also supplied the runners-up (Glasgow Rangers twice and Liverpool).

The enormous success of the Champions' Cup clearly indicated scope for another European competition, and in 1959 the organizers of the Mitropa Cup succeeded in their campaign to launch a knock-out competition for national cup-winners.

It started the following year with only ten entries, the initial problem being that in few Continental countries was the domestic cup greeted with the same enthusiasm and regarded with the same seriousness as the F.A. and Scottish Cups. For instance, Spain played their F.A. Cup at the end of the season, Italy in mid-week (like the Football League Cup), France on neutral grounds and Portugal on a home-and-away basis.

By the third season (1962–63), however, 24 clubs took part in the Cup-Winners' Cup and last season (1971–72) brought an entry of 34 teams. Not only had the Cup of Cups grown to full maturity; its development pepped up the national cup competitions in many countries, because success brought prospects of a lucrative campaign in Europe.

After the first final, in which Fiorentina triumphed for Italy by beating Rangers home and away, U.E.F.A. took over the competition and one of their first decisions was to do away with two-leg finals. But two matches were still needed to decide the 1962 winners—Atletico Madrid, who held the holders Fiorentina 1–1 in Glasgow and, four months later, triumphed 3–0 in Stuttgart.

In 1963 Tottenham Hotspur put themselves, and the Cup-Winners' Cup, truly on the European map. At the Feyenoord

Stadium in Rotterdam a capacity 65,000 crowd saw them take the trophy from Atletico in tremendous style by 5–1, scorers Greaves (2), Dyson (2) and White.

The following year Sporting Lisbon won the cup for Portugal, but in 1965 it was back in England, with Wembley housing the first 100,000 crowd in the history of the competition and West Ham celebrating the occasion by 2–0 against TSV Munich (scorer Sealey, 2).

Britain also supplied a finalist in each of the next two seasons, but twice West German opposition proved too powerful, Liverpool losing 2–1 to Borussia Dortmund in Glasgow in 1966 and a year later, Rangers going down by the only goal to Bayern Munich in Nuremberg.

Season 1965–66, the year following West Ham's success, may not have retained the trophy for Britain, but a record was established by providing three of the semi-finalists: Liverpool, West Ham and Celtic. But in 1970 the Cup-Winners' Cup did return to England . . . and stayed for two seasons.

Manchester City's 2–1 victory over the Polish mining team Gornik Zabrze in Vienna was earned with goals from Young and Lee, who celebrated his 25th birthday with what proved to be the winner from the penalty spot. Thus City completed a spectacular cup double, for they had already won the Football League Cup that season.

On the night they lifted the Cup-Winners' Cup in the rain-lashed Prater Stadium in Vienna, Chelsea were in Manchester, winning the F.A. Cup in the replayed final against Leeds United —a success that paved the way for them to take over the Cup of Cups from Manchester City in 1971. To reach the final they had to eliminate City home and away and did so by 1–0 in both legs of a semi-final in which injuries played havoc with team selection in both camps.

Some 4000 supporters journeyed to Athens to cheer Chelsea in the final against the old masters of Europe, Real Madrid. Osgood's lone goal looked all over the winner until, in the most dramatic climax to any European final, Zoco equalized with the last kick of normal time. Webb's goal-line clearance kept Chelsea alive in extra time, and two nights later in the same Karaiskaki Stadium it began all over again.

This time Chelsea, putting the emphasis on attack from the start, took a two-goal lead through Demsey and Osgood, and although Real Madrid replied 15 minutes from the end, the experience and tradition of eight previous European finals was not enough to save them.

So Chelsea won their first European prize, but the possibility of them becoming the first club to lift the Cup of Cups in successive seasons was quickly shattered in the 1971–72 season. In the first round Chelsea smashed the scoring record for all three

European tournaments by beating Luxembourg Cup-holders Jeunesse Hautcharage 21—0 on aggregate (8—0 away, 13—0 at home). The next hurdle seemed to be there for Chelsea's taking when they were paired with the Swedish part-timers Atvidaberg, but after being kept to a goalless draw in Luxembourg, Chelsea became victims of one of the biggest shocks in European football. They could only draw 1—1 at home, missing a penalty in the process, and Atvidaberg went through on the away goals rule.

Unbelievable, yes. But proof also, and not for the first-time, that the Cup-Winners' Cup has the giantkiller touch that is comparatively unknown in the other big European tournaments.

Results of European Cup-Winners' Cup Finals

Year	Venue	Winners	Runners-up	Score
1961	—	Fiorentina	Rangers	4—1 aggregate

(Fiorentina won first leg 2—0 in Glasgow, second leg 2—1 in Florence)

Year	Venue	Winners	Runners-up	Score
1962	Stuttgart	Atletico Madrid	Fiorentina	3—0

(In replay after 1—1 draw in Glasgow)

Year	Venue	Winners	Runners-up	Score
1963	Rotterdam	Tottenham Hotspur	Atletico Madrid	5—1
1964	Antwerp	Sporting Lisbon	MTK Budapest	1—0

(In replay after 3—3 draw in Brussels)

Year	Venue	Winners	Runners-up	Score
1965	Wembley	West Ham United	TSV Munich	2—0
1966	Glasgow	Borussia Dortmund	Liverpool	2—1
1967	Nuremberg	Bayern München	Glasgow Rangers	1—0
1968	Rotterdam	AC Milan	Hamburg	2—0
1969	Basle	Slovan Bratislava	CF Barcelona	3—2
1970	Vienna	Manchester City	Gornik Zabrze	2—1
1971	Athens	Chelsea	Real Madrid	2—1

(In replay after 1—1 draw, also in Athens)

The U.E.F.A. Cup

Season 1971–72 marked the innovation of the U.E.F.A. Cup in succession to the European Fairs Cup, which was originally known as the European Inter-City Industrial Fairs Cup. This was the forerunner of the three major European football competitions, although in Britain at least it is ranked No. 3 behind the European Cup and Cup-Winners' Cup.

For many years before the Fairs Cup was launched in 1955 matches were played between cities on the Continent, but it was not until 1950 that Ernst B. Thommen, of Switzerland, suggested a competition for cities regularly holding industrial and trade fairs.

Thommen, a vice-president of F.I.F.A., had to wait four years for his idea to take shape because there was no suitable organizing body at the time. The competition got off the ground largely through the initiative of F.I.F.A. president Sir Stanley Rous, and until 1971 it ran independently of U.E.F.A. under an organizing committee.

Some cities (e.g. London) at first entered representative teams but others preferred to nominate club sides, and as the competition grew in prestige and popularity, club sides took over.

Although the first Fairs Cup tournament was begun in 1955, it was not completed until 1958. The reason for staggering the schedule was to avoid a clash with long-standing domestic fixtures. But interest could not be sustained over such a long period, and the competition almost ground to a halt.

The organizers, recognizing this weakness, staged the second series over two years, and since season 1960–61 the competition has been an annual event on the football calendar.

Spain provided five of the first six winners, starting with two triumphs for Barcelona. They won the drawn-out 1955–58 series, beating a representative London side 6–0 in Barcelona and by what was to remain the record aggregate of 8–2. In the 1958–60 series Barcelona went through to the finals without losing a single game and won the trophy again by defeating Birmingham City 5–2 on aggregate.

Birmingham were also the losing finalists in the 1960–61 series, when they held AS Roma to a 2–2 draw in Birmingham, but lost 2–0 in Rome.

Valencia were the high-scoring winners in 1961–62, defeating Barcelona 7–3 on aggregate. They won the trophy again the following season and went close to completing a hat-trick in 1963–64, when for the first time it was decided to play a one-match final on a neutral ground. In an all-Spanish decider they lost 2–1 to Real Zaragoza in Barcelona.

But single-leg finals were not a success and after Ferencvaros had beaten Juventus 1–0 in Turin in 1965—Hungary's first Fairs Cup conquest—the 1965–66 final reverted to two matches. It was held over until the following season and, when it was eventually played, Barcelona became the only team to win the Fairs Cup three times, beating their Spanish rivals Real Zaragoza after losing the home leg.

In 1967 Leeds United became the first British team to reach the final for six years. The toss of a coin took them through the quarter-finals against Bologna after the teams had deadlocked 1–1. In the final, again delayed until the next season, Leeds went down 2–0 on aggregate to Dynamo Zagreb.

A year later, however, Leeds became the first British winners of the trophy. In the first leg they gained a slender 1–0 lead and then held Ferencvaros to a goalless draw in Budapest.

In the last competition under the original title of Inter-Cities Fairs Cup, another British team took the prize—Newcastle United in season 1968–69. It was Newcastle's first venture into Europe, and the Geordies' theme song, 'Blaydon Races', rang out as the crowds thronged St James's Park to see the Tyne-siders beat crack Continental clubs Feyenoord, Sporting Lisbon, Real Zaragoza and Vitoria Setubal.

There was an all-British semi-final between Newcastle and Rangers. United fought a rearguard action to hold Rangers 0–0 at Ibrox and then won 2–0 at St James's Park. With their team two down in the second leg, Rangers followers invaded the field intent on getting the game abandoned and play was held up for 18 minutes. There were 31 arrests, 60 spectators were taken to hospital and the match was played out with 1000 police surrounding the pitch.

In the final, Newcastle beat the Hungarians Ujpest Dozsa 3–0 in the home leg, but even that advantage began to look inadequate when Ujpest quickly pulled back two goals in the return game in Budapest. A storming rally by Newcastle, however, produced three goals and an impressive 6–2 victory on aggregate.

In 1970 Arsenal scored a dramatic victory over Belgium's Anderlecht which kept the Fairs Cup in England for the third successive season. They lost the first leg of the final 3–1 in Brussels, but the second match was won 3–0, and a 51,000 Highbury crowd went wild at Arsenal's first success of any sort for 17 years.

A year later Leeds United made it four consecutive triumphs

for England in the Fairs Cup and became the first British club to win the competition twice. In what was the last European Fairs Cup tournament, they were its first winners on the 'away goals' rule, drawing 2–2 against Juventus in Turin and 1–1 at Elland Road.

Results of Fairs Cup Finals (now U.E.F.A. Cup)

1955–58   **Barcelona** beat *London* 8–2 on aggregate (London 2, Barcelona 2; Barcelona 6, London 0)

1958–60   **Barcelona** beat *Birmingham* 5–2 on aggregate (Birmingham 1, Barcelona 1; Barcelona 4, Birmingham 1)

1961   **AS Roma** beat *Birmingham City* 4–2 on aggregate (Birmingham 2, AS Roma 2; AS Roma 2, Birmingham 0)

1962   **Valencia** beat *Barcelona* 7–3 on aggregate (Valencia 6, Barcelona 2; Barcelona 1, Valencia 1)

1963   **Valencia** beat *Dynamo Zagreb* 4–1 on aggregate (Dynamo Zagreb 1, Valencia 2; Valencia 2, Dynamo Zagreb 0)

1964   **Real Zaragoza** 2, *Valencia* 1 (in Barcelona)

1965   **Ferencvaros** 1, *Juventus* 0 (in Turin)

1966   **Barcelona** beat *Real Zaragoza* 4–3 on aggregate (Barcelona 0, Real Zaragoza 1; Real Zaragoza 2, Barcelona 4)

1967   **Dynamo Zagreb** beat *Leeds United* 2–0 on aggregate (Dynamo Zagreb 2, Leeds 0; Leeds 0, Dynamo Zagreb 0)

1968   **Leeds United** beat *Ferencvaros* 1–0 on aggregate (Leeds 1, Ferencvaros 0; Ferencvaros 0, Leeds 0)

1969   **Newcastle United** beat *Ujpest Dozsa* 6–2 on aggregate (Newcastle 3, Ujpest Dozsa 0; Ujpest Dozsa 2, Newcastle 3)

1970   **Arsenal** beat *Anderlecht* 4–3 on aggregate (Anderlecht 3, Arsenal 1; Arsenal 3, Anderlecht 0)

1971   **Leeds United** beat *Juventus* on away goals after 3–3 draw on aggregate (Juventus 0, Leeds 0—abandoned 51 min., rain; Juventus 2, Leeds 2; Leeds 1, Juventus 1).

The World Club Championship

This unofficial inter-continental tournament, played home and away each season between the winners of the European Cup and the winners of the South American Cup, has been notable for more ill-feeling than any other club contest in the world. It began in 1960, and until 1969 the title was decided on results—not on goal aggregate—so that in cases where each club had won one match, a play-off was necessary. Results:

1960 Real Madrid (Spain) beat *Penarol* (Uruguay). (In Montevideo—Penarol 0, Real Madrid 0; in Madrid—Real Madrid 5, Penarol 1).

1961 Penarol (Uruguay) beat *Benfica* (Portugal). (In Lisbon—Benfica 1, Penarol 0; in Montevideo—Penarol 5, Benfica 0; play-off in Montevideo—Penarol 2, Benfica 1).

1962 Santos (Brazil) beat *Benfica* (Portugal). (In Rio de Janeiro—Santos 3. Benfica 2; in Lisbon—Benfica, 2 Santos 5).

1963 Santos (Brazil) beat *AC Milan* (Italy). (In Milan—AC Milan 4, Santos 2; in Rio de Janeiro—Santos 4, AC Milan 2; play-off in Rio—Santos 1, AC Milan 0).

1964 Internazionale Milan (Italy) beat *Independiente* (Argentina). (In Buenos Aires—Independiente 1, Internazionale 0; in Milan—Internazionale 2, Independiente 0; play-off in Madrid—Internazionale 1, Independiente 0, after extra time).

1965 Internazionale Milan (Italy) beat *Independiente* (Argentina). (In Milan—Internazionale 3, Independiente 0; in Buenos Aires—Independiente 0, Internazionale 0).

1966 Penarol (Uruguay) beat *Real Madrid* (Spain). (In Montevideo—Penarol 2, Real Madrid 0; in Madrid—Real Madrid 0, Penarol 2).

1967 Racing Club (Argentina) beat *Celtic* (Scotland). (In Glasgow—Celtic 1, Racing Club 0; in Buenos Aires—Racing Club 2, Celtic 1; play-off in Montevideo—Racing Club 1, Celtic 0).

1968 Estudiantes (Argentina) beat *Manchester United* (England) (In Buenos Aires—Estudiantes 1, Manchester United 0; in Manchester—Manchester United 1, Estudiantes 1).

1969 AC Milan (Italy) beat *Estudiantes* (Argentina) 4—2 on aggregate. (In Milan—AC Milan 3, Estudiantes 0, in Buenos Aires—Estudiantes 2, Milan 1).

1970 Feyenoord (Holland) beat *Estudiantes* (Argentina) 3—2 on aggregate. (In Buenos Aires—Estudiantes 2, Feyenoord 2; in Rotterdam—Feyenoord 1, Estudiantes 0).

1971 Nacional (Uruguay) beat *Panathinaikos* (Greece) 3—2 on aggregate. European Champions Ajax (Holland) declined to take part in World Club Championship and were replaced by European runners-up Panathinaikos. (In Athens—Panathinaikos 1, Nacional 1; in Montevideo—Nacional 2, Panathinaikos 1).

Records Section
ENGLAND'S COMPLETE RECORD IN FULL INTERNATIONALS

Key: WC = World Cup proper; WCQ = World Cup qualifying round; EC = European Championship proper; ECQ = European Championship qualifying round.

Date	Opponents	Venue	Result
Season 1872–73			
Nov. 30	Scotland	Glasgow	D 0–0
Mar. 8	Scotland	Oval	W 4–2
Season 1873–74			
Mar. 7	Scotland	Glasgow	L 1–2
Season 1874–75			
Mar 6	Scotland	Oval	D 2–2
Season 1875–76			
Mar. 4	Scotland	Glasgow	L 0–3
Season 1876–77			
Mar. 3	Scotland	Oval	L 1–3
Season 1877–78			
Mar. 2	Scotland	Glasgow	L 2–7
Season 1878–79			
Jan. 18	Wales	Oval	W 2–1
Apr. 5	Scotland	Oval	W 5–4
Season 1879–80			
Mar. 13	Scotland	Glasgow	L 4–5
Mar. 15	Wales	Wrexham	W 3–2
Season 1880–81			
Feb. 26	Wales	Blackburn	L 0–1
Mar. 12	Scotland	Oval	L 1–6
Season 1881–82			
Feb. 18	Ireland	Belfast	W 13–0
Mar. 11	Scotland	Glasgow	L 1–5
Mar. 13	Wales	Wrexham	L 3–5
Season 1882–83			
Feb. 3	Wales	Oval	W 5–0
Feb. 24	Ireland	Liverpool	W 7–0
Mar. 10	Scotland	Sheffield	L 2–3
Season 1883–84			
Feb. 23	Ireland	Belfast	W 8–1
Mar. 15	Scotland	Glasgow	L 0–1
Mar. 17	Wales	Wrexham	W 4–0

166

Date	Opponents	Venue	Result
		Season 1884–85	
Feb. 28	Ireland	Manchester	W 4–0
Mar. 14	Wales	Blackburn	D 1–1
Mar. 21	Scotland	Oval	D 1–1
		Season 1885–86	
Mar. 13	Ireland	Belfast	W 6–1
Mar. 29	Wales	Wrexham	W 3–1
Mar. 31	Scotland	Glasgow	D 1–1
		Season 1886–87	
Feb. 5	Ireland	Sheffield	W 7–0
Feb. 26	Wales	Oval	W 4–0
Mar. 19	Scotland	Blackburn	L 2–3
		Season 1887–88	
Feb. 4	Wales	Crewe	W 5–1
Mar. 17	Scotland	Glasgow	W 5–0
Mar. 31	Ireland	Belfast	W 5–1
		Season 1888–89	
Feb. 23	Wales	Stoke	W 4–1
Mar. 2	Ireland	Everton	W 6–1
Apr. 13	Scotland	Oval	L 2–3
		Season 1889–90	
Mar. 15	Wales	Wrexham	W 3–1
Mar. 15	Ireland	Belfast	W 9–1
Apr. 5	Scotland	Glasgow	D 1–1
		Season 1890–91	
Mar. 7	Wales	Sunderland	W 4–1
Mar. 7	Ireland	Wolverhampton	W 6–1
Apr. 6	Scotland	Blackburn	W 2–1
		Season 1891–92	
Mar. 5	Ireland	Belfast	W 2–0
Mar. 5	Wales	Wrexham	W 2–0
Apr. 2	Scotland	Glasgow	W 4–1
		Season 1892–93	
Feb. 25	Ireland	Birmingham	W 6–1
Mar. 13	Wales	Stoke	W 6–0
Apr. 1	Scotland	Richmond	W 5–2
		Season 1893–94	
Mar. 3	Ireland	Belfast	D 2–2
Mar. 12	Wales	Wrexham	W 5–1
Apr. 7	Scotland	Glasgow	D 2–2
		Season 1894–95	
Mar. 9	Ireland	Derby	W 9–0
Mar. 18	Wales	Kensington	D 1–1
Apr. 6	Scotland	Everton	W 3–0

Date	Opponents	Venue	Result
Season 1895—96			
Mar. 7	Ireland	Belfast	W 2—0
Mar. 16	Wales	Cardiff	W 9—1
Apr. 4	Scotland	Glasgow	L 1—2
Season 1896—97			
Feb. 20	Ireland	Nottingham	W 6—0
Mar. 29	Wales	Sheffield	W 4—0
Apr. 3	Scotland	Crystal Palace	L 1—2
Season 1897—98			
Mar. 5	Ireland	Belfast	W 3—2
Mar. 28	Wales	Wrexham	W 3—0
Apr. 2	Scotland	Glasgow	W 3—1
Season 1898—99			
Feb. 18	Ireland	Sunderland	W 13—2
Mar. 20	Wales	Bristol	W 4—0
Apr. 8	Scotland	Birmingham	W 2—1
Season 1899—1900			
Mar. 17	Ireland	Dublin	W 2—0
Mar. 26	Wales	Cardiff	D 1—1
Apr. 7	Scotland	Glasgow	L 1—4
Season 1900—01			
Mar. 9	Ireland	Southampton	W 3—0
Mar. 18	Wales	Newcastle	W 6—0
Mar. 30	Scotland	Crystal Palace	D 2—2
Season 1901—02			
Mar. 3	Wales	Wrexham	D 0—0
Mar. 22	Ireland	Belfast	W 1—0
May 3	Scotland	Birmingham	D 2—2
Season 1902—03			
Feb. 14	Ireland	Wolverhampton	W 4—0
Mar. 2	Wales	Portsmouth	W 2—1
Apr. 4	Scotland	Sheffield	L 1—2
Season 1903—04			
Feb. 29	Wales	Wrexham	D 2—2
Mar. 12	Ireland	Belfast	W 3—1
Apr. 9	Scotland	Glasgow	W 1—0
Season 1904—05			
Feb. 25	Ireland	Middlesbrough	D 1—1
Mar. 27	Wales	Liverpool	W 3—1
Apr 1	Scotland	Crystal Palace	W 1—0
Season 1905—06			
Feb. 17	Ireland	Belfast	W 5—0
Mar. 19	Wales	Cardiff	W 1—0
Apr 7	Scotland	Glasgow	L 1—2

168

Date	Opponents	Venue	Result
Season 1906–07			
Feb. 16	Ireland	Everton	W 1–0
Mar. 18	Wales	Fulham	D 1–1
Apr. 6	Scotland	Newcastle	D 1–1
Season 1907–0			
Feb. 15	Ireland	Belfast	W 3–1
Mar. 16	Wales	Wrexham	W 7–1
Apr. 4	Scotland	Glasgow	D 1–1
June 6	Austria	Vienna	W 6–1
June 8	Austria	Vienna	W 11–1
June 10	Hungary	Budapest	W 7–0
June 13	Bohemia	Prague	W 4–0
Season 1908–09			
Feb. 13	Ireland	Bradford	W 4–0
Mar. 15	Wales	Nottingham	W 2–0
Apr. 3	Scotland	Crystal Palace	W 2–0
May 29	Hungary	Budapest	W 4–2
May 31	Hungary	Budapest	W 8–2
June 1	Austria	Vienna	W 8–1
Season 1909–10			
Feb. 12	Ireland	Belfast	D 1–1
Mar. 14	Wales	Cardiff	W 1–0
Apr. 2	Scotland	Glasgow	L 0–2
Season 1910–11			
Feb. 11	Ireland	Derby	W 2–1
Mar. 13	Wales	Millwall	W 3–0
Apr. 1	Scotland	Everton	D 1–1
Season 1911–12			
Feb. 10	Ireland	Dublin	W 6–1
Mar. 11	Wales	Wrexham	W 2–0
Mar. 23	Scotland	Glasgow	D 1–1
Season 1912–13			
Feb. 15	Ireland	Belfast	L 1–2
Mar. 17	Wales	Bristol	W 4–3
Apr. 5	Scotland	Chelsea	W 1–0
Season 1913–14			
Feb. 14	Ireland	Middlesbrough	L 0–3
Mar. 16	Wales	Cardiff	W 2–0
Apr. 4	Scotland	Glasgow	L 1–3
Season 1919–20			
Oct. 25	Ireland	Belfast	D 1–1
Mar. 15	Wales	Highbury	L 1–2
Apr. 10	Scotland	Sheffield	W 5–4

Date	Opponents	Venue	Result
Season 1920–21			
Oct. 23	Ireland	Sunderland	W 2–0
Mar. 14	Wales	Cardiff	D 0–0
Apr. 9	Scotland	Glasgow	L 0–3
May 21	Belgium	Brussels	W 2–0
Season 1921–22			
Oct. 22	Ireland	Belfast	D 1–1
Mar. 13	Wales	Liverpool	W 1–0
Apr. 8	Scotland	Aston Villa	L 0–1
Season 1922–23			
Oct. 21	Ireland	West Bromwich	W 2–0
Mar. 5	Wales	Cardiff	D 2–2
Mar. 19	Belgium	Highbury	W 6–1
Apr. 14	Scotland	Glasgow	D 2–2
May 10	France	Paris	W 4–1
May 21	Sweden	Stockholm	W 4–2
May 24	Sweden	Stockholm	W 3–1
Season 1923–24			
Oct. 20	Ireland	Belfast	L 1–2
Nov. 1	Belgium	Antwerp	D 2–2
Mar. 3	Wales	Blackburn	L 1–2
Apr. 12	Scotland	Wembley	D 1–1
May 17	France	Paris	W 3–1
Season 1924–25			
Oct. 22	Ireland	Everton	W 3–1
Dec. 8	Belgium	West Bromwich	W 4–0
Feb. 28	Wales	Swansea	W 2–1
Apr. 4	Scotland	Glasgow	L 0–2
May · 21	France	Paris	W 3–2
Season 1925–26			
Oct. 24	Ireland	Belfast	D 0–0
Mar. 1	Wales	Crystal Palace	L 1–3
Apr. 17	Scotland	Manchester	L 0–1
May 24	Belgium	Antwerp	W 5–3
Season 1926–27			
Oct. 20	Ireland	Liverpool	D 3–3
Feb. 12	Wales	Wrexham	D 3–3
Apr. 2	Scotland	Glasgow	W 2–1
May 11	Belgium	Brussels	W 9–1
May 21	Luxembourg	Luxembourg	W 5–2
May 26	France	Paris	W 6–0
Season 1927–28			
Oct. 22	Ireland	Belfast	L 0–2
Nov. 28	Wales	Burnley	L 1–2
Mar. 31	Scotland	Wembley	L 1–5

170

Date	Opponents	Venue	Result
May 17	France	Paris	W 5–1
May 19	Belgium	Antwerp	W 3–1

Season 1928–29

Date	Opponents	Venue	Result
Oct. 22	Ireland	Everton	W 2–1
Nov. 17	Wales	Swansea	W 3–2
Apr. 13	Scotland	Glasgow	L 0–1
May 9	France	Paris	W 4–1
May 11	Belgium	Brussels	W 5–1
May 15	Spain	Madrid	L 3–4

Season 1929–30

Date	Opponents	Venue	Result
Oct 19	Ireland	Belfast	W 3–0
Nov. 20	Wales	Chelsea	W 6–0
Apr. 5	Scotland	Wembley	W 5–2
May 10	Germany	Berlin	D 3–3
May 14	Austria	Vienna	D 0–0

Season 1930–31

Date	Opponents	Venue	Result
Oct 20	Ireland	Sheffield	W 5–1
Nov. 22	Wales	Wrexham	W 4–0
Mar. 31	Scotland	Glasgow	L 0–2
May 14	France	Paris	L 2–5
May 16	Belgium	Brussels	W 4–1

Season 1931–32

Date	Opponents	Venue	Result
Oct. 17	Ireland	Belfast	W 6–2
Nov. 18	Wales	Liverpool	W 3–1
Dec. 9	Spain	Highbury	W 7–1
Apr. 9	Scotland	Wembley	W 3–0

Season 1932–33

Date	Opponents	Venue	Result
Oct. 17	Ireland	Blackpool	W 1–0
Nov. 16	Wales	Wrexham	D 0–0
Dec. 7	Austria	Chelsea	W 4–3
Apr. 1	Scotland	Glasgow	L 1–2
May 13	Italy	Rome	D 1–1
May 20	Switzerland	Berne	W 4–0

Season 1933–34

Date	Opponents	Venue	Result
Oct. 14	Ireland	Belfast	W 3–0
Nov. 15	Wales	Newcastle	L 1–2
Dec. 6	France	Tottenham	W 4–1
Feb. 6	Ireland	Everton	W 2–1
Apr. 14	Scotland	Wembley	W 3–0
May 10	Hungary	Budapest	L 1–2
May 16	Czechoslovakia	Prague	L 1–2

Season 1934–35

Date	Opponents	Venue	Result
Sept. 29	Wales	Cardiff	W 4–0
Nov. 14	Italy	Highbury	W 3–2
Apr. 6	Scotland	Glasgow	L 0–2

Date	Opponents	Venue	Result
Season 1935–36			
Oct. 19	Ireland	Belfast	W 3–1
Dec. 4	Germany	Tottenham	W 3–0
Feb. 5	Wales	Wolverhampton	L 1–2
Apr. 4	Scotland	Wembley	D 1–1
May 6	Austria	Vienna	L 1–2
May 9	Belgium	Brussels	L 2–3
May 18	Holland	Amsterdam	W 1–0
Season 1936–37			
Oct. 17	Wales	Cardiff	L 1–2
Nov. 18	Ireland	Stoke	W 3–1
Dec. 2	Hungary	Highbury	W 6–2
Apr. 17	Scotland	Glasgow	L 1–3
May 14	Norway	Oslo	W 6–0
May 17	Sweden	Stockholm	W 4–0
May 20	Finland	Helsinki	W 8–0
Season 1937–38			
Oct. 23	Ireland	Belfast	W 5–1
Nov. 17	Wales	Middlesbrough	W 2–1
Dec. 1	Czechoslovakia	Tottenham	W 5–4
Apr. 9	Scotland	Wembley	L 0–1
May 14	Germany	Berlin	W 6–3
May 21	Switzerland	Zürich	L 1–2
May 26	France	Paris	W 4–2
Season 1938–39			
Oct. 22	Wales	Cardiff	L 2–4
Oct. 26	F.I.F.A.	Highbury	W 3–0
Nov. 9	Norway	Newcastle	W 4–0
Nov. 16	Ireland	Manchester	W 7–0
Apr. 15	Scotland	Glasgow	W 2–1
May 13	Italy	Milan	D 2–2
May 18	Yugoslavia	Belgrade	L 1–2
May 24	Rumania	Bucharest	W 2–0
Season 1946–47			
Sept. 28	Ireland	Belfast	W 7–2
Sept. 30	Republic of Ireland	Dublin	W 1–0
Nov. 13	Wales	Manchester	W 3–0
Nov. 27	Holland	Huddersfield	W 8–2
Apr. 12	Scotland	Wembley	D 1–1
May 3	France	Highbury	W 3–0
May 18	Switzerland	Zurich	L 0–1
May 25	Portugal	Lisbon	W 10–0

Date	Opponents	Venue	Result
	Season 1947–48		
Sept. 21	Belgium	Brussels	W 5–2
Oct. 18	Wales	Cardiff	W 3–0
Nov. 5	Ireland	Everton	D 2–2
Nov. 19	Sweden	Highbury	W 4–2
Apr. 10	Scotland	Glasgow	W 2–0
May 16	Italy	Turin	W 4–0
	Season 1948–49		
Sept. 26	Denmark	Copenhagen	D 0–0
Oct. 9	Ireland	Belfast	W 6–2
Nov. 10	Wales	Villa Park	W 1–0
Dec. 2	Switzerland	Highbury	W 6–0
Apr. 9	Scotland	Wembley	L 1–3
May 13	Sweden	Stockholm	L 1–3
May 18	Norway	Oslo	W 4–1
May 22	France	Paris	W 3–1
	Season 1949–50		
Sept. 21	Republic of Ireland	Everton	L 0–2
Oct. 15	Wales	Cardiff	W 4–1 WCQ
Nov. 16	Ireland	Manchester	W 9–2 WCQ
Nov. 30	Italy	Tottenham	W 2–0
Apr. 15	Scotland	Glasgow	W 1–0 WCQ
May 14	Portugal	Lisbon	W 5–3
May 18	Belgium	Brussels	W 4–1
June 25	Chile	Rio de Janeiro	W 2–0 WC
June 29	U.S.A.	Belo Horizonte	L 0–1 WC
July 2	Spain	Rio de Janeiro	L 0–1 WC
	Season 1950–51		
Oct. 7	Ireland	Belfast	W 4–1
Nov. 15	Wales	Sunderland	W 4–2
Nov. 22	Yugoslavia	Highbury	D 2–2
Apr. 14	Scotland	Wembley	L 2–3
May 9	Argentina	Wembley	W 2–1
May 19	Portugal	Everton	W 5–2
	Season 1951–52		
Oct. 3	France	Highbury	D 2–2
Oct. 20	Wales	Cardiff	D 1–1
Nov. 14	Ireland	Villa Park	W 2–0
Nov. 28	Austria	Wembley	D 2–2
Apr. 5	Scotland	Glasgow	W 2–1
May 18	Italy	Florence	D 1–1
May 25	Austria	Vienna	W 3–2
May 28	Switzerland	Zürich	W 3–0

Date	Opponents	Venue	Result
Season 1952–53			
Oct. 4	Ireland	Belfast	D 2–2
Nov. 12	Wales	Wembley	W 5–2
Nov. 26	Belgium	Wembley	W 5–0
Apr. 18	Scotland	Wembley	D 2–2
May 17	Argentina	Buenos Aires	0–0
	(Abandoned after 23 min.—rain)		
May 24	Chile	Santiago	W 2–1
May 31	Uruguay	Montevideo	L 1–2
June 8	U.S.A.	New York	W 6–3
Season 1953–54			
Oct. 10	Wales	Cardiff	W 4–1 WCQ
Oct. 21	F.I.F.A.	Wembley	D 4–4
Nov. 11	Ireland	Everton	W 3–1 WCQ
Nov. 25	Hungary	Wembley	L 3–6
Apr. 3	Scotland	Glasgow	W 4–2 WCQ
May 16	Yugoslavia	Belgrade	L 0–1
May 23	Hungary	Budapest	L 1–7
June 17	Belgium	Basle	D 4–4 WC
June 20	Switzerland	Berne	W 2–0 WC
June 26	Uruguay	Basle	L 2–4 WC
Season 1954–55			
Oct. 2	Ireland	Belfast	W 2–0
Nov. 10	Wales	Wembley	W 3–2
Dec. 1	Germany	Wembley	W 3–1
Apr. 2	Scotland	Wembley	W 7–2
May 15	France	Paris	L 0–1
May 18	Spain	Madrid	D 1–1
May 22	Portugal	Oporto	L 1–3
Season 1955–56			
Oct. 2	Denmark	Copenhagen	W 5–1
Oct. 22	Wales	Cardiff	L 1–2
Nov. 2	Ireland	Wembley	W 3–0
Nov. 30	Spain	Wembley	W 4–1
Apr. 14	Scotland	Glasgow	D 1–1
May 9	Brazil	Wembley	W 4–2
May 16	Sweden	Stockholm	D 0–0
May 20	Finland	Helsinki	W 5–1
May 26	Germany	Berlin	W 3–1
Season 1956–57			
Oct. 6	Ireland	Belfast	D 1–1
Nov. 14	Wales	Wembley	W 3–1
Nov. 28	Yugoslavia	Wembley	W 3–0
Dec. 5	Denmark	Wolverhampton	W 5–2 WCQ
Apr. 6	Scotland	Wembley	W 2–1

Date	Opponents	Venue	Result
May 8	Republic of Ireland	Wembley	W 5–1 WCQ
May 15	Denmark	Copenhagen	W 4–1 WCQ
May 19	Republic of Ireland	Dublin	D 1–1 WCQ

Season 1957–58

Date	Opponents	Venue	Result
Oct. 19	Wales	Cardiff	W 4–0
Nov. 6	Ireland	Wembley	L 2–3
Nov. 27	France	Wembley	W 4–0
Apr. 19	Scotland	Glasgow	W 4–0
May 7	Portugal	Wembley	W 2–1
May 11	Yugoslavia	Belgrade	L 0–5
May 18	Russia	Moscow	D 1–1
June 8	Russia	Gothenburg	D 2–2 WC
June 11	Brazil	Gothenburg	D 0–0 WC
June 15	Austria	Boras	D 2–2 WC
June 17	Russia	Gothenburg	L 0–1 WC

Season 1958–59

Date	Opponents	Venue	Result
Oct. 4	Ireland	Belfast	D 3–3
Oct. 22	Russia	Wembley	W 5–0
Nov. 26	Wales	Villa Park	D 2–2
Apr. 11	Scotland	Wembley	W 1–0
May 6	Italy	Wembley	D 2–2
May 13	Brazil	Rio de Janeiro	L 0–2
May 17	Peru	Lima	L 1–4
May 24	Mexico	Mexico City	L 1–2
May 28	U.S.A.	Los Angeles	W 8–1

Season 1959–60

Date	Opponents	Venue	Result
Oct. 17	Wales	Cardiff	D 1–1
Oct. 28	Sweden	Wembley	L 2–3
Nov. 18	Ireland	Wembley	W 2–1
Apr. 9	Scotland	Glasgow	D 1–1
May 11	Yugoslavia	Wembley	D 3–3
May 15	Spain	Madrid	L 0–3
May 22	Hungary	Budapest	L 0–2

Season 1960–61

Date	Opponents	Venue	Result
Oct. 8	Ireland	Belfast	W 5–2
Oct. 19	Luxembourg	Luxembourg	W 9–0 WCQ
Oct. 26	Spain	Wembley	W 4–2
Nov. 23	Wales	Wembley	W 5–1
Apr. 15	Scotland	Wembley	W 9–3
May 10	Mexico	Wembley	W 8–0
May 21	Portugal	Lisbon	D 1–1 WCQ
May 24	Italy	Rome	W 3–2
May 27	Austria	Vienna	L 1–3

Date	Opponents	Venue	Result
Season 1961–62			
Sept. 28	Luxembourg	Highbury	W 4–1 WCQ
Oct. 14	Wales	Cardiff	D 1–1
Oct. 25	Portugal	Wembley	W 2–0 WCQ
Nov. 22	Ireland	Wembley	D 1–1
Apr. 4	Austria	Wembley	W 3–1
Apr. 14	Scotland	Glasgow	L 0–2
May 9	Switzerland	Wembley	W 3–1
May 20	Peru	Lima	W 4–0
May 31	Hungary	Rancagua	L 1–2 WC
June 2	Argentina	Rancagua	W 3–1 WC
June 7	Bulgaria	Rancagua	D 0–0 WC
June 10	Brazil	Vina del Mar	L 1–3 WC
Season 1962–63			
Oct. 3	France	Sheffield	D 1–1 ECQ
Oct. 20	Ireland	Belfast	W 3–1
Nov. 21	Wales	Wembley	W 4–0
Feb. 27	France	Paris	L 2–5 ECQ
Apr. 6	Scotland	Wembley	L 1–2
May 8	Brazil	Wembley	D 1–1
May 29	Czechoslovakia	Bratislava	W 4–2
June 2	East Germany	Leipzig	W 2–1
June 5	Switzerland	Basle	W 8–1
Season 1963–64			
Oct. 12	Wales	Cardiff	W 4–0
Oct. 23	F.I.F.A.	Wembley	W 2–1
Nov. 20	Ireland	Wembley	W 8–3
Apr. 11	Scotland	Glasgow	L 0–1
May 6	Uruguay	Wembley	W 2–1
May 17	Portugal	Lisbon	W 4–3
May 24	Republic of Ireland	Dublin	W 3–1
May 27	U.S.A.	New York	W 10–0
May 30	Brazil	Rio de Janeiro	L 1–5
June 4	Portugal	Sao Paulo	D 1–1
June 6	Argentina	Rio de Janeiro	L 0–1
Season 1964–65			
Oct. 3	Ireland	Belfast	W 4–3
Oct. 21	Belgium	Wembley	D 2–2
Nov. 18	Wales	Wembley	W 2–1
Dec. 9	Holland	Amsterdam	D 1–1
Apr. 10	Scotland	Wembley	D 2–2
May 5	Hungary	Wembley	W 1–0
May 9	Yugoslavia	Belgrade	D 1–1
May 12	West Germany	Nuremberg	W 1–0
May 16	Sweden	Gothenburg	W 2–1

Date	Opponents	Venue	Result
Season 1965–66			
Oct. 2	Wales	Cardiff	D 0–0
Oct. 20	Austria	Wembley	L 2–3
Nov. 10	Ireland	Wembley	W 2–1
Dec. 8	Spain	Madrid	W 2–0
Jan. 5	Poland	Everton	D 1–1
Feb. 23	West Germany	Wembley	W 1–0
Apr. 2	Scotland	Glasgow	W 4–3
May 4	Yugoslavia	Wembley	W 2–0
June 26	Finland	Helsinki	W 3–0
June 29	Norway	Oslo	W 6–1
July 3	Denmark	Copenhagen	W 2–0
July 5	Poland	Chorzow	W 1–0
July 11	Uruguay	Wembley	D 0–0 WC
July 16	Mexico	Wembley	W 2–0 WC
July 20	France	Wembley	W 2–0 WC
July 23	Argentina	Wembley	W 1–0 WC
July 26	Portugal	Wembley	W 2–1 WC
July 30	West Germany	Wembley	W 4–2 WC
Season 1966–67			
Oct. 22	Ireland	Belfast	W 2–0 ECQ
Nov. 2	Czechoslovakia	Wembley	D 0–0
Nov. 16	Wales	Wembley	W 5–1 ECQ
Apr. 15	Scotland	Wembley	L 2–3 ECQ
May 24	Spain	Wembley	W 2–0
May 27	Austria	Vienna	W 1–0
Season 1967–68			
Oct. 21	Wales	Cardiff	W 3–0 ECQ
Nov. 22	Ireland	Wembley	W 2–0 ECQ
Dec. 6	Russia	Wembley	D 2–2
Feb. 24	Scotland	Glasgow	D 1–1 ECQ
Apr. 3	Spain	Wembley	W 1–0 EC
May 8	Spain	Madrid	W 2–1 EC
May 22	Sweden	Wembley	W 3–1
June 1	West Germany	Hanover	L 0–1
June 5	Yugoslavia	Florence	L 0–1 EC
June 8	Russia	Rome	W 2–0 EC
Season 1968–69			
Nov. 6	Rumania	Bucharest	D 0–0
Dec. 11	Bulgaria	Wembley	D 1–1
Jan. 15	Rumania	Wembley	D 1–1
Mar. 12	France	Wembley	W 5–0
May 3	Ireland	Belfast	W 3–1
May 7	Wales	Wembley	W 2–1
May 10	Scotland	Wembley	W 4–1
June 1	Mexico	Mexico City	D 0–0

Date	Opponents	Venue	Result
June 8	Uruguay	Montevideo	W 2–1
June 12	Brazil	Rio de Janeiro	L 1–2

Season 1969–70

Date	Opponents	Venue	Result
Nov. 5	Holland	Amsterdam	W 1–0
Dec. 10	Portugal	Wembley	W 1–0
Jan. 14	Holland	Wembley	D 0–0
Feb. 25	Belgium	Brussels	W 3–1
Apr. 18	Wales	Cardiff	D 1–1
Apr. 21	Ireland	Wembley	W 3–1
Apr. 25	Scotland	Glasgow	D 0–0
May 20	Colombia	Bogota	W 4–0
May 24	Ecuador	Quito	W 2–0
June 2	Rumania	Guadalajara	W 1–0 WC
June 7	Brazil	Guadalajara	L 0–1 WC
June 11	Czechoslovakia	Guadalajara	W 1–0 WC
June 14	West Germany	Leon	L 2–3 WC

Season 1970–71

Date	Opponents	Venue	Result
Nov. 25	East Germany	Wembley	W 3–1
Feb. 3	Malta	Valletta	W 1–0 ECQ
Apr. 21	Greece	Wembley	W 3–0 ECQ
May 12	Malta	Wembley	W 5–0 ECQ
May 15	Ireland	Belfast	W 1–0
May 19	Wales	Wembley	D 0–0
May 22	Scotland	Wembley	W 3–1

Season 1971–72

Date	Opponents	Venue	Result
Oct. 13	Switzerland	Basle	W 3–2 ECQ
Nov. 10	Switzerland	Wembley	D 1–1 ECQ
Dec. 1	Greece	Athens	W 2–0 ECQ

FOOTBALL LEAGUE CHAMPIONS
AND THEIR RECORDS

Season	Champions	P	W	D	L	F	A	Pts
1888–89	Preston N.E.	22	18	4	0	74	15	40
1889–90	Preston N.E	22	15	3	4	71	30	33
1890–91	Everton	22	14	1	7	63	29	29
1891–92	Sunderland	26	21	0	5	93	36	42
1892–93	Sunderland	30	22	4	4	100	36	48
1893–94	Aston Villa	30	19	6	5	84	42	44
1894–95	Sunderland	30	21	5	4	80	37	47
1895–96	Aston Villa	30	20	5	5	78	45	45
1896–97	Aston Villa	30	21	5	4	73	38	47
1897–98	Sheffield Utd.	30	17	8	5	56	31	42
1898–99	Aston Villa	34	19	7	8	76	40	45
1899–1900	Aston Villa	34	22	6	6	77	35	50
1900–01	Liverpool	34	19	7	8	59	35	45
1901–02	Sunderland	34	19	6	9	50	35	44
1902–03	Sheffield Wed.	34	19	4	11	54	36	42
1903–04	Sheffield Wed.	34	20	7	7	48	28	47
1904–05	Newcastle Utd.	34	23	2	9	72	33	48
1905–06	Liverpool	38	23	5	10	79	46	51
1906–07	Newcastle Utd.	38	22	7	9	74	46	51
1907–08	Manchester Utd.	38	23	6	9	81	48	52
1908–09	Newcastle Utd.	38	24	5	9	65	41	53
1909–10	Aston Villa	38	23	7	8	84	42	53
1910–11	Manchester Utd.	38	22	8	8	72	40	52
1911–12	Blackburn Rov.	38	20	9	9	60	43	49
1912–13	Sunderland	38	25	4	9	86	43	54
1913–14	Blackburn Rov.	38	20	11	7	78	42	51
1914–15	Everton	38	19	8	11	76	47	46
1915–19	No competition—First World War							
1919–20	West Brom. Albion	42	28	4	10	104	47	60
1920–21	Burnley	42	23	13	6	79	36	59
1921–22	Liverpool	42	22	13	7	63	36	57
1922–23	Liverpool	42	26	8	8	70	31	60
1923–24	Huddersfield Town	42	23	11	8	60	33	57
1924–25	Huddersfield Town	42	21	16	5	69	28	58
1925–26	Huddersfield Town	42	23	11	8	92	60	57
1926–27	Newcastle Utd.	42	25	6	11	96	58	56
1927–28	Everton	42	20	13	9	102	66	53
1928–29	Sheffield Wed.	42	21	10	11	86	62	52
1929–30	Sheffield Wed.	42	26	8	8	105	57	60
1930–31	Arsenal	42	28	10	4	127	59	66
1931–32	Everton	42	26	4	12	116	64	56
1932–33	Arsenal	42	25	8	9	118	61	58
1933–34	Arsenal	42	25	9	8	75	47	59
1934–35	Arsenal	42	23	12	7	115	46	58

Season	Champions	P	W	D	L	F	A	Pts
1935–36	Sunderland	42	25	6	11	109	74	56
1936–37	Manchester City	42	22	13	7	107	61	57
1937–38	Arsenal	42	21	10	11	77	44	52
1938–39	Everton	42	27	5	10	88	52	59
1939–46	No competition—Second World War							
1946–47	Liverpool	42	25	7	10	84	52	57
1947–48	Arsenal	42	23	13	6	81	32	59
1948–49	Portsmouth	42	25	8	9	84	42	58
1949–50	Portsmouth	42	22	9	11	74	38	53
1950–51	Tottenham Hotspur	42	25	10	7	82	44	60
1951–52	Manchester Utd.	42	23	11	8	95	52	57
1952–53	Arsenal	42	21	12	9	97	64	54
1953–54	Wolverhampton W.	42	25	7	10	96	56	57
1954–55	Chelsea	42	20	12	10	81	57	52
1955–56	Manchester Utd	42	25	10	7	83	51	60
1956–57	Manchester Utd	42	28	8	6	103	54	64
1957–58	Wolverhampton W.	42	28	8	6	103	47	64
1958–59	Wolverhampton W	42	28	5	9	110	49	61
1959–60	Burnley	42	24	7	11	85	61	55
1960–61	Tottenham Hotspur	42	31	4	7	115	55	66
1961–62	Ipswich Town	42	24	8	10	93	67	56
1962–63	Everton	42	25	11	6	84	42	61
1963–64	Liverpool	42	26	5	11	92	45	57
1964–65	Manchester Utd.	42	26	9	7	89	39	61
1965–66	Liverpool	42	26	9	7	79	34	61
1966–67	Manchester Utd.	42	24	12	6	84	45	60
1967–68	Manchester City	42	26	6	10	86	43	58
1968–69	Leeds United	42	27	13	2	66	26	67
1969–70	Everton	42	29	8	5	72	34	66
1970–71	Arsenal	42	29	7	6	71	29	65
1971–72	Derby County	42	24	10	8	69	33	58

Summary of Champions

Arsenal	8	Sheffield Wed.	4	Preston	2
Everton	7	Huddersfield	3	Tottenham	2
Liverpool	7	Wolves	3	Chelsea	1
Manchester Utd.	7	Blackburn	2	Derby County	1
Aston Villa	6	Burnley	2	Ipswich	1
Sunderland	6	Manchester City	2	Leeds	1
Newcastle	4	Portsmouth	2	Sheffield Utd.	1
				West Bromwich	1

F.A. CUP WINNERS

Cup Final venues:

1872–92	Kennington Oval (except 1873— at Lillie Bridge, London)	1895–1914 1915	Crystal Palace Old Trafford, Manchester
1893	Fallowfield, Manchester	1920–22 1923 to date	Stamford Bridge Wembley
1894	Anfield, Liverpool		

* = Replay; † = After extra time

Season	Winners	Runners-up	Result	Attend-dance
1871–72	Wanderers	Royal Engineers	1–0	2,000
1872–73	Wanderers	Oxford University	2–0	3,000
1873–74	Oxford University	Royal Engineers	2–0	2,500
1874–75	Royal Engineers	Old Etonians	*2–0 (after 1–1 draw)	3,000
875–76	Wanderers	Old Etonians	*3–0 (after 0–0 draw)	4,000
1876–77	Wanderers	Oxford University	†2–0	3,000
1877–78	Wanderers	Royal Engineers	3–1	5,000
1878–79	Old Etonians	Clapham Rovers	1–0	5,000
1879–80	Clapham Rovers	Oxford University	1–0	6,000
1880–81	Old Carthusians	Old Etonians	3–0	4,000
1881–82	Old Etonians	Blackburn R	1–0	7,000
1882–83	Blackburn Olympic	Old Etonians	†2–1	8,000
1883–84	Blackburn R	Queen's Park, Glasgow	2–1	4,000
1884–85	Blackburn R.	Queen's Park Glasgow	2–0	12,500
1885–86	Blackburn R.	W.B.A.	*2–0	15,000
	(Replay at Derby—after 0–0 draw)			
1886–87	Aston Villa	W.B.A.	2–0	16,000
1887–88	W.B.A.	Preston N.E	2–1	19,000
1888–89	Preston N.E.	Wolves	3–0	22,000
1889–90	Blackburn R.	Sheffield Wed.	6–1	20,000
1890–91	Blackburn R.	Notts County	3–1	23,000
1891–92	W.B.A.	Aston Villa	3–0	25,000
1892–93	Wolves	Everton	1–0	45,000
1893–94	Notts County	Bolton W.	4–1	37,000
1894–95	Aston Villa	W.B.A.	1–0	42,500

Season	Winners	Runners-up	Result	Attend-ance
1895–96	Sheffield Wed.	Wolves	2–1	49,000
1896–97	Aston Villa	Everton	3–2	66,000
1897–98	Nott'm Forest	Derby County	3–1	62,000
1898–99	Sheffield Utd	Derby County	4–1	74,000
1899–1900	Bury	Southampton	4–0	69,000
1900–01	Tottenham H.	Sheffield Utd.	*3–1	30,000

(Replay at Bolton—after 2–2 draw, att: 110,820)

1901–02	Sheffield Utd.	Southampton	*2–1	33,000

(Replay at Crystal Palace—after 1–1 draw, att: 77,000)

1902–03	Bury	Derby County	6–0	63,000
1903–04	Manchester C.	Bolton W.	1–0	61,000
1904–05	Aston Villa	Newcastle U.	2–0	101,000
1905–06	Everton	Newcastle U.	1–0	76,000
1906–07	Sheffield Wed.	Everton	2–1	84,500
1907–08	Wolves	Newcastle U.	3–1	75,000
1908–09	Manchester U.	Bristol City	1–0	68,000
1909–10	Newcastle U.	Barnsley	*2–0	69,000

(Replay at Goodison Park, Everton—after 1–1 draw, att: 78,000)

1910–11	Bradford City	Newcastle U.	*1–0	58,000

(Replay at Old Trafford, Manchester—after 0–0 draw, att: 69,000)

1911–12	Barnsley	W.B.A.	*1–0	38,500

(Replay at Bramall Lane, Sheffield—after 0–0 draw, att: 54,500)

1912–13	Aston Villa	Sunderland	1–0	120,000
1913–14	Burnley	Liverpool	1–0	73,000
1914–15	Sheffield U	Chelsea	3–0	50,000
1915–19	No competition—First World War			
1919–20	Aston Villa	Huddersfield T.	†1–0	50,000
1920–21	Tottenham H.	Wolves	1–0	73,000
1921–22	Huddersfield T.	Preston N.E.	1–0	53,000

Results, with scorers, since the F.A. Cup Final has been played at Wembley

Season	Winners	Runners-up	Result	Attend-ance
1922–23	Bolton W (Jack, J. R. Smith)	West Ham U.	2–0	126,047
1923–24	Newcastle U (Harris, Seymour)	Aston Villa	2–0	92,000
1924–25	Sheffield Utd. (Tunstall)	Cardiff City	1–0	92,000
1925–26	Bolton W. (Jack)	Manchester C.	1–0	91,500
1926–27	Cardiff City (Ferguson)	Arsenal	1–0	91,000
1927–28	Blackburn R. (Roscamp 2, McLean)	Huddersfield T. (Jackson)	3–1	92,000

Season	Winners	Runners-up	Result	Attend-ance
1928–29	Bolton W *(Butler, Blackmore)*	Portsmouth	2–0	92,500
1929–30	Arsenal *(James, Lambert)*	Huddersfield T.	2–0	92,500
1930–31	W.B.A. *(W. G. Richardson)*	Birmingham *(Bradford)*	2–1	92,500
1931–32	Newcastle U. *(Allen 2)*	Arsenal *(John)*	2–1	92,000
1932–33	Everton *(Stein, Dean, Dunn)*	Manchester City	3–0	93,000
1933–34	Manchester C. *(Tilson 2)*	Portsmouth *(Rutherford)*	2–1	93,500
1934–35	Sheffield Wed. *(Rimmer 2, Palethorpe, Hooper)*	W.B.A. *(Boyes, Sandford)*	4–2	93,000
1935–36	Arsenal *(Drake)*	Sheffield Utd.	1–0	93,500
1936–37	Sunderland *(Gurney, Carter, Burbanks)*	Preston N.E. *(F. O'Donnell)*	3–1	93,500
1937–38	Preston N.E. *(Mutch—pen.)*	Huddersfield T.	†1–0	93,500
1938–39	Portsmouth *(Parker 2, Barlow, Anderson)*	Wolves *(Dorsett)*	4–1	99,000
1939–45	No competition—Second World War			
1945–46	Derby County *(H. Turner own goal, Doherty, Stamps 2)*	Charlton A. *(H. Turner)*	†4–1	98,000
1946–47	Charlton A. *(Duffy)*	Burnley	†1–0	98,000
1947–48	Manchester U. *(Rowley 2, Pearson, Anderson)*	Blackpool *(Shimwell—pen., Mortensen)*	4–2	99,000
1948–49	Wolves *(Pye 2, Smyth)*	Leicester City *(Griffiths)*	3–1	100,000

Season	Winners	Runners-up	Result	Attend-ance
1949–50	Arsenal *(Lewis 2)*	Liverpool	2–0	100,000
1950–51	Newcastle U. *(Milburn 2)*	Blackpool	2–0	100,000
1951–52	Newcastle U. *(G. Robledo)*	Arsenal	1–0	100,000
1952–53	Blackpool *(Mortensen 3, Perry)*	Bolton W. *(Lofthouse, Moir, Bell)*	4–3	100,000
1953–54	W.B.A. *(Allen 2—1 pen., Griffin)*	Preston N.E. *(Morrison, Wayman)*	3–2	100,000
1954–55	Newcastle U. *(Milburn, Mitchell, Hannah)*	Manchester C. *(Johnstone)*	3–1	100,000
1955–56	Manchester C. *(Hayes, Dyson, Johnstone)*	Birmingham C. *(Kinsey)*	3–1	100,000
1956–57	Aston Villa *(McParland 2)*	Manchester U. *(Taylor)*	2–1	100,000
1957–58	Bolton W. *(Lofthouse 2)*	Manchester U.	2–0	100,000
1958–59	Nott'm Forest *(Dwight, Wilson)*	Luton Town *(Pacey)*	2–1	100,000
1959–60	Wolves *(McGrath own goal, Deeley 2)*	Blackburn R.	3–0	100,000
1960–61	Tottenham H. *(Smith, Dyson)*	Leicester C.	2–0	100,000
1961–62	Tottenham *(Greaves, Smith, Blanchflower *pen.)*	Burnley *(Robson)*	3–1	100,000
1962–63	Manchester U. *(Law, Herd 2)*	Leicester C. *(Keyworth)*	3–1	100,000
1963–64	West Ham U. *(Sissons, Hurst, Boyce)*	Preston N.E. *(Holden, Dawson)*	3–2	100,000
1964–65	Liverpool *(Hunt, St. John)*	Leeds United *(Bremner)*	†2–1	100,000

184

Season	Winners	Runners-up	Result	Attendance
1965–66	Everton (Trebilcock 2, Temple)	Sheffield Wed. (McCalliog, Ford)	3–2	100,000
1966–67	Tottenham H. (Robertson, Saul)	Chelsea (Tambling)	2–1	100,000
1967–68	W.B.A. (Astle)	Everton	†1–0	100,000
1968–69	Manchester C. (Young)	Leicester City	1–0	100,000
1969–70	Chelsea	Leeds United	*†2–1	62,000

(Replay at Old Trafford, Manchester—after †2–2 draw at Wembley—att:—100,000)

Scorers at Wembley Chelsea: *Houseman, Hutchinson.* Leeds: *Charlton, Jones.*

Scorers in replay Chelsea: *Osgood, Webb.* Leeds: *Jones.*

Season	Winners	Runners-up	Result	Attendance
1970–71	Arsenal (Kelly, George)	Liverpool (Heighway)	†2–1	100,000
1971–72	Leeds Utd. (Clarke)	Arsenal	1–0	100,000

Summary of F.A. Cup Winners

Aston Villa	7	Sheffield Wed.	3	Chelsea	1
Blackburn	6	Bury	2	Clapham Rovers	1
Newcastle	6	Nottingham F.	2	Derby	1
Tottenham	5	Old Etonians	2	Huddersfield	1
Wanderers	5	Preston	2	Leeds Utd.	1
West Bromwich	5	Barnsley	1	Liverpool	1
Arsenal	4	Blackburn Olympic	1	Notts Co.	1
Bolton	4	Blackpool	1	Old Carthusians	1
Manchester City	4	Bradford C.	1	Oxford	1
Sheffield Utd.	4	Burnley	1	Portsmouth	1
Wolves	4	Cardiff	1	Royal Engineers	1
Everton	3	Charlton	1	Sunderland	1
Manchester U.	3			West Ham Univ.	1

FOOTBALL LEAGUE CUP WINNERS

For the first six seasons, before the fixture was taken to Wembley, the Football League Cup Final was played on a home-and-away basis.

Season	Winners	Runners-up	Aggregate	Home	Away
1960–61	Aston Villa	Rotherham U.	3–2	3–0	0–2
1961–62	Norwich City	Rochdale	4–0	1–0	3–0
1962–63	Birmingham	Aston Villa	3–1	3–1	0–0
1963–64	Leicester	Stoke City	4–3	3–2	1–1
1964–65	Chelsea	Leicester	3–2	3–2	0–0
1965–66	West Brom.	West Ham	5–3	4–1	1–2

Results, with scorers, of League Cup Finals at Wembley:

			Result	Attendance
1966–67	Q.P.R. (R. Morgan, Marsh, Lazarus)	W.B.A. (Clark 2)	3–2	97,952
1967–68	Leeds United (Cooper)	Arsenal	1–0	100,000
1968–69	Swindon (Rogers 2, Smart)	Arsenal (Gould)	†3–1	100,000
1969–70	Man. City (Doyle, Pardoe)	W.B.A. (Astle)	†2–1	100,000
1970–71	Tottenham (Chivers 2)	Aston Villa	2–0	100,000
1971–72	Stoke City (Conroy, Eastham)	Chelsea (Osgood)	2–1	100,000

(† = After extra time)

SCOTTISH LEAGUE CHAMPIONS

Season		Points	Season		Points
1890–91	Rangers Dumbarton	29	1927–28	Rangers	60
			1928–29	Rangers	67
1891–92	Dumbarton	37	1929–30	Rangers	60
1892–93	Celtic	29	1930–31	Rangers	60
1893–94	Celtic	29	1931–32	Motherwell	66
1894–95	Hearts	31	1932–33	Rangers	62
1895–96	Celtic	30	1933–34	Rangers	66
1896–97	Hearts	28	1934–35	Rangers	55
1897–98	Celtic	33	1935–36	Celtic	66
1898–99	Rangers	36	1936–37	Rangers	61
1899–1900	Rangers	32	1937–38	Celtic	61
			1938–39	Rangers	59
1900–01	Rangers	35	1939–46	*No competition*	
1901–02	Rangers	28	1946–47	Rangers	46
1902–03	Hibernian	37	1947–48	Hibernian	48
1903–04	Third Lanark	43	1948–49	Rangers	46
1904–05	Celtic	41	1949–50	Rangers	50
1905–06	Celtic	49	1950–51	Hibernian	48
1906–07	Celtic	55	1951–52	Hibernian	45
1907–08	Celtic	55	1952–53	Rangers	43
1908–09	Celtic	51	1953–54	Celtic	43
1909–10	Celtic	54	1954–55	Aberdeen	49
1910–11	Rangers	52	1955–56	Rangers	52
1911–12	Rangers	51	1956–57	Rangers	55
1912–13	Rangers	53	1957–58	Hearts	62
1913–14	Celtic	65	1958–59	Rangers	50
1914–15	Celtic	65	1959–60	Hearts	54
1915–16	Celtic	67	1960–61	Rangers	51
1916–17	Celtic	64	1961–62	Dundee	54
1917–18	Rangers	56	1962–63	Rangers	57
1918–19	Celtic	58	1963–64	Rangers	55
1919–20	Rangers	71	1964–65	Kilmarnock	50
1920–21	Rangers	76	1965–66	Celtic	57
1921–22	Celtic	67	1966–67	Celtic	58
1922–23	Rangers	55	1967–68	Celtic	63
1923–24	Rangers	59	1968–69	Celtic	54
1924–25	Rangers	60	1969–70	Celtic	57
1925–26	Celtic	58	1970–71	Celtic	56
1926–27	Rangers	56	1971–72	Celtic	60

Summary of Scottish League Champions

Rangers	*34		Aberdeen	1
Celtic	27		Dundee	1
Hearts	4		Kilmarnock	1
Hibernian	4		Motherwell	1
Dumbarton	*2		Third Lanark	1

(*Includes one shared title)

SCOTTISH F.A. CUP WINNERS

(* = Replay)

Season	Winners	Runners-up	Result
1873–74	Queen's Park	Clydesdale	2–0
1874–75	Queen's Park	Renton	3–0
1875–76	Queen's Park	Third Lanark	*2–0
			(after 1–1 draw)
1876–77	Vale of Leven	Rangers	*3–2
			(after 0–0, 1–1 draws)
1877–78	Vale of Leven	Third Lanark	1–0
1878–79	Vale of Leven	(Rangers did not appear for replay after 1–1 draw)	
1879–80	Queen's Park	Thornlibank	3–0
1880–81	Queen's Park	Dumbarton	3–1
1881–82	Queen's Park	Dumbarton	*4–1
			(after 2–2 draw)
1882–83	Dumbarton	Vale of Leven	*2–1
			(after 2–2 draw)
1883–84	Queen's Park	(Vale of Leven did not appear for Final)	
1884–85	Renton	Vale of Leven	*3–1
			(after 0–0 draw)
1885–86	Queen's Park	Renton	3–1
1886–87	Hibernian	Dumbarton	2–1
1887–88	Renton	Cambuslang	6–1
1888–89	Third Lanark	Celtic	2–1
1889–90	Queen's Park	Vale of Leven	*2–1
			(after 1–1 draw)
1890–91	Hearts	Dumbarton	1–0
1891–92	Celtic	Queen's Park	5–1
1892–93	Queen's Park	Celtic	2–1
1893–94	Rangers	Celtic	3–1
1894–95	St Bernard's	Renton	2–1
1895–96	Hearts	Hibernian	3–1
1896–97	Rangers	Dumbarton	5–1
1897–98	Rangers	Kilmarnock	2–0
1898–99	Celtic	Rangers	2–0
1899–1900	Celtic	Queen's Park	4–3
1900–01	Hearts	Celtic	4–3
1901–02	Hibernian	Celtic	1–0
1902–03	Rangers	Hearts	*2–0
			(after 1–1, 0–0 draws)
1903–04	Celtic	Rangers	3–2
1904–05	Third Lanark	Rangers	*3–1
			(after 0–0 draw)

Season	Winners	Runners-up	Result
1905–06	Hearts	Third Lanark	1–0
1906–07	Celtic	Hearts	3–0
1907–08	Celtic	St Mirren	5–1
1908–09	*Cup withheld because of riot following two drawn games (2–2, 1–1) between Celtic and Rangers.*		
1909–10	Dundee	Clyde	*2–1
			(after 2–2, 0–0 draws)
1910–11	Celtic	Hamilton	*2–0
			(after 0–0 draw)
1911–12	Celtic	Clyde	2–0
1912–13	Falkirk	Raith Rovers	2–0
1913–14	Celtic	Hibernian	*4–1
			(after 0–0 draw)
1914–19	*No competition*		
1919–20	Kilmarnock	Albion Rovers	3–2
1920–21	Partick Thistle	Rangers	1–0
1921–22	Morton	Rangers	1–0
1922–23	Celtic	Hibernian	1–0
1923–24	Airdrieonians	Hibernian	2–0
1924–25	Celtic	Dundee	2–1
1925–26	St Mirren	Celtic	2–0
1926–27	Celtic	East Fife	3–1
1927–28	Rangers	Celtic	4–0
1928–29	Kilmarnock	Rangers	2–0
1929–30	Rangers	Partick Thistle	*2–1
			(after 0–0 draw)
1930–31	Celtic	Motherwell	*4–2
			(after 2–2 draw)
1931–32	Rangers	Kilmarnock	*3–0
			(after 1–1 draw)
1932–33	Celtic	Motherwell	1–0
1933–34	Rangers	St Mirren	5–0
1934–35	Rangers	Hamilton	2–1
1935–36	Rangers	Third Lanark	1–0
1936–37	Celtic	Aberdeen	2–1
1937–38	East Fife	Kilmarnock	*4–2
			(after 1–1 draw)
1938–39	Clyde	Motherwell	4–0
1939–46	*No competition*		
1946–47	Aberdeen	Hibernian	2–1
1947–48	Rangers	Morton	*1–0
			(after 1–1 draw)
1948–49	Rangers	Clyde	4–1
1949–50	Rangers	East Fife	3–0
1950–51	Celtic	Motherwell	1–0
1951–52	Motherwell	Dundee	4–0

Season	Winners	Runners-up	Result
1952–53	Rangers	Aberdeen	*1–0
			(after 1–1 draw)
1953–54	Celtic	Aberdeen	2–1
1954–55	Clyde	Celtic	*1–0
			(after 1–1 draw)
1955–56	Hearts	Celtic	3–1
1956–57	Falkirk	Kilmarnock	*2–1
			(after 1–1 draw)
1957–58	Clyde	Hibernian	1–0
1958–59	St Mirren	Aberdeen	3–1
1959–60	Rangers	Kilmarnock	2–0
1960–61	Dunfermline	Celtic	*2–0
			(after 0–0 draw)
1961–62	Rangers	St Mirren	2–0
1962–63	Rangers	Celtic	*3–0
			(after 1–1 draw)
1963–64	Rangers	Dundee	3–1
1964–65	Celtic	Dunfermline	3–2
1965–66	Rangers	Celtic	*1–0
			(after 0–0 draw)
1966–67	Celtic	Aberdeen	2–0
1967–68	Dunfermline	Hearts	3–1
1968–69	Celtic	Rangers	4–0
1969–70	Aberdeen	Celtic	3–1
1970–71	Celtic	Rangers	*2–1
			(after 1–1 draw)
1971–72	Celtic	Hibernian	6–1

Summary of Scottish F.A. Cup Winners

Celtic	22	Falkirk	2	Dumbarton	1
Rangers	19	Hibernian	2	Dundee	1
Queen's Park	10	Kilmarnock	2	East Fife	1
Hearts	5	Renton	2	Morton	1
Clyde	3	Third Lanark	2	Motherwell	1
Vale of Leven	3	St Mirren	2	Partick	1
Aberdeen	2	Airdrieonians	1	St Bernard's	1
Dunfermline	2				

SCOTTISH LEAGUE CUP WINNERS

(* = Replay)

Season	Winners	Runners-up	Result
1945–46	Aberdeen	Rangers	3–2
1946–47	Rangers	Aberdeen	4–0
1947–48	East Fife	Falkirk	*4–1
			(after 1–1 draw)
1948–49	Rangers	Raith Rovers	2–0
1949–50	East Fife	Dunfermline	3–0
1950–51	Motherwell	Hibernian	3–0
1951–52	Dundee	Rangers	3–2
1952–53	Dundee	Kilmarnock	2–0
1953–54	East Fife	Partick Thistle	3–2
1954–55	Hearts	Motherwell	4–2
1955–56	Aberdeen	St Mirren	2–1
1956–57	Celtic	Partick Thistle	*3–0
			(after 0–0 draw)
1957–58	Celtic	Rangers	7–1
1958–59	Hearts	Partick Thistle	5–1
1959–60	Hearts	Third Lanark	2–1
1960–61	Rangers	Kilmarnock	2–0
1961–62	Rangers	Hearts	*3–1
			(after 1–1 draw)
1962–63	Hearts	Kilmarnock	1–0
1963–64	Rangers	Morton	5–0
1964–65	Rangers	Celtic	2–1
1965–66	Celtic	Rangers	2–1
1966–67	Celtic	Rangers	1–0
1967–68	Celtic	Dundee	5–3
1968–69	Celtic	Hibernian	6–2
1969–70	Celtic	St Johnstone	1–0
1970–71	Rangers	Celtic	1–0
1971–72	Partick Thistle	Celtic	4–1

Summary of Scottish League Cup Winners

Celtic	7	East Fife	3	Motherwell	1
Rangers	7	Aberdeen	2	Partick	1
Hearts	4	Dundee	2		